# The Strategic Project Leader

*Mastering Service-Based Project Leadership*

CENTER FOR BUSINESS PRACTICES

Editor
James S. Pennypacker
Director
Center for Business Practices
Havertown, Pennsylvania

ADDITIONAL VOLUMES IN PREPARATION

# The Strategic Project Leader

*Mastering Service-Based Project Leadership*

## Jack Ferraro

## Auerbach Publications
Taylor & Francis Group
Boca Raton  New York

Auerbach Publications is an imprint of the
Taylor & Francis Group, an **informa** business

Auerbach Publications
Taylor & Francis Group
6000 Broken Sound Parkway NW, Suite 300
Boca Raton, FL 33487-2742

© 2008 by Taylor & Francis Group, LLC
Auerbach is an imprint of Taylor & Francis Group, an Informa business

No claim to original U.S. Government works
Printed in the United States of America on acid-free paper
10 9 8 7 6 5 4 3 2 1

International Standard Book Number-13: 978-0-8493-8794-4 (Hardcover)

**Library of Congress Cataloging-in-Publication Data**

Ferraro, Jack, 1964-
   The strategic project leader : mastering service-based project leadership / Jack Ferraro.
      p. cm. -- (Center for Business Practices ; 8)
      Includes bibliographical references and index.
      ISBN 978-0-8493-8794-4 (alk. paper)
      1. Project management. 2. Leadership. I. Title.

HD69.P75F47 2008
658.4'092--dc22                                                    2007017847

**Visit the Taylor & Francis Web site at**
**http://www.taylorandfrancis.com**

**and the Auerbach Web site at**
**http://www.auerbach-publications.com**

# Dedication

**To My Son Jonathan,**

Believe, Live . . . and Follow Your Dreams

# Contents

## SECTION IV: UNDERSTANDING ASSESSMENTS
*By Roberta F. Hill, MBA, MCC*

# Foreword

What does the typical, highly trained and experienced project manager have in common with a sack of coffee beans? More than you might think. Apart from the fact that you're likely to find either in all reaches of the world, the project manager is becoming yet another commodity in the global marketplace, taking his place alongside sacks of coffee, wheat, rice, and laptop computers. This is the downside of the tremendous advancements of the last twenty years in codifying the work of the project manager and in training people to be effective project managers. Project management has become less like art and more like science, and professional associations like the Project Management Institute are cranking out newly minted project managers just as fast as they can get them trained and certified.

There's some evidence that the process is working. Despite the fact that project work is becoming more complex, and that there is greater pressure to deliver better results sooner and cheaper, the percentage of projects that are deemed "successful" is actually increasing, though the rate is still disturbingly lower than it ought to be.

More and more of the world's work is being cast as projects and the resulting demand for project managers will be addressed by further standardization and codification of project management processes. Project sponsors will look to the profession to meet the demand, and the profession will oblige by supplying project managers who are adequately trained and certified in these standardized and codified processes.

This ***commoditization*** is the first harsh reality that the project manager must face.

It wasn't all that long ago that a project manager working for top dollar in a North American or European IT company thought him or herself to be immune from offshoring, believing (and it was true for a brief while) that the difficulty of the craft would guarantee that his employer would want to keep project management "in house." The present reality looks different. As more and more of the work gets chunked up and sent overseas, more and more of the management of the work needs to take place overseas. As the offshore corporations mature, their employees gain experience and are themselves becoming trained and certified in standardized and codified project management processes. The project manager working in North America or Europe, as a commodity, faces being shipped to where the work is, or being replaced by less expensive local commodities.

That's the second harsh reality the project manager must face.

One of the many consequences of these two realities is that the project manager is becoming an administrator and, in fact, as would be expected, the price for the project manager as a commodity is being bid down in world markets.

There's another reality as well. Despite all the advances in making a science of the art of project management, there's one aspect of project management that seems to defy standardization and codification, and that is **leadership.** Here is where opportunity is to be found. For all the good that standardization and codification, training and certification have done, little progress has been made in the profession in the area of cultivating the leadership abilities of project managers. This is, in my view, why so many projects still fail.

Ultimately, all project work gets done by people—by people on project teams—and people need to be led. In sports, both amateur and professional, and in the military, leadership is given its due. In business, it seems, we want to manage rather than to lead. It's very telling that we call what we do *project* **management** and we call ourselves *project* **managers.** In point of fact, this is what we are and this is what all of this standardization, codification, education and certification are all about—**management**—the **management** of **projects**, and not the **leadership** of **people**.

In business, as in sports and in the military, victory goes to the team with the most capable leader. A person who sees him or herself as merely **a manager of projects** will only ever be a manager of projects, a commodity in the global marketplace, who should never expect to have better success rates than contemporary statistics would indicate. On the other hand, by focusing on and cultivating leadership skills, by becoming a **leader of project teams,** one can avoid being commoditized, and can reliably, predictably, repeatedly lead project teams to succeed. Such a **project leader** will not only survive but prosper.

The decision to **lead** forces one to also consider what type of leader to become, and this is at heart of what Jack has to teach us. Jack's philosophy of leadership is one of service. Jack proposes that we go beyond being mere **project managers,** and even beyond being **project leaders,** to become **service-based project leaders.** It's a broad leap, in a profession that seems to be driving itself more and more toward "administration and management," rather than anything as bold as service-based leadership. Jack goes beyond merely articulating the imperative. He provides the insights and inspiration to make us want to make the transition, and also the tools to help us do so.

One can argue that service-based leadership makes good hard-headed, pragmatic business sense, and it does. It will keep the price for what you do from being bid down, and it will increase your ability to lead project teams to success. That ought to be reason enough. But my reasons for embracing and endorsing Jack's philosophy transcend the pragmatic and speak to who Jack is and who I am. It has to do with our world view, and our view of the people whom we serve when we lead project teams. It has to do with having a profound respect for each and every stakeholder, and our view of the role we strive to play in balancing competing interests while seeking to challenge and inspire our teams. Service-based project leadership is about creating and nurturing relationships and a sense of common purpose and commitment within the entire project stakeholder community.

Most importantly, Jack encourages and helps us all to begin or continue a fulfilling lifelong journey of personal growth, focusing, as leaders, on the human aspects of project work. He provides the roadmap, the vehicle and food for the journey—a journey that is in itself a destination. A journey we must start individually and collectively as a profession if we are to be relevant in the future.

The world is changing around us. We have an important choice to make. Become service-based project leaders . . . or coffee beans.

**Jim De Piante PMP**
*Executive Project Manager, IBM*

# Acknowledgments

Writing a book is project, and just like any project, you need to rely on people to do great work with dedication, attention to detail and a passion for what you are attempting to achieve. I have been blessed to have the assistance of many such people.

First, I would like to thank Jeannette Cabanis-Brewin of the Center for Business Practices, who first proposed the idea of writing a book to me back in 2004. Jeannette's knowledge of the project management industry and its literature has helped craft this book to meet the needs of readers. Her vision and commitment to this book were unending. Being my first book, I was very fortunate to have her edit the manuscript and coach me through the process. Besides editing the manuscript, Jeannette injected ideas, provided a sounding board and constant encouragement. Thank you, Jeannette!

I am also grateful for the help of Olivia Lucas who has been working with me for several years and has been a great editor and contributor of my writing. Olivia found time between college classes and exams to conduct numerous edits on this manuscript and made substantial contributions to Chapter 23 on Communities of Practice.

I would also like to thank Aaron Miller who provided value input to the chapter on building subject matter expertise quickly. Aaron is one of the brightest project team members I have ever worked with and embodies the qualities of a service-based project leader.

I would like to thank Roberta Hill for her commitment to write Section IV on the tools and assessments. Roberta is a leading expert on coaching and assessments. Her input was instrumental in rounding out this manuscript and providing project managers with the tools and information needed to navigate their leadership journey.

I would like to thank all my customers and sponsors from whom I have learned so much over the years, on good projects and bad projects. In particular I would like mention a customer and friend, Jim Wadkins, with whom I worked on a great, successful transformational project, as well as Jack Case and John Bollman, who trusted me to lead their strategic initiatives.

I am grateful to all my team members whom I have had the privilege to lead on many strategic initiatives for your patience, your commitment to getting something meaningful done, and for what you taught me.

I would like to thank all the project management practitioners for whom I have conducted workshops and presentations. You were so receptive to these concepts as they went from ideas to workshops and course curriculum to this book.

Lastly, I would like to thank my wife Sonia and my son Jonathan for their enduring patience.

# How to Use This Book

There are plenty of workbooks on leadership, many of which provide great value and insight to help people. What makes this book different? First, the book is aimed at people running projects and programs. Second, it addresses the challenges of any transformational process. One formidable challenge to the service-based project leader is this continual state of personal transformation. Focus and energy are required to accept and endure this challenge over extended periods of time. Another requirement is applying leadership material in a practical way. Leadership material is voluminous, the concepts often similar but the application of them difficult. A lack of a meaningful framework makes leadership concepts difficult to implement. The relationship between leadership competencies—such as trust, credibility, visioning, and motivation—has an impact on their implementation.

The other formidable challenge is the development of a self-directed plan for building leadership competencies on a daily basis in one's job. The framework must be translated into clear actions to increase the chances of being successful as a service-based project leader.

To help practitioners face these challenges, I have written a book designed to motivate project managers, program managers, team members, and organizational change leaders to not only take ownership of their leadership agenda, but also provide a usable framework for building leadership skills and a plan to begin implementing them on your projects.

The book consists of four sections; the first three sections are meant to be read in the order they are presented. The last section, Section IV, written by Roberta Hill, MBA, MCC, can be used as a reference for team and self-assessments. In addition, the appendices include a short leadership theory primer for those who are new to leadership theory and a workbook that you should begin after reading Section III.

Section I, "The New Project Leader," defines the service-based project leader and examines the trends calling you to be one. Service-based project leaders continually transform themselves and initiate transformation in others. Certifications, industry trends, and professionalism are discussed to give the reader a view of the bigger forces at work within our industry. Consider how these forces are impacting you today and how they will impact you in the future.

The remaining chapters in Section I describe the serious nature of becoming a service-based project leader through self-directed leadership development. This is an inner journey that proceeds from the inside out. Understanding topics such as self-actualization, transcendence, and confidence is critical prior to embarking on this self-directed leadership journey. Before a project or program manager can jump into the service-based project leader's role through self-directed leadership, he must first discover and align his core convictions and belief system with his profession. He must see the need for the service-based project leader and feel the inherent desire first to serve, and then to consciously lead. This creates a designation for the project manager seeking to become a leader. Hopefully, by the end of Section I, you will have a desire to become a service-based project leader.

Section II begins with a review of competency in project management, including what it means to be competent, and an exploration of key project characteristics and the needs of the customer that drive the requirements from the leadership competency framework, the MyProjectAdvisor® Leadership Competency Pyramid. The remainder of this section provides the framework for leadership competencies. The framework provides an intuitive model that can be applied to project managers at any level. The framework is depicted by five layers of a pyramid, and each layer of the pyramid must exist to some extent for any project manager. This section elaborates on each layer, its relationship with other layers, and the components of those layers. The five layers to the MyProjectAdvisor® Leadership Competency Pyramid are:

- Knowledge, skills, and experience
- Subject matter expertise
- Trust-based relationships
- Consultative leadership
- Courage

A chapter is dedicated to each layer of the pyramid, with supporting evidence for the necessity of each of these layers, as well as practical advice on how to build and practice these component layers.

Once the framework has been presented, Section III is devoted to the process for self-directed leadership for the service-based project leader. This is the model for becoming a service-based project leader.

The model draws from my own personal growth experiences as well as Richard Boyatzis's intentional change theory. The process has been used successfully with project managers and team members in organizations. The project management leadership development experience consists of continual commitment and establishment of direction, assessment, and acquisition of leadership capabilities, the practicing of these capabilities, and service to one's community at large.

These steps are not linear steps that, once completed, end the process. Rather, they often occur simultaneously, feeding off each other. These steps occur on the perimeter of supportive relationships that allow the project manager to grow in a healthy environment. Chapter 24 and its appendix include a workbook for a project manager to use in developing his own personal leadership plan and exercises—to guide him through the self-directed leadership process. These formatted templates allow you to track your development and progress, which will teach you how to align timeframes with reasonable goals and help you track and visualize progress over time.

The last section focuses on tools and assessments typically used by leadership development today. The first step to begin using assessments is to become educated on the theories and research behind them. A detailed glossary and explanation of various theories supporting the numerous personality, preference, and behavior assessments are provided by Roberta F. Hill.

A thorough review of assessment tools and case studies is presented to enable project managers to better understand what the history and theories behind these assessments are, how they work, and what potential benefits one can gain from them.

A note about the way gender is handled in this book: rather than calling all project managers "he" and expecting my female readers—an increasingly large segment of the project management profession—to assume they are included, I've opted to alternate between male and female pronouns in chapters of the book. This in itself can be a "transformational" experience for male readers, I realize! But it's only fair: as the population of project managers becomes more balanced between the genders, so should the language we use to speak to and about them. Also, where appropriate, some of the names used in the stories have been changed out of respect for privacy.

Writing this book has been an intense personal journey for me; I never imagined myself writing a book, much less a leadership book. It is simply a result of following my instincts, the courage and confidence to believe I have something valuable to share, and the support from practitioners, co-workers, and friends. I hope this book is a rewarding journey for you and I pledge my faith and confidence in you to realize your full leadership potential and the importance of living it out every day.

# Introducing: A New Kind of Project Leader

If you are a project manager or practitioner in this rapidly growing project management industry, you need to know this: *Your project management services compete on a global basis.* Yes, project management is a service. Project management is also a tool, of course, but your application of it is a service to your customers. And—here's where it gets sticky—your service is becoming, if it is not already, a commodity for organizations to purchase when and where they want it.

Think about it: a service is an economic activity driven by interaction between producers and consumers. Consumers—your stakeholders—are willing to purchase this activity, and producers—project managers like you and me—are willing to render it, for a fee.

As practitioners providing a service, we must ensure that our services—in style, content, and quality—differentiate us from the pack and provide unique value. This is a tough challenge for several reasons.

One trend driving the commoditization of project management is the conversion of individually held tacit knowledge into organizational knowledge by means of standard terminology and processes. Such standardization is a catch-22 for project management. On one hand, it means the discipline is spreading like wildfire and is increasingly accessible. On the other hand, standardization and accessibility make project management less mysterious—and project managers more easily replaceable.

Another driving force is globalization, with the resulting availability of low-cost, highly educated workers, as well as cheaper, faster communication methods that redefine how we interact with our stakeholders.

Though the demand for project management is strong and growing stronger—certifications have grown exponentially and jobs in project management have expanded—project managers rarely reap the benefits. Salary increases have been held in check by the flood of new talent and the fact that more project management jobs are contract positions controlled by staffing firms. Organizations are now often looking for specialists that they can "rent" to perform planning, execution, and control of project tasks. Job descriptions read like personal classified ads—looking for Project Manager with Agile, SAP PM 3–4 yrs. experience, Project Manager with Earned Value, or Senior Project Manager with Change Management. To make matters worse, barriers to decent-paying project management jobs have increased. Many jobs requiring only 3 to 5 years of experience now also require a certification, which just a few years ago was aligned with senior-level project jobs!

The squeeze is on: project managers are viewed as a bureaucratic cost of managing change. Many organizations' approach is to reduce the cost of project management while maintaining basic services. This is having a dramatic impact on the future of new practitioners jumping into the job-rich project management market, as well as on the careers of those who have been there for a while.

If any of this is as much a concern to you as it is to me, then we better figure out a way to rise above the pack, and provide value to our customers that far exceeds their expectations!

The commoditization and specialization of project management functions are here to stay. It is not hard to imagine any project management function becoming specialized, leaving little for the project manager to do … except lead!

To separate from the pack, we must move from tactic to strategic, from departmental projects to enterprise projects and programs, from tools and techniques to people and relationships, from manager to leader—a strategic project leader. If we are to survive and prosper in our project careers, we must redefine ourselves—before others do it for us—as critical components to our organizations.

Experience has shown me that there is a new role for us: the service-based project leader. This role serves the entire project organization by creating *a meaningful experience* for team members, customers, and critical stakeholders. This experience initiates the transformation of people—including yourself—and the transformation, through people, of systems and organizations. This service encompasses a duty to initiate and sustain transformation, because of our unique position as a spearhead of change.

Some assume that team leaders are now less critical as organizations flatten their structures attempting to increase knowledge sharing and collaboration. The problem is that few organizations are aware of the need for this critical role. Instead, they roll the dice on the standard processes, methodologies, and technology to achieve nirvana in strategic programs and projects. However, they are foolishly ignoring the critical role you—the leader—can play in determining a project's lasting benefits.

If you feel the tremendous urgency to become this kind of transformative service-based project leader, self-directed leadership development, as described in this book, will be required. Self-directed leadership development is the process by which an individual, inspired by personal convictions and a purpose, develops and carries out a plan to improve his leadership competencies. This plan must be your own, not something produced by a corporate training department, human resource organization, boss, or coach. Self-directed leadership development is about *you*, not about others. The results of this journey are not contingent on others; there are no excuses.

## A Transforming Story

I recently became reacquainted with one of my former students when a new assignment brought our paths together once again after several years. As I performed due diligence on the assignment, I noticed a constant theme emerging concerning her work. Every colleague and team member on the program marveled at her performance. "Wow! She is an amazing person," commented a team member.

Only a few years ago, she was still figuring out how to spell "project management," and now she is leading a high-performance team on a multi-million dollar strategic initiative. Her colleagues universally notice her drive, passion, and unsurpassed energy. It would be an understatement to call her a player in a hugely complex, strategic technology project; she is the key player!

Talking on the phone one afternoon, something she said struck me: "I am having so much fun on this project." Probing a bit more on this subject, I concluded that she is someone who has connected with her work on both a professional and personal level. She is following, though perhaps unknowingly, a self-directed leadership plan. After a few meetings and a lengthy dinner with her, I jotted down the following observations. She fully recognizes the magnitude and significance of this project and the role it serves to the future of her company, her coworkers, and community. She has sought responsibility, fully comprehending the associated personal risks. Realizing the magnitude of the situation and her role in it, she is actively transforming her personal behaviors. By seeking out a coach, destructive negative behaviors are being replaced by positive ones that feed energy to her high-performance team. Finally, her job function on this project is "business leader," not project manager, but she relies on project management to do her job.

Although self-directed, this kind of journey is not taken alone. Of course, you must help yourself to truly change; but self-directed project leadership is an avenue through which you grow internally through project life with your team members, sponsors, and even customers.

Self-directing puts you in control of your call to lead, but by becoming a service-based project leader, you give up control by serving the best interests of others, not yourself. This seemingly diametrically opposed paradigm works to put meaning and significance back into your project work. This significance is the springboard to professional growth.

In the end, projects tell us much about who we are as individuals and how well we work with others. Projects don't fail; people fail! Potential causes of failure are many, but ultimately it is not the projects that fail, but rather the people who initiate, plan, execute, and control them. People are the common denominator across all projects. Without people, projects don't exist.

Teams are central to an organization's ability to drive change and achieve specific business results. These organizations' teams are synonymous with projects. Teams increasingly work on strategic projects and programs that involve a tremendous investment of financial, material, and human resources, and positively or negatively impact the future of the organization's health.

As organizations increasingly strive to align projects with strategic objectives, the future of these organizations is deeply impacted by teams' ability to produce positively disruptive, mission-critical, enterprisewide implementations of technology, business processes, and change management initiatives.

Success requires unprecedented collaboration across an organization's lines of business, and even across the entire enterprise.

It is becoming increasingly apparent that a strategic team leader, in addition to project management skills, needs leadership competencies such as courage, self-knowledge, and a sense of purpose, to be effective in his role. But combining competent project management knowledge, skill, and experience with leadership competencies is difficult to cultivate within organizations. Leaders often see project management as costly bureaucracy and project managers see leaders as monarchs who "just don't understand" project management.

So today you stand on the edge of a steep cliff, saddled with project office methodologies and mandates on how to proceed down into the treacherous dark valley and back up the other side. Far off in the distance is your sponsor or leader waiting eagerly for the expected results. You know the journey all too well.

All of the hype over project management—portfolio management, advanced degrees, and certifications—increases customers', sponsors', and general stakeholders' expectations of your project and your team. They expect you to journey through the valley more quickly and arrive with more benefits. You'll be satisfied just to make it out alive.

But today there is a rare opportunity to combine your project management discipline with leadership competencies that allow you to serve your sponsors and customers with distinction, creating greater value for them and increasing your career growth and satisfaction. If you can make this dramatic, risky leap to being a service-based project leader, you will find a much more meaningful—and lucrative—career in project management.

As people who are passionate about project management, we are obligated to unleash the potential power of project management knowledge to reshape our organizations into better ones that serve society and their employees. We all benefit greatly from the combination of both authentic leadership capability and competent project management. Whether it's a home project or the transformation of an entire business, project management is an essential life skill as well as a valuable skill for any C-level position. Continued, meaningful leadership development experiences starting within the project management ranks can enhance and accelerate your career, and provide substantial benefits to your organization as global markets continue to accelerate organizational change.

Unfortunately, the leaders in charge today are taking the safe route of selling "the process," not "the people." We must develop ourselves as strategic leaders if we are to grow professionally and fully realize our individual and collective potential to impact the world around us.

My goal for this book is to instigate change through *you*, by providing a practical guide through which to move from project manager to service-based project leader, using self-directed leadership development. My hope is that you will take ownership of the tremendous potential of combining project management capability with a purpose you believe in. I hope that this will lead you to move beyond project management knowledge and tools to true service-based project leadership and to position yourself for greater leadership opportunities within and outside of project management. In the end, this is a call to action for project managers to mobilize into customer-focused, service-based leaders who will leave a legacy of positive change in the world.

# Author

**Jack Ferraro** is the founder of MyProjectAdvisor®, a project management services company and a PMI® Registered Education Provider (REP), which provides project management training and leadership development. He has 15 years of adult training and education experience and has conducted training sessions and developed leadership workshops for project managers. He has 18 years of experience working with project teams and extensive experience managing complex enterprise technology and business process improvement projects.

A consultant, trainer, and mentor for project managers and teams seeking to excel at strategic project management, he has designed a leadership development program to help project managers build their leadership skills and important personal competencies. He conducts workshops and coaches project managers and teams in a dynamic fashion.

A PMI member since 1999, he is also a member of the PMI chapter in Washington, D.C. He was a volunteer on the PMI's OPM3 project, a volunteer PMP prep course trainer for the PMI Washington, D.C. chapter, and a project management presenter for the American Management Association (AMA).

A frequent writer and lecturer on project management leadership trends, he has had numerous articles published in *PM Network*, PMI's monthly magazine, including:

- "Successful Sourcing," April, 2002
- "Begin with the End," February, 2003
- "A Question of Trust," December, 2004
- "Self-Directed Leadership Development," May, 2006

His speaking engagements have included:

- PMI Global Congress North America 2004 – "Do You Trust That Project Manager in the Mirror?"
- PMI Global Congress EMEA 2005 – "Self-Directed Leadership Development – Beyond the PMP!"
- PMI Global Congress EMEA 2006 – "Recharge Your PM Battery!"
- PMI Global Congress North America 2006 – "Project Manager as Generalist: Project Manager as Obsolete"

# THE NEW PROJECT LEADER   1

*Chapter 1*

# Leadership in Project Management: A Defining Moment

## Introduction

Practicing and teaching project management have left numerous impressions on me. One is that many project managers today don't seem very satisfied. Some are experiencing doubt as to whether this career is for them. Others are permanently changed from being caught up in an extraordinary project that went sour, ruining careers and reputations. Surprising? No, we know the statistics. On the other hand, projects often positively influence the lives of project managers, their customers, and their extended communities. Those critical projects seem to have moments when a few people make remarkable contributions that positively alter the direction of the project. Their unique fingerprints cover the project, and they have left their individual, personal mark and influence behind. Any forensic project scientist can see the positive impact these leaders have had. These leaders' fingerprints indelibly cover their project work.

### Bob's Story

Success is a wonderful thing in any discipline; success on projects is unique in the number of people it benefits in various ways. Bob began his career with some relatively straightforward system integration projects. He was young, had lots of energy, took on anything thrown his way, and quickly established himself as a project manager with a proven reputation. He took a hands-on approach to his projects and managed every detail. His customers seemed very satisfied, which usually meant they paid their invoices on time. His management was content because his projects delivered revenue and better-than-expected profits to the bottom line. Bob quickly won praise from his peers and gained additional responsibilities for large projects and new customer engagements. For him, it seemed that success bred success. As demands for Bob's skills grew, his projects grew in size and number, and he poured more energy into managing the details of each project, which together spanned time zones from Europe to California to Australia. As time passed, stress levels grew, energy levels sank, and Bob became frustrated with customers, teammates, and management as he began to lose his prized control. Project profits failed to meet expectations and customer acceptance turned into an arm wrestling match. Success had stopped breeding success. Bob became so stressed, angry, and temperamental that eventually he lost the confidence of his customers, management, peers, and himself.

## Are We Better Off?

Let's step back for a moment. Almost anyone in project management is aware of the enormous growth, maturity, and recognition that have swept the industry over the past 15 years. Certifications of project managers have skyrocketed; organizations are funding project management offices and methodologies at record high levels. Educational activities and professional communities have sprung up around the world, making project management a globally recognized skill for individuals and organizations of all sizes. Success is breeding success. Or is it?

Remember when President Ronald Reagan, during his 1984 reelection campaign, asked the electorate, "Are you better off today than you were four years ago?" Project managers should ask themselves the same question. The pace of change in project management is rapid; new standards and research hit the market each year. New tools and project management information systems help us manage information better. More structure and process have been developed to enhance project organizations, allowing them to become more mature in executing programs and portfolios. Organizations are more attentive to realizing actual benefits and holding sponsors and project teams accountable for those benefits. Projects and programs are being formally initiated by executives who realize that projects are the vehicles for executing their strategic plans. The expectations of sponsors, stakeholders, and even team members are increasing at a rapid pace. High expectations are desirable for the growth of the project management industry, as these are what make the profession a relevant and valuable contributor to organizations' strategic goals and objectives.

However, project managers still operate in a treacherous environment. They have accountability, but little authority. Project structures are more closely defined, leaving less leeway for entrepreneurship. There is more complexity and information, but less time and resources for execution. Project managers must balance the daily stress of project management—demanding customers, ambiguity, high expectations, unreasonable work loads, the chaotic pace of change—and also manage their personal lives.

## Trend Toward Specialization

Increased standardization of project processes, codification of tacit knowledge, globalization of project management, enhanced technologies, information overload, and greater project complexity are driving increased specialization of project management functions. **The industry is poised for dramatic changes in how it views project practitioners.**

Many customers require specialized experts in areas such as risk, scheduling, budgeting, procurement, and so on. Others require experts in control and reporting, while still others need leaders. Specialization increases competition within the profession. Some skills will be viewed as more valuable than others, depending on customer needs and project characteristics.

Project professionals will experience rapid commoditization of skills as the pressure to control escalating project costs intensifies. Emerging are three generic roles for practitioners: Administrator, Knowledge Expert, and Leader, each with its own potential for additional specialization based on project characteristics. All three of these roles respond to unique customer needs and are critical to industry growth.

**Program or Project Administrators** are specialists serving the information needs of stakeholders: reporting, tracking, and budgeting. This role is being driven by increased regulatory and financial reporting requirements from government bodies. Executives need accurate, timely information to report to oversight boards. The value proposition for such informational services is sound project initiation and control processes with timely and accurate reporting.

**Project Knowledge Experts** are practitioners who specialize in particular industries or subject areas of project management, such as procurement, risk analysis, scheduling, scope planning, or resource management. Educational programs are increasing in number and depth to provide specific knowledge in important project management knowledge areas. Specialty training courses are common in IT niches such as telecommunications, software development, financial management, and vendor management. Demand for these knowledge experts expands significantly as project and program complexity increases. The value proposition is deep vertical knowledge and experience that provides efficient, expert service.

**Project Leaders spearhead the unique solution to extraordinary organizational problems.**[1] They make it happen and bear the burden of expectations about results. Of course, they motivate, communicate, set examples, plan, set goals, listen, persuade, align, adapt, and create, and so on, within a temporary work organization.

But the crucial activity of a project leader is facilitated decision making. Decision making drives momentum and good decisions drive toward success. A project leader's connection to the sponsor's vision and the reality of the work being performed by his team makes his role as decision facilitator of utmost importance to all stakeholders.

The project leader is arguably a unique animal—operating within a temporary organization, with limited authority and much accountability—and requires skills related to personal effectiveness, project management, and intuition about the situation at hand. His value proposition lies in leading projects and programs that do not have ready-made solutions.

You are probably reading this book because the role that is most relevant to you, now or in the future, is the project leadership role.

# Understanding Leadership

What is project leadership and how do we achieve it? There is no simple answer, but the first step is to understand the various leadership theories and how they relate to project management. It is common for senior management to ask an ordinary manager to take a leadership role in a corporate strategic initiative often overlooking a project manager poised to lead. This usually requires an individual to dedicate a significant portion, if not all, of his time to the initiative. Most project managers would love to be dedicated to just one project. The downside of this situation is that everyone from the CEO to the administrative assistant knows who is driving the initiative and whose reputation is at stake. Consequently, the outcome of the initiative is likely to have a significant impact on the individual's career.

## *Carol's Story*

Such was the case with Carol, a vice president who was tapped to lead an organizational change initiative associated with a new business model and technology. The project would affect over 5,000 employees. Readiness required significant changes in job functions, consolidation of positions, restructure of geographic territories, and $50 million in new technology. To meet senior management's benefits expectations, Carol would lead a team in implementing new processes and change the ingrained mindset of the business unit managers who had operated independently for years. In defining the readiness activity, management offered Carol some needed coaching to help her adjust to this new high-profile leadership role. In my first conversation with Carol, she said, "Jack, I know my strengths and weaknesses; I have taken a 360-degree and various other assessments. Besides, there are thousands of books on leadership available—who is to say which one is better than any other?"

Carol's point is a valid one: who *is* to say which one holds the answers? So I asked her, "Which ones do you like? Which authors do you gravitate toward: Bennis,

Bass, Blanchard, or Goleman? Which theories make the most sense—the trait, behavioral, participative, situational, or transformational? Maybe we can discuss them." Carol stumbled a bit, and then confessed she had not read much on leadership, but felt she did need some help. The point is: anyone serious about project leadership must have a broad base of leadership knowledge because it will allow a better understanding of oneself and one's environment, and help define the kind of leader one aspires to be. Just as project managers must continuously build project management knowledge, skills, and experience, if one desires to become a project leader, one must continuously build leadership knowledge, skills, and experience. This base allows the sharpening of awareness, application of natural or learned skills, and experimentation with leadership skills on projects you lead today.

There is extensive research on how one becomes an effective leader. All of the competing theories flow from either the Trait theories or Behavioral theories.

The Trait Theory states that leadership is inherited. Many people still believe that leaders are born with innate qualities that make them more likely to be good leaders. The Behavioral Theory of leadership takes the position that by observing the actions and behaviors of leaders and mimicking them, one can learn to be an effective leader. Behaviorists attempt to measure the actions and behaviors of leaders by observation to determine how they lead.[2] Then, aspiring leaders can mimic or learn these actions and become effective.

But these theories are really just the beginning of understanding leadership. Appendix A covers many of the leadership theories applicable to project management. Project managers must also have insight into an extended project environment. They must still have keen insight into a situation and how it impacts their customer, team members, and themselves. Some environments foster top-down decision-making while others prefer consensus-driven decisions. Either one will influence and impact the effectiveness of the project leader. The unique circumstances of the situation play an enormous role in leader effectiveness and team behavior. What is at stake? Who is impacted by the outcome? Who is accountable? What are the perceptions of influential stakeholders? These questions and many more create a myriad of circumstances that influence a project leader.

Leadership is complex; there is no set formula and project leadership is uniquely problematic due to the lack of authority inherent in the project manager title. Success is often temporary at best. **Attempting to lead in project management requires knowledge of self, awareness of stakeholder preferences and their messages, and the ability to quickly interpret, synthesize, and act upon the continually changing situational dynamics of the project environment.**

Leadership is also changing. It is becoming more dynamic due to greater reliance on interdependent workers instead of a dominant leader and follower model. Leadership competencies are also changing; decisiveness, resourcefulness, and "doing what it takes" are being replaced by participative management, relationship building, and the creation of an environment in which teams flourish. Leadership is being viewed as a collective and shared process rather than as a top-down one.[3]

A practitioner once asked me after a presentation where the practice field for this stuff could be found. I answered, "It's in your office or place of work, Monday through Friday. There is no real practice field; we learn this by experiential on-the-job-training." You have to create your own classroom for leadership experiences.

Time is too scarce to randomly try quick fixes or the latest leadership fad. **Leadership is learned from the inside out as you absorb the outside—your environment—into your heart and mind.**

## Challenges for Practitioners

Transforming yourself into a project leader is not a quick or easy process. The journey is unique for everyone, but the road is filled with common experiences. **You must overcome the reasons why you will not act to become a project leader. There are real challenges, but there are also excuses. These excuses are usually rooted in fear.** Most of the excuses are related to the lack of authority, the inability to lead, and organizational resistance. Let's discuss each excuse briefly and provide a rationale for dismissing it as a reason for you not to become a project leader.

### *"I Don't Have the Authority"*

Successful leaders do not attain their leadership positions by waiting for superiors to appoint them. **Leaders don't wait for someone to tell them to lead.** They start the process; reach for more responsibility, and create opportunities for themselves by serving the interests of others.

There is often more implied authority in helping others, and it is sometimes easier to help someone else than it is to help oneself. But helping others can create fear. What if you cannot help them? What if they rebuke your offer?

If you think you don't have the authority to lead, start by reaching out to serve. Reaching for more authority can be done in subtle ways that positively impact the stakeholder community, as opposed to overt plays for power.

Opportunities appear every day in which a project manager can create a better experience for customers and team members. With openness to selfless service to others, opportunities for subtle positive changes in people, systems, and your organization will begin to appear. Ask a team member, "How can I help?" One does not need authority to do that. On the contrary, some people are desperately waiting for your help.

### *"I Don't Have the Ability"*

Another common excuse is lack of leadership competencies. Some convince themselves their brain is not wired for leadership work. Fear is often at the heart of this excuse, unless one truly believes leaders are only born.

Because leadership opportunities are abundant and come in all shapes and sizes, developing leadership competencies should be a life-long goal for any professional. Leadership competencies can be improved through the proper feedback mechanisms and use of emotional intelligence skills. The journey is unique since everyone has different formation experiences.

It is also possible to learn new ways of thinking. Project managers, as individuals, have different learning styles—the optimum method of acquiring and retaining knowledge—just like everyone else. **Through practice and repetition, we can learn to use our brains differently.** A project manager whose strengths are technical in nature can learn to correlate these details into strategy, a competency of a leader. It can be the fear of leadership that creates a mental block. More often than not, project managers consciously choose to look away and not lead, rather than be limited by their lack of ability.

## *"The Organizational Culture Must Change First"*

Some convince themselves the organizational culture will not allow them to be a successful leader even if they had the authority. Waiting for the organizational culture to change is too risky. Opportunities are floating past you every day, and you must act upon them. Organizational cultures are changed by change agents, who first transform themselves. People transform organizations; organizations don't transform people.

Project managers often complain that their organizational culture will not accept project managers as leaders. They recite, "Project managers in our company only perform certain types of activities, take notes in meetings, write a charter, develop a project plan, and schedule meetings." If you can't change what a project manager does, then you can change your title, take your project skills, and start the journey as a project leader in the role of a functional manager or whatever title is needed to make it happen.

If the culture is so bad, why are you working there in the first place? Get out of there. But again, the fear of leaving a well-paying job for unknown pastures can be gripping. The capabilities of a project manager have too much to offer. **A dysfunctional corporate culture slowly eats away at one's heart and mind, so do something about it, now!**

The reality remains that change is difficult. Personal change includes challenging existing thought processes that have been ingrained from early on in life. We must confront our own fears. These are serious challenges to one's desire to change. These challenges are unique to each individual.

A young professional raising and supporting three young children is at a different place in life than someone who may have been in the workplace for 20 years and accomplished most of his or professional and personal goals.

One can also slip into a sense of normalcy. Many jobs, including project management, give workers a routine to rely on. This routine establishes a sense of normalcy, which is desirable, but too much normalcy can dull the senses. Society helps create an expectation for people to accept a normalcy. Go to school, get a degree, go to work for someone, accept what is given. Acceptance of these expectations dampens the practitioner's expectations of himself.

Practitioners are also at risk of falling into the "comfort trap." Corporations sometimes fuel this comfort trap by providing long-term incentives to entice employees to stick it out, making it very unattractive to leave pension plans or stock options. An individual propagates this by living beyond his means, taking on debt, not saving enough financial reserves, and restricting the freedom of career choices. Project managers, like others, become slaves to their own lifestyles.

## A Defining Moment

Project managers have an unprecedented opportunity to create leadership opportunities that will provide continual challenge and reward for them and their team members. The scarcity of project leadership talent shifts the balance of power from organizations to the hands of the practitioner. **There has never been a more important time for project leaders to develop project environments that are humane, challenging, and meaningful for their stakeholders.**[4]

Let's return to Bob's story. Bob's rapid rise to success initially generated further success. However, Bob did not adapt to his changing environment and the new demands being placed upon him, guaranteeing that his career projectile could not indefinitely rise. Methods that were more than effective for a handful of small projects did not work well when he had several large, complex ones. Bob's story can act as a microcosm of the entire project management industry; what has served the profession well over the past 10–15 years many prove inadequate in the years to come. Methodologies, standards, and certifications all have made significant and valuable contributions to our industry, but a defining moment for the industry is upon us. Our collective ability to define, develop, and measure project leaders will be a dominant factor in the ability to allow "success to breed success" in our industry. Otherwise, we risk losing valuable customers and the opportunity to leave the world a better place for our children. The response from you must be personal—a response that includes a choice to lead projects that transform our world.

## Summary

This is a defining moment in the industry. Project leadership is desperately needed in organizations. It has become a strategic component of delivering results in an increasingly fast-paced, information intensive, competitively charged, global environment. To be able to consistently lead in this environment, project managers must first become students of self and of leadership, then create a "classroom" of experiences in their professional and social lives. Only then can their leadership potential be fulfilled.

# Endnotes

1. Albert A. Einsiedel, Jr., Ph.D, "Profile of Effective Project Managers," in *Leadership Skills for Project Managers*, Jeffrey Pinto and Jeffrey W. Trailer, Eds., (New Town Square, PA: The Project Management Institute: 1998) 1–7.
2. Arthur G. Bedeian and William F. Gleuck, *Management, 3rd* ed. (Chicago: Dreyden Press, 1983), 498.
3. *The Center for Creative Leadership, s.v. "changing, nature, leadership"* (by Andre Martin), http://www.ccl.org "2005 Changing Nature of Leadership Report," (accessed November 8, 2006).
4. Patricia E. Boverie and Michael Kroth, *Transforming Work–New Perspectives in Organizational Learning*, Performance, and Change (Cambridge, MA: Perseus Publishing, 2001) 1.

# Chapter 2

# Emergence of the Service-Based Project Leader

## Introduction

The new role of the project manager is to serve the project organization, creating a meaningful experience for team members, customers, and critical stakeholders. This experience is the fuel that ignites the transformation of people, systems, and organizations. Such service not only achieves successful projects on time and within budget, while meeting the needs of stakeholders, but also places the project manager in a unique position as a spearhead of transformative change.

However, project leaders cannot bring about transformation on their own. Transformation requires willing participation. Transformation begins with the human and social needs of the project organization, the community of stakeholders, and their relationship to customers' business needs. **The project leader aligns personal aspirations, needs, transformative insight, and leadership to not only satisfy the overall objectives of the project, but also leave behind permanent benefits.**

The new name for those who initiate and sustain transformation through the alignment of the human and social needs of stakeholders is the service-based project leader. Her burning spirit to change herself and the world communicates itself through human relationships characterized by mutual respect, honesty, and trust. Service-based project leaders consider the purpose of project work and the value being created. They define their success not just by traditional project metrics and

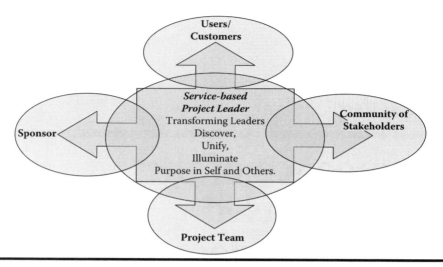

**Figure 2.1    Service model for the service-based project leader.**

rewards, but by the net social outcomes and the intrinsic value of the work itself. Service-based project leaders create work that is transformative for the individual and the project organization; they lead work that illuminates individual identities and discovery of purpose. Their leadership unites stakeholders, enabling their rapid self-organization in pursuit of a common goal. Figure 2.1 illustrates the service model of the service-based project leader.

## Importance of Transformation

Transformation means "change" or "alter," from the Latin word "mutation." It's a popular word in leadership today. Why? Maybe it is because modern life, with all of its conveniences, hastened pace, and constant disruptions, leaves us without the quiet internal experiences we need to reach our full potential. I truly believe that deep within ourselves, we long to become significant contributors to society, rather than just cope with or survive our jobs and routines.

Though projects are temporary and unique, the results are meant to be lasting; this is especially true of the larger, strategic projects that are so critical to today's organizations. Projects also require progressive elaboration, implying incremental change through planned, persistent, and coordinated steps. This progressive work is essentially transformational work: projects instigate and drive change, creating results that alter appearance or form. This change is more likely to be successful, take root, and be meaningful when the stakeholders actively participate in their own transformational process. This transformation must be initiated by someone, and the position aligned with creating and sustaining transformation is the project leader.

Stakeholders must be willing to participate, and conditions must be conducive to participation. These conditions are influenced by the leadership competencies of the project leader.

**Service-based project leaders consciously initiate and sustain transformation first through people, beginning with themselves, then through systems, processes, and finally through the organization.** Only when approached in that order does transformational project work take root and grow. A service-based project leader lives in a continuous state of transformation.

# Separating from the Pack

To step out of the role of project manager into that of a service-based project leader, a project manager must see herself as a professional whose primary purpose is to generate value through personal performance and services provided to customers. A service-based project leader has many customers: team members, critical stakeholders, sponsors, and end users. The key to value in services is creating a recognizable value proposition through performance, finding new creative services to satisfy that proposition, and emphasizing quality and the experience of the service.[1] These services must overcome the forces of commoditization. **These new project leaders do not compete on price but on value, created through unique customized services that provide meaningful experiences and initiate transformation.** Let's review the qualities that differentiate these leaders from those of project managers.

## *Efficiency*

Service-based project leaders create efficiency by focusing on high-value work rather than becoming bogged down in repetitive tasks with low value or minimal impact on project goals. Instead, they quickly master those procedural, repetitive tasks and then coach, train, and promote other resources to do them, thereby elevating both themselves and others to higher levels of performance. These leaders have a sense of where high-value work rests. They invest their personal time in learning, comprehending, and mastering these tasks and situations. This efficiency creates a superior value proposition for stakeholders, without the need to work ridiculous hours. A sense of moral and ethical purpose, their primary motivation, differentiates these leaders and is at the heart of their efficiency.

A service-based project leader creates value that exceeds her cost by several multipliers. Whether the acting leader is a contractor or a full-time employee, the customer normally has a sense of the accrued cost versus the accrued benefits to the project. For contractors, it may be as simple as the summation of their hourly or daily fees. A full-time employee's accrued costs include salary and benefits, such as vacation, training, or other perks. Sponsors, team members, and customers quickly develop perceptions about the cost-to-value relationship of project managers and leaders.

Efficiency differentiates service-based leaders by their ability to make the best use of project resources, first by starting with their own time and talents. Service-based project leaders maximize work days by keeping team members productive, aligned, in sync with each other, and by removing unseen barriers that impede progress. They create more psychological energy than is consumed. This excess energy cascades throughout the project organization; there are no lulls, spinning wheels, or half-hearted efforts.

One of the leader's primary objectives is to develop and maintain healthy teams by allowing members to naturally organize into their best-of-breed roles and facilitate the free exchange of information. She is prudent about excessive meetings that provide little or no value to the customer. Her self-organizing teams stay connected allowing accurate, meaningful, just-in-time information to flow unencumbered. Frequent time-consuming status meetings are not needed. This enables team members, particularly specialists in high demand such as engineers or analysts, to do their work, while at the same time avoid increasing administrative costs.

To accomplish this, a serviced-based project leader uses the customer's peak interacting hours—time unburdened by distractions and daily demands—to execute high-value services. Services such as facilitating critical dialogue, seeking out concerns, listening intensely, and encouraging debate enhance productivity and lift the spirit. **These services connect the disconnected, heal the wounded, inspire the uninspired, and free the encumbered,** and are rendered to stakeholders, team members, and customers with a selfless attitude.

Efficient services eliminate additional work to fix misguided project mistakes that do not serve a customer's best interests. The service-based project leader leverages each customer dollar to its maximum potential because they understand they are trustees of valuable resources that are competitively sought in organizations. Their necessary administrative functions done in off-peak interacting hours—when opportunities for high-value services are limited—are made more efficient through the self-organizing team's unimpeded flow of information.

## *Customization*

A service-based project leader doesn't throw out the proven processes, tools, and techniques she used as a project manager, but rather finds creative ways to adapt these tools and discover new services. She customizes templates and tools to meet the needs of her customers, and continually seeks to discover what is unique about her current engagement and the needs of her constituents. Because of her deep understanding and intense focus on her customers' needs, she continually adapts deliverables to meet those needs and create a better experience for stakeholders.

To create this experience, the service-based project leader recognizes and understands the progression of the economic value chain. Figure 2.2 shows the economic value chain adapted from Pine and Gilmore.[2] The natural progression of economic

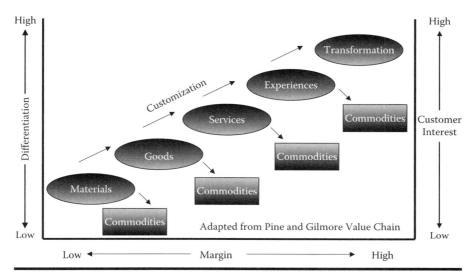

**Figure 2.2 Value chain.**

value requires basic goods and services to be customized to increase their value, differentiation, and price margin. Along this value chain is continual pressure to commoditize as the customization becomes more popular and features become more similar, causing a service provider's price margins to fall.

**Deep within each stakeholder, service-based project leader, customer, and team is the aspiration to grow and change.** Service-based project leaders seek to understand these aspirations and customize experiences to initiate and guide change in themselves and in their respective organizations. Service value is increased when experiences meet or exceed customer expectations, allowing change to become possible.

Project managers often operate at the service level of this chain; project leaders operate at the experience and service-based transformation level.[3] Service-based project leaders are competitively differentiated from their peers, get premium fees for their services, and have the greatest impact on their projects and programs. Their customized services are focused on current customers' needs which enables them to create experiences for the customer and initiate and guide transformations.

Organizations with rigid project management structures, mandated processes and procedures for all customers, unfortunately watch their project managers oscillate between goods and services, and struggle to deliver experiences. Some are able to develop and improve repeatable project processes and create goods and services faster, cheaper, and with better quality. However, practitioners in these environments find their work and subsequent value being commoditized and at risk for outsourcing.

Customized services are most recognized by stakeholders when the leader takes on projects that have a high-value proposition to stakeholders, but simultaneously carry uncomfortable levels of risk and uncertainty. High-value-proposition projects and programs make stakeholders uncomfortable because they are characterized by a history of failure, rely on cutting-edge technology, or require traditional organizational silos to collaborate. These projects and programs are center stage in an organization's strategic project portfolio. These projects gravitate toward performers who have this differentiating skill of customization.

Service-based project leaders find themselves in more strategic, complex projects and programs where an underlying transformation is required for success. In these projects, repeatable processes and templates fail to produce results as they did when lower-value goods and services met stakeholders' expectations and needs.

This emerging role uses creativity to customize and sometimes invent new project management methods and services, which creates experiences for stakeholders and initiates and guides transformation. These experiences are more than elaborate kick-off parties or milestone celebrations. **Customization is embedded into every project activity and ingrained in the mindsets of team members.** Project leaders who understand how to create and execute these experiences will command premium compensation because customers requiring transformation will pay for it.

## *Foresight*

Foresight is the head start the project leader has over her peers; once she relinquishes this advantage, she is no longer leading but is reacting to events. She is a leader in name only, not by action. Events force her hand before she can muster the cognitive instincts to lead.[4] Foresight doesn't mean predicting the future, but it does mean becoming skilled at seeing trends in how people work both individually and collectively, listening to the mood and attitude of stakeholders, and recognizing the ebb and flow of events. This is not accomplished by sitting behind a desk or in meetings. Foresight is accomplished by being close to the project's work, its outputs, and their consumption, without disrupting it.

A project manager works in the present with a plan for the future; a service-based project leader works in the present to bring about the future. **Foresight is necessary to move project teams from reactive to proactive anticipation.** When a project is in trouble, teams find themselves continually reacting to the latest crisis. The project plan becomes outdated as activities and tasks become disconnected from the plan. The crisis comes and goes thanks to heroic efforts of team members, but soon a new crisis erupts because monies were spent outside of the plan, and schedules and resources are out of sync, causing an array of potential new crises.

A service-based project leader's foresight moves the team from surviving crisis after crisis, which erodes trust and ignites fear, to executing with creativity and confidence.

Service-based project leaders distinguish themselves by simultaneously evolving two views of the project organization:

1. They are embedded tightly in the organization and are accurately aware of its tendencies, including strengths and weaknesses.
2. They see the big picture: the project organization and its related entities, the totality, as well as the movement and direction of its collective relationships, progress, and growth.

These two views give the service-based project leader valuable insight into the future. Though they cannot see these evolving conditions with 100 percent certainty, they have better-than-average odds of being in the right place at the right time to add maximum value. Decisions made with uncertainty are easily second-guessed. Even with foresight comes the risk of making the wrong decision, but the courage and intention of their actions ultimately defines the service-based project leader.

**The motivation to act in decisive ways with this foresight becomes a matter of ethics for the service-based project leader, because her conscience does not let opportunities for action slip away only to watch stakeholders pay the price for her inaction.** The service-based project leader's conscience is as alert and alive as her inner life and her ability to discern. By practicing regular discernment, a service-based project leader differentiates herself through the practice of quiet reflection, and listening to her own inner voice, enabling her to release fears and insecurities, comprehend the past, act confidently in the present, and visualize the future with keen intuition and genuine optimism.

Developing this healthy inner life is critical for a project leader's foresight, as she must live on the edge of today looking into the future with the weight of team members', customers', and sponsors' expectations upon her. Anxiety about future decisions, their timing, and confidence in one's information is mentally taxing and eroding to the health of one's inner life. The service-based project leader must trust herself and have the self-esteem and humility to know that she cannot bear this alone. Rather, service-based project leaders have the foresight to seek help from others.

## Connectedness

Work, particularly project work, can quench one's deep internal need for connectedness with self and others. This internal yearning is rooted in the potential for new self-discovery. When one begins to feel the satisfaction brought on by new self-discovery, the constraints of reality seem to be lifted, even if only ever so slightly, giving rise to life-giving energy. Service-based project leaders distinguish themselves by creating a transcendent connection between project team members, stakeholders, and customers to bring forth new, life-giving change. This connectedness displays itself as a kind of intuition among participants.

Efficient, customized services, coupled with foresight, require the harmony of project teams and customers to enable rapid self-organization and the entrance into the zone of peak performance.

Whether working remotely or in a "war room," each member radiates energy, positive and negative, that is contagious. When positive energy is radiated, participants bond together, seemingly anticipating each others' needs and next moves. Negative energy, in contrast, disconnects people from people and accelerates their movement away from each other, creating isolation.

When project organizations are seamlessly connected, leadership is shared and distributed through the project organization, not based on experience, tenure, or status, but rather based on evolving conditions and needs. **With connectedness, team members feel free to push beyond their comfort zones, because failure is not feared.** With connectedness comes the imaginary yoke of interwoven arms forming to catch those who courageously reach beyond themselves and momentarily fall. This yoke, symbolic of human resolve and purpose, strengthens with each stumble and subsequent recovery.

Connected teams create results that are significantly greater than the sum of results achieved independently. That is why these service-based leaders work tirelessly to create connectedness among participants. There is no formula for this natural phenomenon, the essence of system dynamics. Instead, it is allowed to occur naturally.

David Bohm, the architect of quantum theory, described the non-local influences of fields, "fields [which] are forces of unseen connection that are influenced by our intentions and by our ways of being."[5] The foundation of this statement is "Bell's Theorem," which Bohm argues is the most profound discovery in the history of science. It showed how two paired and spinning subatomic particles that were separated allowed one particle's spin to be altered. Bell discovered changing the spin of one particle also immediately changed the spin of its partner regardless of the distance between the two. Fields are connected through unseen forces that are influenced by intentions. Likewise, a field of connectedness among team members allows change to take place speedily, without resistance.

Joseph Jaworski, founder of the American Leadership Forum, calls this "separation in the world without separateness."[6] People, whether collocated or across the world from each other, can stay connected when certain conditions exist.

Service-based project leaders rise above organizational confines; they operate in an environment of principle, purpose, and connectedness that allows them to understand the influence of their intentions on the fields in their projects and programs. Rather than separating and manipulating these project fields in the sterile laboratory of process and control, they allow these unseen forces to work together, connected across space through their energy, sense of purpose, and humanness.

One promotes connectedness first by observing the collective fields and becoming in sync with the environment rather than separate from it. Only by becoming a part of the environment can the service-based project leader propagate a vision and mission statement that accurately represents the collective will of the participants. The service-based project leader embraces the will of the project community, assisting or enabling a new self-organizing environment that brings about new realities. The service-based project leader views the new environment as connected parts of the unified project organization and society rather than disparate groups competing for their own interests.

Efficiency, customization, foresight, and connectedness are a service-based project leader's differentiating qualities. Once the leap has been made from project manager into the new role of a service-based project leader, sustaining this differentiation is achieved by continual alignment of her core values with the purpose of her project work. Though her core values do not often change, they can shift; she must continually find commonality among her values and services.

## Filling the Role of Service-Based Project Leader

The debate goes on: between standardization as the path to excellence and creating superior performers who themselves generate excellence. Most rudimentary projects benefit greatly from standardization, but we live in a project world of unprecedented complexity, interdependence, and uncertainty. At every level in society, traditional political, organizational, and social structures are being ripped apart and reformed by globalization, technology, and conflicts that disrupt markets. **An organization's purpose, reflected in its products and services, must rapidly realign to these new structures. This alignment is riding on the backs of the projects and programs designed to create transformational change. These projects have a dire need for service-based project leaders who are unique, creative, and filled with purpose.**

## The Younger Generation of Workers

Research on the younger generation, sometimes referred to as the entitlement generation because of its desire for instant gratification, shows that this generation has a sincere interest in more meaningful work. They have little interest in building long-term loyalty to an organization, but rather loyalty toward causes. This generation has seen its parents exhaust themselves for their organization, often at the expense of personal fulfillment. Younger workers entering the workforce often have a broader base of experiences than their parents to focus their aspirations and goals for self-fulfillment. Younger workers want more feedback from superiors; they put a high premium on satisfaction and enjoyment of their work rather than on title or even pay. They think of success as "not having a jerk for a boss." They want to make a difference *now*.[7]

## The Volunteer's Story

Before her junior year in college, a young undergraduate woman went overseas to study in Germany and Finland. She has participated in many service projects during both high school and college, absorbing various cultures while helping the poor and unfortunate put their lives back together. Experiences such as these are shaping the leaders of tomorrow. She reflects on these service experiences:

> My generation has realized the value in generating change by addressing the issues they care most about directly, at their roots, with their own two hands. They camp out outside the Office of Student Volunteer Services to sign up for the service trips. All the trips are usually filled in a matter of minutes!

At William and Mary about 70 percent of all students participate in service activities contributing over 150,000 volunteer hours each year. These students find opportunities for service in one-time activities with campus organizations, ongoing volunteerism with local agencies, or as a component of a class that helps to provide an experiential understanding to issues like citizenship, justice, and democracy. As an example, currently over 70 percent of undergraduate students in the Greater Williamsburg, Virginia area volunteer. Seventy-five percent of juniors report that they volunteer weekly as compared with the fifty percent of juniors that report they volunteered at least one time during their junior year twelve years ago.

Last year, a record number of students volunteered in the Greater Williamsburg area. Students explored community needs from a variety of perspectives while gaining an understanding and appreciation of complex social issues. The summer of 2006 over twenty students received funding to volunteer across the globe.[8]

**The leaders of this new workforce spend their summers and spring breaks doing service project work, away from the comforts of home. They work with strangers in self-organizing structures that quickly come together with little supervision for the purpose of making an impact and transforming people's lives while simultaneously transforming themselves.** They are seeking meaningful work now; they are not willing to work mundane jobs to pay their dues. Soon these young people will be leading organizational projects.

It is easy for today's hurried project managers to neglect the needs of the younger work force or the internal needs of existing project workers. Some are stuck in the traditional paradigm of working in a transactional society that rests with the contract mentality that says, "I agreed to do ____ for you for ____ price." Competition for these contractual project management jobs will soon become brutal as these jobs become commoditized and young, highly educated workers from foreign countries continue to flood the market.

There is an untapped opportunity for service-based project leaders to change the world and transform those around them, using their knowledge of project management combined with personal aspirations aligned with their core values. These aspirations and values lie in the crucible next to their heart. Their strength and clarity may determine our future.

## Summary

The new role of the project manager is to serve the project organization by creating meaningful experiences for team members, customers, and critical stakeholders that fuel the transformation of people, systems, and organizations. Service-based project leaders distinguish themselves through efficiency, customization, foresight, and connectedness. Younger generations are primed to fill these positions though their educational service experiences and their desire for meaningful work, but the rewarding opportunities for service-based project leadership are open to all.

## Endnotes

1. Leonard L. Berry, *Discovering the Soul of Service, Nine Drivers of Sustainable Business Success*, (New York: The Free Press, 1999) chap 1.
2. B. Joseph Pine II and James H. Gilmore, *The Experience Economy*, (Boston: Harvard Business School Press, 1999) chap 4.
3. Max B. Smith, "Service Projects in the Evolving Economy," (Paper Presentation Proceedings of the Project Management Institute Annual Seminars and Symposium, San Antonio, 2002).
4. Robert K. Greenleaf, *The Servant as Leader*, The Robert K. Greenleaf Center, 1991, 18.
5. Joseph Jaworski, "Synchronicity and Servant-Leadership," in *Insights on Leadership: Service, Stewardship, Spirit, and Servant-Leadership*, Larry Spears and Michele Lawrence, Eds., (New York: Wiley & Sons 1998) 287–293.
6. Jaworski, Ibid.
7. Nisha Ramachandran, "New Paths at Work," *U.S. News & World Report*, March 20, 2006, 46–47.
8. The College of William & Mary, The Office of Student Activities, http://www.wm.edu/studentactivities/service/ (Accessed December 22, 2006).

# Chapter 3

# Trends in Project Management

## Introduction

Projects exist to meet human needs![1] Through management decisions or the collective will of a group of humans, a decision to fill this need is made and a project is born. These humans make up the heart of the project. Some individual or group of individuals will benefit from this need being filled; they are customers, the driving force behind the sponsor. Various people are impacted by the work of the project or have a stake in the outcome: they are project stakeholders. The initiation of these projects to fill these human needs results in unpredictable integrations of human skills, emotions, and knowledge. This dynamic integration drives continuous evolution of their expectations, expectations of each other, and the project itself. The project leader, visible to these stakeholders, is at the center of all of these expectations and is called to be a service-based project leader.

## *Carmen's Story*

Carmen, a vice president of a pharmaceutical company, had a promising career as a manager and became the go-to person for executives to jump-start key projects. Carmen was adept at pulling together groups of individuals within the organization, articulating the executive's vision and needs while organizing the human capital to get it accomplished. She had no background or formal training in project management. As projects were not her full-time job, she had never created a formal project plan or used any scheduling tools. She set a clear direction, laid out simple milestones, and helped people achieve them. She related to people, listened well, and was caring, articulate, and understood the business. As executives witnessed her ability to jump-start critical strategic projects, each began to request her help on their own project. Her reputation and relationship with executives gave these projects immediate legitimacy. Everyone had the same expectations of Carmen; that she would get results quickly and without excuses.

There are plenty of people who build successful careers in organizations by getting results through project work. Like Carmen, these solo practitioners use projects as launching pads and often are rewarded with accelerated career growth. But as organizations gain more control of project portfolios and establish standard practices for initiating and executing their projects and programs, solo practitioners are being partnered with or even replaced by process-oriented project practitioners skilled at scheduling, planning, and using project management methodologies, tools, and templates. A survey of executives done in 2003 indicated the majority of organizations have established project management offices (PMO) with 76 percent of the executives surveyed saying they have created a PMO within the past three years.[2] These project offices are now entrenched in organizations and this partnership is mired in friction as the freelancing solo and process-oriented practitioners struggle with competing approaches to meet customer needs. As PMO maturity increases, the solo ad hoc practitioner is becoming a relic of the past. But two constants remain: the human element of projects has not changed and sponsors and executives still want results.

## Growing Expectations

The continual maturation of organizational project management processes, along with the investment in project management offices, training, and methodologies, is driving sponsors' and executives' expectations of project leaders higher. Those expectations are about getting project results, not just about reducing costs. One survey found that 74 percent of respondents replied that the implementation of their PMOs had not resulted in cost reduction.[3] Increased investments in project management offices, methodologies, and education will continue to shape the expectations of sponsors and customers. As costs are passed along, so is the increase in expected service value from performing organizations and their members.

## Project Management as a Service

To succeed under increasing expectations of stakeholders, the project leader must view project management as a service. "A service is an economic activity that adds value either directly to another economic unit or to a good belonging to another economic unit." Consequently, a defining feature of a service is *direct interaction between producers and consumers* before the service can be rendered.[4]

How does this relate to project management and the project leader? The economic activity is the project—a temporary, unique endeavor with specific objectives. Traditionally, project management was viewed as an economic activity consisting of the project team's efforts to satisfy the direct needs of the sponsor and community of stakeholders. The primary economic unit is the sponsor whose need initiates the economic activity, or the project. Additional economic units also exist, such as the project team, project office, and support functions that respond to the customer need. There are also goods belonging to other economic units, a community of stakeholders not directly involved in the project, but nonetheless impacted by the project.

Embedded in this model is a subsequent model for service. **The project leader's economic activity is to add value directly to other economic units—the project team, its sponsor, the customers, and interested stakeholders.** For the project leader to add this value, he must have direct interaction with them in order to understand how to best create that value. Figure 3.1 depicts this service model.

**The project leader must regard all of these human stakeholders as consumers of his service. To satisfy their expectations, the project leader must have a strong sense of their needs and expectations.** Project management is a service that adds value to the work of the project, its team, and all of its stakeholders. Understanding the service model of project management helps a project leader understand other trends, often invisible, that are forcing dramatic changes in the project management industry. How practitioners react to these forces will influence their careers for years to come as professional project managers.

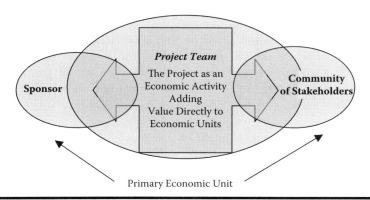

**Figure 3.1   Project management service model.**

# Trends Devaluing Project Management
## *Professional Services Becoming Commodities*

Services are economic activities that add value to economic units, driving interaction between producers and consumers. In the global environment within which we are now accustomed to operating, there are four ways in which this producer and consumer interaction is disrupted from the more traditional interactions between consumers and local service providers.

First, communication between producers and consumers occurs across international borders and continents through technologically driven means such as e-mail, the internet, video conferencing, or telephone. Transportation costs of information have been and continue to be drastically reduced. Increased telecommunication capacity, computer networks, and standard interfaces allow information to move freely across the globe at a fraction of the cost of only 25 years ago. Even airline fares for U.S. carriers have dropped 50 percent from 14.4¢ per mile to 7.89¢ per mile from 1970 to 1997.[5]

Second, the producer relocates his organization to be in closer proximity to the consumer. Organizations establish offices outside their own borders to serve new markets. Many foreign organizations set up U.S.-based offices to serve the U.S. markets; automobile production, travel, and entertainment services are a few examples. Similarly, U.S.-based organizations are extending operations abroad to serve emerging markets, such as fast food.

Third, the individual service provider moves to the consumer's country. Individuals may relocate to be closer to job-rich markets. In 2005, foreign-born workers made up 15 percent of the United States labor force, and 26 percent of those were management or professional.[6] Individuals with technical expertise have been coming to the United States for years. One of India's largest companies, Tata, supplies highly educated skilled labor on a temporary basis to U.S. organizations from their local talent pool. These workers enter the U.S. on temporary visas and perform functions at costs that are often substantially less than those of services attained by local service providers.

Finally, the consumer moves to the supplier's location, typically known as outsourcing. These are not fast food workers, nor are they just software programmers. The median salary for a PMP® in India is $21,000[7] in an IT project management job compared to the median salary of $85,000[8] made by a PMP® and permanent resident in the United States. So the cost incentive to outsource is significant.

Accompanying the decrease in the cost to move information and the associated interaction between producers and consumers of these services, there has been the gradual reduction of protectionist measures, such as tariffs. These measures are fueling more opportunities for the globalization of services that drive down consumer costs and increase service quality through increased competition. This

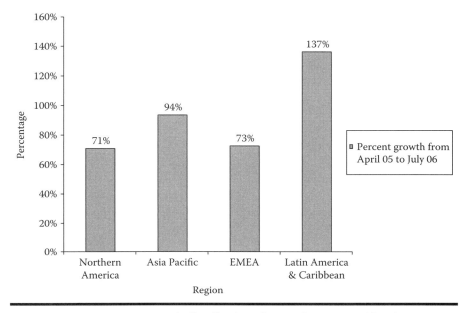

**Figure 3.2  Percentage growth distribution charts of PMP® certifications worldwide.**

increased competition reduces profit margin on services and thus requires these organizations to reduce costs to stay profitable. This also drives cost-cutting measures in the producer's business model. These service providers can procure cheaper labor or reduce labor costs through automation to remain competitive, maintain service quality, and ward off reduced margins on services. However, to distinguish themselves and regain margins, they must create new services that serve niche markets, which have less competition.

Figure 3.2 illustrates that the percentage increase in PMP® certifications in North America is less than in the Asian Pacific, Europe, Middle East, Asia, and Latin America.[9]

## The Optometrist's Story

As an example of an established profession that has become commoditized in our lifetimes, consider the optometrist. By every definition, optometrists are professionals; trained and certified in a specialized discipline, the care of the human eye, one of the most complex organs in the body. And, like project managers, optometrists are in demand. The eye care market is expanding as baby boomers age, increased use of computers strain vision, and the public becomes aware of the benefits of proactive eye care.

For years, the family practice was a mainstay in the eye-care industry, providing professional service providers with premium service fees and margins. However, this industry has undergone dramatic change. The family optometrist may not be completely extinct, but eye-care megastores began popping up in the 1980s, and now take a significant share of the corrective eye-care market. Consumers walk into an eye-care superstore and get a safe, professional eye examination. The same is beginning to happen with delicate niche eye-care services such as laser eye surgery. Only a few years ago, this was state-of-the-art surgery; now doctors perform these surgeries in shopping malls.

Demand for optometrists' services is projected to grow in the coming years. The average optometrist works 40 hours per week but many work weekends and evenings to meet the needs of patients. Emergency calls, once uncommon, have increased with the passage of therapeutic-drug laws expanding optometrists' ability to prescribe medications. A Doctor of Optometry degree requires the completion of a four-year program at an accredited optometry school, preceded by at least three years of pre-optometric study. In 2004, only 17 U.S. schools and colleges of optometry offered programs accredited by the Accreditation Council on Optometric Education of the American Optometric Association. Increasing demand and restricted supply would typically increase optometrists' income. However, median annual earnings of salaried optometrists were $88,410 in May, 2004.[10] This is modest compared to what most doctors earn.

What can we learn from this? Demand for optometrists would be higher if job efficiencies had not been gained, allowing optometrists to see more patients in a day through optical assistants and other personnel. How was this accomplished? The basic eye-care exam has not changed very much in the past twenty years, but eye-care services have standardized and technology has been leveraged. Office assistants can process hundreds of people a day; checking in patients, managing paperwork, and completing purchases, allowing the optometrists to see as many patients as quickly as possible. These efficiencies are evident in large optical superstores.

Optical goods megastores control a significant portion of the corrective eye-care market. Optometrists often work in malls and shopping centers to better serve customers who find spare moments to fit examinations into their busy schedules. Even though demand is increasing for these services, commoditization of optometry services has disrupted the basic law of supply and demand. Customers are the driving force behind these changes.

The project leader should not take much solace in the globalization and commoditization of services, though it may have helped the project management industry to grow. **This commoditization will benefit professionals who have a steadfast commitment to improve themselves through self-directed training and leadership development. Project managers who do not commit to such self-improvement will see their services commoditized.** We may not see project managers providing drop-in services in shopping malls, but the trend toward depressed salaries and greater competition should be a wake-up call.

## Information Technology Case Study

A study of other industries that have been impacted by the availability of reduced communication costs, free-trade policies, and the availability of low-cost, highly-educated labor provides insight as to why project practitioners urgently need to invest in self-directed training opportunities to enhance their skills.

The information technology industry is a recent example of such alarming trends for professional services. The lesson from the IT industry after a decade of seemingly endless growth in the United States during the 1990s is frightening. In 2000, there were 500,000 unfilled IT jobs in the United States, but by 2002, 500,000 IT jobs were lost, 200,000 of which were software engineer positions.[11] Certainly the recession and dot-com bust were significant contributors, but other factors contributed as well. The automobile industry had a similar experience between 1970 and 1990. Both industries experienced similar situations:

- Rapid increase in demand for a product or service
- Foreign competition that emphasized cost and quality
- International competition's early adoption of U.S.-developed quality methods

Since 2002, the IT industry has been growing slowly, but U.S. demand for software expertise is level, and the growth is occurring overseas due to the availability of English-speaking, technically literate, and low-cost workers who are enabled by the adoption of international software quality standards, such as Capability Maturity Model (CMM), Personal Software Process (PSP), and Team Software Process (TSP).[12]

The project management industry is in the early stages of this cycle:

- Rapid increase in demand for project management services is evident. (Growth of project management certifications and project offices)
- A supply of highly-educated foreign workers that emphasizes cost and quality. (Growth of certifications outside the U.S. in places such as India, China, etc.)
- International competition has quickly adopted standards and quality methods. (PMBOK®, ICB Competence Standard, and organizational project management and governence methodologies)

Also, a large number of project management professionals work in finance and telecommunication organizations or in internal information technology jobs. These certified project managers are working in non-billable pay structures, as opposed to professional services such as consulting and systems integration, where project management services are billed to the customer with a multiplier that includes overhead, benefits, and profit margin. These non-billable project managers are a cost of doing business for organizations. In difficult economic conditions, management typically seeks cost reductions of non-revenue activities before they tinker with revenue-producing activities.

## "What" versus "How" Work Gets Done

**Project management growth has been predominantly centered around the IT industry, which gives a practitioner more reason to take service commoditization very seriously.** When project management is viewed as a service, the work product is measured not by just the output or results, "the what," but also by the experience created for the sponsors, customers, and team members, "the how." Project office methodologies often limit their focus to "the what," such as requirements, specifications, and work product. The creation of these outputs can be standardized and even automated to some extent; for example, software test results.

When the focus is solely on "the what," or project output, the stakeholder's experience, "the how," of the leader's service is not measured. But finding opportunities to enhance this experience creates distinction and separation. These experiences set a project leader apart from a potential influx of project managers who have certifications and some practical experience. The ability of the practitioner to define these experiences, create, and measure them will substantially increase their value to the organization.

## Vertical Disintegration

Another trend that is starting to emerge in the project management industry is the natural evolution of industries to vertical integration, and then vertical disintegration into their components. Researchers have studied the evolution and reversal of knowledge-based industries. A classic example is the computer industry, in which providers such as IBM once controlled all components of the product or service. But as research increased, standards emerged, and components became more interoperable, industry maturity accelerated, and niche components suppliers grew rapidly in countries where labor was cheap. The increased competition drove costs down rapidly.

Most have first-hand knowledge of the price pressures on computer manufacturers and their component suppliers as the explosion of interchangeable components swamped consumer markets. To maintain price margins, a provider, instead of competing with these low-cost providers, focuses on high-margin knowledge-based services or integrating services and components as an end-to-end solution.

This process of disintegration is also emerging in project management. Four conditions drive this disintegration process:[13]

- The increased codification or dissemination of formerly tacit knowledge within the industry's value chain
- The development of technical standards that promote stability and codification
- The reduction of barriers to market entry
- A growing market that attracts large numbers of these *de novo* entrants, intensifying competition

## Implications for Project Management Practitioners

This process of disintegration impacts the project management practitioner. The definition of a project manager has always varied significantly within and across organizations. But as project management matures, with a focus on methodologies and certifications, the industry has propagated a view of the project manager as the central component of the project team. A project manager is viewed as a provider of services that relate to the core knowledge areas in project management, such as scheduling, cost, risk, procurement, communication, integration, etc. PMI's Project Management Body of Knowledge (*PMBOK® Guide*), defines nine knowledge areas in which the project manager performs value-added services to the project as a whole.[14] The International Project Management Association's Competence Baseline has 46 competence factors across technical, contextual, and behavioral domains.

The project manager is responsible for managing the project and leading the team through the respective process. This strongly implies a holistic level of accountability and responsiblity for planning, execution, control, and closure of this initiative. Thus, **the project manager plays the leading role in providing comprehesive services to the project stakeholders.**

Project management knowledge that was once tacit is now much more formally documented and distributed across the diverse project management industry. Industry standards are widely accepted and available. Each have processes, knowledge components, and techniques that promote the codification of project management.

The techniques for calculating a critical path, quantifying risk, or measuring earned value have been standardized, which supports the trend toward the disintegration of project management services. This allows specialists to enter the market and provide specialized project management services that threaten the general functions of today's project manager.

Technical standards within project management are also maturing; project management information systems have continued to evolve with sophisticated technologies to manage projects, programs, and portfolios. The technical definitions and standards for critical tools used with the project management industry are becoming increasingly more stable, allowing for interoperability between systems.

Few political or commercial barriers restrict the entry of supplier countries into the market. Where strong educational systems allow the teaching of the discipline of project management, it can be exported cheaply. According to Craig Barrett, CEO of Intel, "India, China, Russia and the Eastern Bloc joined the world's free economic system: three billion people. We've never had anything approaching that before."[15]

Table 3.1 depicts the relationship between natural vertical disintegration conditions and conditions appearing in the project management industry.

Project management is being branded as critical for organizational success. **A trend toward unbundling all of the responsibilities of the project manager**

**Table 3.1   Examples of Disintegration of PM Services.**

| Conditions for Disintegration | Project Management Industry |
| --- | --- |
| Codification of tacit knowledge | Standard terminology<br>Standard project management processes<br>  (i.e., PMBOK® Guide)<br>Establishment of best practices; work<br>  breakdown structure, scheduling, risk, etc. |
| Technical standards | Project management information system<br>  standards<br>Database and interface standards<br>Internet and network communication<br>  standards<br>Higher education degrees and certifications |
| Reduction of market barriers | Reduction of trade barriers (i.e., China)<br>Increase globalization trends |
| Growing markets | Growing markets and countries with low-cost,<br>  educated work forces<br>Global humanitarian and social causes |

**is evidenced on large projects and programs.** In time, these conditions for disintegration of project management services will begin to appear in the more typical organizational project work that most project managers wake up to every day.

For example, organizations are beginning to rely on specialists to create complex integrated project schedules, conduct estimating sessions to identify program costs and budgets, or perform quality checks on project deliverables. Procurement specialists are used to define vendor statements of work with payment milestones, proper language for requirements, and service descriptions to ensure the risk of procuring these services from outside the organization is properly mitigated.

# New Managerial Work

In the early 1990s, leading management authors began to write about the "New Managerial Work" being brought about by information technology. The trend is not new, but its impacts are still being felt across management, as evidenced by technology companies' inventing more personal information gadgets that allow an abundance of information to follow workers everywhere they go. Traditional decision-making theory promotes a rigid hierarchical approach to decision-making in which management makes all the decisions because average employees have insufficient capacity or information to make them.[16] But today's information technology has led to information overload; management has access to an abundance of information that it cannot process quickly enough for effective decision-making. The constraints are not the information itself, but the human brain and its capacity to process information. This constraint drives the decentralization of decision-making, since one person alone cannot process all the information.

In order to deal with this situation, companies have spent millions of dollars to combine knowledge-based job functions and processes in massive centers, striving to push decision-making capability out and down to knowledge workers in all areas of the "flattened," decentralized organization.

Technology has successfully enabled centralization only where the tasks and decisions are relatively simple. Take, for instance, Mrs. Fields® Cookies, with shops in malls and highway restaurants all around the country, whose growth without using a franchise model was a tremendous success. Mrs. Fields® Cookies controls all decision-making from a central headquarters using information technology to disseminate critical decisions and information to workers in stores across the country.[17] This is effective because the work is relatively straightforward. Compare this to processing a mortgage, which could have thousands of variables for each transaction.

As projects become more strategically aligned with organizational objectives, they inherently become more enterprisewide as well. Strategic projects can span across many or all of an organization's business units, impacting more stakeholders, both internally and externally. Thus, projects are more like complex mortgage transactions than cookie-cutter initiatives. Within the context of the New Managerial Work, more and more decisions are made at the project or team level, and project leaders must act less as mere employees, and more as liaisons between project knowledge workers and executives who need project realities translated into high-level, actionable information nuggets. This requires more business knowledge and managerial skill than the traditonal project manager role.

## Practitioner Information Overload

The project leader, of course, also suffers from information overload. A study on trends in project management conducted in Germany[18] found that the top reasons why project management was being introduced into organizations was:

- Increasing project complexity—projects becoming less linear, more complex, and more international
- Time pressure for projects—the expected timeline to complete projects is continually shortening
- Number of projects—the number of projects people must manage is increasing
- Quality—stakeholder expectations for quality project outputs are increasing

**After spending much of the day in meetings, practitioners have to work grueling hours that cut into their personal lives in order to catch up on e-mails,**

**review the latest revisions to specifications or requirements, approve timesheets, incorporate the latest PMO templates for the next round of budgeting, or read meeting minutes that are 24-hours old and already out-of-date.**

This is the life of a project professional trying to hold onto the old managerial methods without embracing the new managerial work. The new managerial work trumps the "first law of scientific management" that states the superior must have complete knowledge of the work that needs to be done and prepare detailed instructions for its completion before the work is started. Instead, negiotation and salesmanship characterize the new managerial work.[19]

## New Work, Old Model

Successful leaders in knowledge-intensive jobs create structures and processes for information that flows freely so workers can use the information to do the job as they see fit. These leaders then provide incentives for good decisions. **Unfortunately, many project management consultants and trainers still promote the old-fashioned "scientific management" view: they train project managers to control decision-making and plan out every detail of the task so workers can complete it in a timely manner without asking questions.** Although this style of management, appropriate to the early Industrial Age, has been largely discredited in the information and knowledge era, project management literature has traditionally emphasized this kind of centralized control and decision making structure for project processes. However, the evidence suggests that a program or project manager is limited in ability to process all the information available, assess its accuracy and relevancy, and determine the best course of project action in a timely manner. This model, when applied to strategic, complex projects results either in indecision or in poor quality decisions, leading to frustration among team members, customers, sponsors, and stakeholders.

One industry standard on project manager competency encourages the centralization of decision-making. The standard aligns project management knowledge with specific performance criteria and measurable outcomes. Among the hundreds of observable performance criteria described in this standard, the word "determine" is used approximately 45 times.[20] (The definition of determine is, "to make a decision about."[21])

To achieve competency according to this standard, a project manager must determine the project plan development methodology, determine product and service characteristics, insurance coverage needs, project quality outcomes, and quality policy. The list goes on and on, and among all the decision-making criteria, there are hundreds of additional performance criteria in which the project manager is creating, identifying, documenting, and developing.

Table 3.2 illustrates the verb usage in the performance criteria for project manager competency standard. The performance criteria implied by this verb usage

**Table 3.2   A Definition of Competency Based on Doing the Work … Instead of Leading the Work.**

| Performance Criteria Terms(Number of occurrences) | Examples |
|---|---|
| Determine (45) | ■ Determine the project plan development methodology<br>■ Determine product or service characteristics using expert judgment as needed<br>■ Determine need for a schedule change<br>■ Determine and quantify resource needs using planning inputs<br>■ Determine the benefits or costs of quality efforts<br>■ Determine that work product and results are completely correct |
| Identify or Select (52) | ■ Identify constraints and assumptions<br>■ Identify the relationships between project activities and activity sequencing<br>■ Identify reasons behind corrective actions<br>■ Identify potential project risk events |
| Create or Develop (42) | ■ Develop a project charter<br>■ Develop cost benefit analysis<br>■ Develop rewards and recognition plan<br>■ Develop schedule management plan<br>■ Create workarounds for unplanned risk events<br>■ Develop a procurement statement of work |
| Communicate (6) | ■ Communicate designated staff responsibilities, authority, and performance criteria<br>■ Communicate inputs to the procurement planning process |

is aligned with a command-and-control management model: a model that information overload and enterprise information systems have rendered increasingly unsuccessful.

The standard does state that a project manager's role is to lead the project through the project management processes. However, the performance criteria is skewed toward "the what" instead of "the how," as illustrated by the table. This criteria is more easily achieved on less complex projects where previous work products and templates can be reused.

**As projects get more complex, the project manager's ability to process all the information required to make good decisions can be severely limited, making this type of performance criteria unrealistic.**

## Summary

The adoption of a service view of project management offers practitioners the opportunity to distinguish themselves from their peers. But a practitioner must be aware of the trends that are reducing the value of project management services and of the profession as a whole. Globalization, the commoditization of services, the natural disintegration of services, the explosion of information and its ability to overload project managers are all risks to a project manager's value proposition to stakeholders. These risks, if left alone, will surely impact the careers and lives of many project practitioners. Leadership is the one competency of project managers that cannot be standardized, codified, or commoditized. So what should *you* be concentrating on?

## Endnotes

1. J. Davidson Frame, *Managing Projects in Organizations*, revised ed., (San Francisco: Jossey-Bass, 1995), 109.
2. Lorraine Cosgrove Ware, "Best Practices for Project Management Offices," CIO Research Reports, July 2, 2003, http://www2.cio.com/research/surveyreport.cfm?id=58 (accessed November 8, 2006).
3. Megan Santosus, "Office Discipline: Why You Need a Project Management Office," CIO Magazine, July 1, 2003, http://www.cio.com/archive/070103/office.html (assessed November 8, 2006).
4. Gary Hufbauer and Tony Warren, "The Globalization of Services: What Has Happened? What Are The Implications?" Peter G. Peterson Institute of International Economics, October 1999, http://iie.com/publications/wp/99-12.pdf.
5. Ibid.
6. U.S. Department of Labor Bureau of Labor Statistics, "Labor Force Characteristics of Foreign-Born Workers," http://www.bls.gov/news.release/forbrn.nr0.htm (accessed December 5, 2006).
7. *Payscale*, s.v. "PMP, India," http://www.payscale.com/rccountries.aspx (accessed November 8, 2006).
8. *Payscale*, s.v. "PMP, U.S," http://www.payscale.com/rccountries.aspx (accessed November 8, 2006).
9. The Project Management Institute, s.v. "April 2005, July 2006" http://www.pmi.org/info/GMC_MemberFACTSheet.asp (access November 8, 2006).
10. U.S. Department of Labor Bureau of Labor Statistics, "Occupational Outlook Handbook," http://www.bls.gov/oco/ocos073.htm (accessed February 20, 2006).

11. Galen B.Crow and Balakrishnan Muthuswamy, "International Outsourcing in the Information Technology Industry: Trends and Implications," *International Information Management Association*, 3, no. 1, (2003): 25–34.
12. Ibid.
13. Jeffrey T. Macher and David Mowery, "Vertical Specialization and Industry Structure in High Technology Industries," *Business Strategy Over the Industry Lifecycle, Advances in Strategic Management*, 21, (2004) 317–356. Elsevier, Ltd.
14. Project Management Institute. *A Guide to the Project Management Body of Knowledge, 3rd ed.* New Town Square, PA: Project Management Institute, 2004.
15. David Baker, John Shinal, and Matthew Yi, "Intel Corp. On The Record: Craig Barrett," *San Francisco Chronicle*, September 26, 2004, http://www.sfgate.com/cgi-bin/article. cgi?f=/c/a/2004/09/26/BUGV88SI8T1.DTL (accessed November 8, 2006).
16. Frederick Winslow Taylor, *The Principles of Scientific Management* (1911; repr., Mineola, New York: Dover Publications 1998) 9–10.
17. Erik Brynjolfsson, "Information Technology and the 'New Managerial Work'" (working paper, *MIT Sloan School of Management Center for Coordination Science*, Cambridge, MA 1991) http://ideas.repec.org/p/mit/sloanp/2467.html .
18. Sebastian Dworatschek, Alexander Pruschoff, and Arne Kruse, "Expert Survey on State and Trends in Project Management, PM Study Germany and PM World Study" (Paper presentation, Project Management Institute Global Congress North America, Baltimore, MD 2003).
19. Brynjolfsson, ibid.
20. Project Management Institute. *Project Manager Competency Development Framework.* New Town Square, PA: Project Management Institute, 2002.
21. *Roget's II The New Thesaurus*, (Boston: Houghton Mifflin 1988).

## Chapter 4

# Project Management Certifications: The Leadership Angle

## Introduction

Project managers who face the strong, chaotic undercurrents in the project management industry require a compass and craft to keep their careers afloat and heading in the right direction. Many are reaching for certifications to safely navigate these turbulent waters. Certifications are a point-in-time measure of one's knowledge and intent to apply that knowledge. But several factors devalue these certifications and their ability to provide buoyancy in the real world of project job performance.

## The Value of Certifications

Make no mistake, certifications provide great value in knowledge-intensive industries where the knowledge possessed by the workforce is the industry's greatest asset. Many of today's most popular certifications are technical in nature, and serve the information technology industry in which many project management practitioners can be found. Practitioners as well as vendors and organizations that employ knowledgeable, workers certainly benefit from these certifications.

Organizations benefit from certifications because they inform employers about the knowledge they are acquiring when they employ or contract human capital. Organizations compete vigorously for this knowledge, and certifications allow workers' knowledge to be formally recognized, giving them an advantage in competitive job markets, particularly in knowledge-based services. **A certification can mean the difference in a hiring decision where most other qualifications—experience, education, and references—are equal.** Certifications motivate knowledge workers to increase their formal and tacit knowledge. Benefits such as advancement opportunities, increased pay, and job security accrue through the increased availability of knowledge-based certifications. The presence of a respected standard of knowledge lends much status to a profession. A survey from a certification magazine aligned with Microsoft® showed that 47 percent of respondents indicated their salary increase was positively affected by their Microsoft® certification.[1]

Vendors also benefit from certifications. Vendor-sponsored IT certifications ensure they have enough talent to install, configure, and maintain their technologies across industries and thousands of client sites. With rapid changes in technology, vendor certifications allow human capital to keep pace, and technical certifications in the hardware and software industry have increased significantly over the past ten years.

For instance, changes to security and wireless technologies have driven additional certifications, both vendor independent and vendor sponsored, through their broad implementation and commercialization. Many of these certifications have been promoted by the vendors with a dominant market share, such as Microsoft®, Cisco®, and Oracle®, or by vendor independent organizations such a Computer Technology Industry Association (CompTIA).

## Project Management Certifications

Project management certifications are similar to technology certifications in that they attempt to measure a project manager's knowledge, skill, and experience. The most popular industry certification by sheer numbers is PMI's Project Management Professional (PMP®) certification. The most represented specific areas of interest for continuing education among PMPs are information systems.[2] This is not surprising, since the project management industry has grown up alongside the information technology industry.

Project management certifications have been beneficial to both practitioners and employers. Many practitioners are motivated by the competitive edge presented by certifications, as they can lead to advancement, increased pay, and job security.

The trade organizations that support project management certifications have seen continued growth as project management expands. These certifications are vendor independent. Figure 4.1 shows the increase in the total number of certifications from 2000 to 2006.

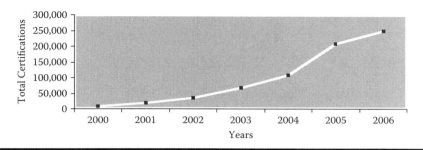

**Figure 4.1    Global project management certifications.**

Project management certifications all use a body or framework of knowledge as a basis for the certification. However, some certifications focus on knowledge and level of experience, while others include more emphasis on assessments and performance-related criteria. In other words, some certifications focus not just on what a practitioner knows, but how he performs.

## Australian Institute of Project Management

The Australian Institute of Project Management (AIPM) has three levels of certification for project managers, which are aligned with the Australian Qualifications Framework (AQF) and are based on individual assessments.

■ Qualified Project Practitioner
■ Register Project Manager (RegPM)
■ Master Project Director

The primary certification is a RegPM, which stands for registered project manager and takes 3–12 months to achieve. The RegPM is a competency assessment completed by a qualified assessor and based on a compilation of documentation and the assessment of an individual's project management competency. Project documentation and interviews with team members and peers are taken into account. The assessment is done under the guidance of the Australian National Training Authority and National Competency Standards for Project Management developed with input from AIPM. The AIPM has adopted PMI's *PMBOK® Guide* and its nine knowledge areas as a structure for the knowledge-based components. The assessor deems the candidate competent or non-competent, and provides documented feedback to the practitioner. Once certification has been achieved, it must be renewed every three years. There are over 5,000 RegPM certified practitioners in Australia.[3]

## International Project Management Association

The International Project Management Association (IPMA) has four levels of certification.

- Certified Project Management Associate—Level D
- Certified Project Manager—Level C
- Certified Senior Project Manager—Level B
- Certified Projects Director—Level A

Level A, certified projects director, must have at least five years of experience, and core competence in managing portfolios or programs. Level B, certified senior project managers, must have at least three years of experience leading complex projects, five years of project management experience, and core competence in managing complex projects. Level C, certified project managers, must have at least three years of project management experience, and core competence in managing projects with limited complexity. Level D, certified project management associate, should have some general project experience and core competence in knowledge of all competence elements.[4]

The associate exam is purely a knowledge-based certification. The remaining certifications combine technical project management knowledge, contextual experience, and personal effectiveness as the criteria for certification. The certification process includes a variety of mechanisms including self-assessments, written examinations, proven experience, and independent assessments. IPMA certification is growing rapidly around the world, with over 60,000 certified professionals at the end of 2006.[5]

## Project Management Institute

The Project Management Institute has two levels of certifications as of this writing, but work is underway to add certifications for program managers. The entry level certification is the CAPM®, a certified associate in project management. To be eligible for the CAPM, one must have 1,500 hours of project team experience or 23 contact hours of formal project management education.

The most popular certification by pure numbers is the PMP®, the project management professional. PMI has over 200,000 registered PMPs around the globe. The PMP credential demonstrates education and project experience, the completion of an examination, and a commitment to a professional code of conduct. To maintain their active credentials, one must meet continuing education requirements. PMPs must earn 60 professional development units (PDUs) every three years. Table 4.1 depicts PMI's current and future certification plans.

Another type of qualification, the certificate, has a more academic spin. Many academic institutions offer certificates in project management, which require the

**Table 4.1    PMI's Current and Future Certification Plans.**

| Certification | Description |
|---|---|
| CAPM® | Overview of what project management is, benefits of project management, why it is different than general management, overview of knowledge areas, basic initiation, planning, controlling, executing, and closing processes. Tests for basic knowledge. |
| PMP® | Detailed knowledge and experience of project management processes and knowledge areas; scheduling, cost, scope, risk, communication, human resources, etc. Tests for advanced project management knowledge and validates experience. |
| PgMP^SM | Detailed knowledge and experience associated with PMP® with additional financial, stakeholder management, communication, and leadership effectiveness skills. Tests for advanced program knowledge, validates experiences, and requires peer review of personal effectiveness. |

participant to attend and pay for a series of educational sessions that meet predetermined learning objectives. If these learning objectives are met, usually measured by an exam at the end of the class, the participants receive a certificate. Unlike certifications, certificates do not communicate any level of experience, quality of performance, or assessment of capabilities.

Certifications are continuing to adjust to market demands. In addition to measuring a practitioner's knowledge, skill, and experience, performance and personal effectiveness must be taken into consideration. Without an accurate assessment of one's capability and actual job performance, certifications will continue to be subject to criticism.

## Problems with Certification

The standards represented by a certification give an employer a quick reference to a job applicant's raw skills and knowledge, and can make all the difference in landing highly competitive positions. **However, as certifications grow in popularity as a measurement of knowledge, their potential for abuse also grows. Certifications are limited in what they can tell an employer or a practitioner.** Multiple-choice tests can evaluate knowledge and comprehension of methodologies, but they struggle to measure how a person will perform in the future.

In 1956, Benjamin Bloom created a taxonomy for categorizing learning skills by level of complexity (See Table 4.2).[6] The taxonomy provides a useful structure through which to categorize what a student is learning based on the characteristics of the questions.

**Table 4.2    Bloom's Taxomony of Learning. (Source: Adapted from http://
www.businessballs.com/bloomstaxonomyoflearningdomains.htm).**

Level 1—Knowledge–observing and recalling information, knowledge of dates,
events, places, knowledge of major ideas, mastery of subject matter.

Level 2—Comprehension–translating knowledge into new context,
interpreting facts, comparing, contrasting, ordering, grouping, inferring
causes, predicting consequences.

Level 3—Application–using information, methods, concepts, theories in new
situations, to solve problems using required skills or knowledge.

Level 4—Analysis–observing patterns, recognition of hidden meanings,
identification of components.

Level 5—Synthesis–using old ideas to create new ones, relating knowledge from
several areas, predicting, drawing conclusions.

Level 6—Evaluation–comparing and discriminating between ideas, assessing the
value of theories, choosing based on reasoned argument.

Knowledge certifications use Levels 1 and 2 to validate learning. Questions
may ask students to recall information by identifying and listing information. More
advanced certifications also use Levels 3 and 4 validation techniques in their questions.
Exam questions may include problem solving, calculations such as calculating earned
value, or solving the critical path of a network diagram. However, most of these
questions are simple in that potential variables are controlled to fit the constraints
of testing. These questions validate whether a student understands the concept, but
do not necessarily validate whether or not he can apply it in a more complex project
environment. Levels 5 and 6 are associated with advanced degrees and graduate-level
learning and often require an extensive assessment of performance. None of these
measure the personal effectiveness associated with leadership success.[7]

With the explosive growth of certification came innumerable handbooks and
guides on passing the test, opening up the issue of "brain dumping," a phenomenon in which the participants transfer test material to a written format after they
complete the actual exam.[8] **Regardless of the legality or illegality of this action,
brain dumping devalues certifications by making them easier to obtain.**
A legitimate series of questions can be purchased from a vendor or other illicit
means, which claims to be similar or even actual test questions. Vendors sell their
promise of success by using their tightly refined tools to increase the certainty of
passing the certification exam on the first try with minimal effort. This eventually
reduces the credibility of the certification.

Certifications are popular because the demand for knowledge-based expertise
moves practitioners in droves to earn the hottest certification in the hopes of making more money or increasing job security. As the sheer number of certified practitioners increases, the probability that lower quality candidates will be certified also

increases, diluting the expectations of employers and further eroding the appeal of certifications.

Associations or vendors administrating certifications continually renew their content and apply strict quality guidelines to ensure the integrity of their certifications. But even when these precautions are taken, they still risk dilution.

## Jacque's Story

Jacque, a consultant and certified project manager, reflects on her certification process:

After working on projects for about eight years, I became sick and tired of them. I enrolled in a few project management courses sponsored by my employer and came to learn what project management was really about. Learning about the discipline opened my interest in project management. Maybe there was more to projects than just gloom and doom. I attended several project management courses and digested the theory, the tools, and applicability of them in my job. After two more years of contemplating whether I should choose to make projects my career, I decided to invest in a certification. Feeling like I had found work that suited my strengths, a community and best practices that could support me, I eagerly applied for the exam. Once accepted, I traveled out-of-state to take a prep course for the exam.

The first day of class, an IT professional from a large corporation was sitting next to me. I remember vividly, as I sat waiting for the instructor to begin, hearing him state emphatically that he was there for one thing and one thing only. All he wanted was to learn enough to take the exam and pass. No more, no less. **Ever since, I have been leery of what these other practitioners really know.**

## Summary

Certifications empower workers with the opportunity to have their knowledge formally assessed and recognized. They are popular and allow workers to distinguish themselves. However, a certification's ability to measure future job performance is limited and certifications risk dilution through legal and illegal brain dumping. Certifications are big business, and like any business activity, subject to having their original intentions warped by inappropriate pressure from the profit motive.

## Endnotes

1. Michael Domingo, "10th Annual Salary Survey: Movin' on Up!," *Redmondmag*.com, September 2005, http://redmondmag.com/salarysurveys/article.asp?EditorialsID=82 (accessed November 8, 2006).

2. Michael Price, "Learning Preferences and Trends of Project Management Professionals (PMP): A Preliminary Report," (Paper Presentation Project Management Institute Global Congress Europe, Prague, 2004).
3. *Australian Institute of Project Management*, s.v. "RegPM," http://www.aipm.com.au/html/default.cfm (accessed November 8, 2006).
4. International Project Management Association, ICB IPMA Competence Baseline Version 3.0. The Netherlands: International Project Management Association, 2006.
5. *International Project Management Association*, s.v. "Certification Growth," http://www.ipma.ch/asp/default.asp?p=107 (accessed November 8, 2006).
6. *Businessballs.com* s.v. "Bloom," http://www.businessballs.com/bloomstaxonomyoflearningdomains.htm (accessed November 8, 2006).
7. Frank J. Cesario, "Educating Project Managers in the 21st Century," (Paper Presentation Project Management Institute Global Congress North America, Baltimore, 2003).
8. Michael Woznicki, "Brain Dumps, Study Guides, and Certifications," *Certification Magazine*, May 2003, http://www.certmag.com/articles/templates/cmag_webonly.asp?articleid=218&zoneid=29 (accessed November 8, 2006).

# Chapter 5

## Professionalism and the Project Manager

### Introduction

Projects are an invitation to change the world we live in, and ourselves! This potential for individual and community transformation crystallizes the difference between just having a job and having a profession.

To "certify" is to confirm formally as true, accurate, or genuine, or to guarantee as meeting a standard.[1] Food products are certified as safe; nurses are certified as competent. Project managers may be certified, but how does this relate to the notion of project management being a profession?

A professional project manager is a source of expertise to customers, sponsor, and teams, an invaluable aid to the execution of critical projects. Professional project managers supply the knowledge, planning, and execution tactics, along with the energy to inspire team members to great achievement in the midst of ambiguity. They are known for both technical excellence as well as their personal effectiveness. Are all certified project managers also professional project managers?

The National Association of Workforce Development Professionals provides a working definition of "professional" against which the project management industry can examine this question. According to this definition, the following qualities are what together make up a professional:[2]

- A commitment to advancement of knowledge
- An organized and systematic body of knowledge
- Standards of excellence

- A "higher purpose" or public interest
- A responsibility of the practitioner to the profession and the client
- A common bond based on abilities and commitment
- Public recognition as a profession

The first two requirements are easily satisfied by industry standards and frameworks such as PMI's Project Management Body of Knowledge. Responsibility to the profession and client is seen within a code of ethics and a common bond that can be found among practitioners. Public recognition is enhanced by the mere existence of professional associates such PMI, IPMA or AIPM. However, a higher purpose and standards of excellence seem to be left unaccounted for.

Certifications attempt to ensure technical competency, but cannot ensure the leadership competency necessary to influence, achieve excellence, or serve a higher purpose. Striving for professionalism encourages project managers to align themselves with a higher goal, intent, and purpose, and to pursue excellence in themselves, their project teams, and their fellow project managers. **Self-imposed standards of excellence and pursuit of a higher purpose determine whether a practitioner can become and remain truly professional.**

Individual professionalism can be pursued independently from trade professionalism. Superior performers rely less on organized professional associations because they create their own professional brand. For example, Tiger Woods is a member of the Professional Golfers' Association (PGA) but does he need the PGA, or does the PGA need him? Most average performers or newcomers will benefit more from this professional trade association, but superior performers like Tiger do not.

The question remains whether or not project management can be a profession, similar to other recognized professions such as doctors, lawyers, registered nurses, or teachers. Over 65 percent of PMI members identify project management as a profession.[3] The reality is that establishing a profession in today's environment is an arduous task. Professions-to-be must convince the public and government entities that it is in the long-term public interest to grant this status in exchange for the guarantee of increased standards of practice and better service to the public.[4]

# Obstacles to Professionalism

Significant obstacles stand in the way of project managers claiming the privileged status of a profession. Most project managers work in large organizations or in organizations that contract with large organizations to provide professional services. These organizations traditionally align their thinking with short-term goals, such as quarterly profits or revenue. They often do not think in terms of long-term social benefits, though more organizations are becoming socially conscious. Project managers normally don't have individuals as clients like a doctor would, but rather work for large groups of stakeholders. These stakeholders often relate the project initiative to a sponsor rather than a project manager.[5] These conditions separate the project manager from the specific outcomes of the work, unlike the close accountability of a doctor or lawyer for the clients' well-being or success.

To achieve professional status, the industry must also gain control over use of the names "project manager" and "project leader." As we know, today anyone can be called a project manager or leader. The industry must define exactly where the casual project manager transitions to the professional project manager. What specific services distinguish professional from casual project services? How do quality, price, and customer satisfaction define these services that are intended for long-term public good?

For project management to become a recognized profession, a body of knowledge must clearly exist to unite all professionals and hold them accountable to a standard of best practices. The *PMBOK® Guide* and IPMA's Competency Baseline are a start. But the industry is fragmented even though international frameworks are similar. Governing bodies hold their knowledge framework close, creating a lack of worldwide unity.

The reasons supporting project management as a profession are as numerous as the reasons skeptics say this status cannot be achieved. Education in project management is growing at a strong rate as evidenced by the recognition of advanced degrees in project management. Associations, growing in numbers and strength, actively promote project management as a competency applicable to every organization and walk of life. But does the average practitioner really want this organized professional status?

Along with the cachet of belonging to a profession, practitioners must accept the burden of regulation and potential liability claims. In addition, although professional associations bring benefits, they can also be self-limiting when they too narrowly define a profession or when, by establishing salary guidelines, they inadvertently impose a cap on compensation growth.[6]

To establish project management as a profession, governments, associations, consumers, and practitioners must unite and define the long-term common good associated with achievement of professional status. Whether or not this will happen cannot be predicted, but project managers should not wait for it to happen.

**Anyone working in project management today has the opportunity to align their own profession with tangible benefits to society.** The key to this accomplishment is self-driven initiative to brand one's project skills as professional and back it up with measured performance, aligned with a moral purpose and the common good.

But today's environment that produces mass certifications has been both beneficial and detrimental to the profession. The presence of a respected standard of competency lends much status to the profession. However, organizations, such as local chapters, sponsor and train individuals to become certified and focus their training on passing an exam, rather than training project managers in how to manage and lead.

In project management, certifications that boost the status of the practitioners offer an excellent method for testing basic proficiency. They provide a useful tool for people and organizations interested in acquiring and developing technical knowledge. However, it is important to remember the associated limitations, and to avoid confusing certifications with professionalism. A certification in project management does not measure one's ability to lead in today's project management environment. Leadership competency is a critical component of the true professional.

## The Leadership Void

At best, project certifications and project professionalism have three common traits. Both require continual accumulation of knowledge of project management, relevant experience in the profession, and demonstrable skills. **These traits fall woefully short of solving the crisis in project management today**.

Most are familiar with the Chaos survey (2004) by The Standish Group, which reports 71 percent of all projects are challenged. The news is full of specific projects that fall within that percentage. What about a $10 billion cost overrun—Royal Dutch Shell's liquefied gas facility project costs increased from $10 to $20 billion, unbeknownst to the CEO. In 2004, Price Waterhouse Coopers surveyed 10,640 projects valued at $7.2 million and found only 2.5 percent of businesses achieved 100 percent success in their projects. The Ontario government paid out $63 million to settle litigation with their vendor. In fact not only are the projects failing, the governance bodies—Project Management Offices (PMO)—are failing. Seventy-five percent of organizations that set up a PMO shut them down within three years because they did not add value.[7]

Surely this state of crisis cannot all be laid at the feet of project managers, though it is probable that a lack of leadership on these initiatives was a contributing factor. Organizational project maturity, management support of project management, and a myriad of other factors contribute to this crisis. **Getting out of this crisis is going to require leadership at all levels—including the practitioner level.**

A sponsor initiating a strategic project or program is aware of future career opportunities associated with the results. A project team member realizes his reputation will be tied to the outcome of the project. What kind of project manager does he want leading the initiative?

These stakeholders *want* relevant knowledge, experience, and skill, but they *need* attitudes and behaviors that enable team performance. They *need* a leader anxious for new challenges, not a play-it-safe mentality, seeking a comfortable work environment.

A highly visible project with complexity, constant change, diverse personalities, demanding deadlines, shrinking budgets, and constrained resources creates a stress-filled environment that people will naturally move away from to protect themselves from being associated with failure. **These projects *need* courageous project managers who reach for leadership opportunities, put aside their own self-interests, and focus on the communal and societal benefits for all.** If you are not extending yourself to grasp these opportunities to lead, you are a contributor to the leadership void that produces the miserable project failure rates.

## Performance and Expectations Gap

Project management is being recognized as a core competency for organizations and the demand for project management throughout organizations is increasing. Sponsors of project management either recognize the opportunity to increase benefits using better project management, or they recognize the wasted investment of resources that failed to produce the expected benefits using poor project management practices.

In either case, the expected performance of a project management practitioner, group of project managers, or project management office is less than the actual perceived performance. This gap creates an impetus for an investment in project management resources including training, education infrastructure, and methodologies. **This investment increases performance expectations of a practitioner, group of project managers, or performing organization.**

Figure 5.1 shows the hypothetical performance and expectation gap, which creates the impetus for an investment in project management. As project management maturity increases through the investment of capital, there is a resulting increase in stakeholder expectations.

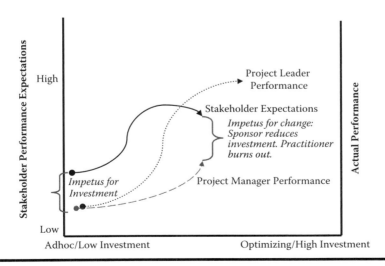

**Figure 5.1    Investment in project management creates higher expectations.**

The challenge for practitioners and performing organizations is to overcome this gap in light of the challenges of increasing social and technical complexity, shortened deadlines, limited and constrained resources, information overload, and increased workloads. Among all of these challenges, increasing the investment in project management may result in the performing organizations and practitioners improving their actual performance, as represented by the dashed line, but not enough to reach the stakeholder's expectation. Failure to overcome this gap will result in another impetus to change. Sponsors of project management may withdraw their investments and practitioners may become burnt out. To overcome this expectation gap, fresh approaches to practitioner development are needed. The new approach must ignite the dramatic leap to overcome performance expectations in today's challenging environment represented by the project leader performance line.

A study of the project management training industry in 2004 found that over 500,000 individuals participated in project management training through PMI's Registered Education Providers.[8] The monies being spent on training, certifications, project methodologies, and project offices fuel management expectations. The tremendous growth of knowledge, experience, and skills-based certifications alone do not fill the leadership development and professionalism void experienced in today's demanding environment.

## Contributors to Leadership Void

Many project management industry constituents have some accountability in the creation of this leadership void, and it is certain that all constituent groups—practitioners, sponsors, organizations, associations, customers, vendors—have a huge stake in its resolution.

### *Organizations*

Organizations have propagated this void by attempting to build mature project organizations solely through process and methodology. They resist investing in project management leadership development for a variety of reasons. Sponsors view project managers as tacticians with little business knowledge, who use institutionalized project management knowledge and best practices to complete their duties. Leadership is costly and the results are often suspect. Good leadership is hard to hold onto; with today's free-market mentality, knowledgeable workers will leave if they can earn more money elsewhere. Project managers roam from project to project, without recognition from management, because they are not permanently aligned with a traditional functional group, such as operations, marketing, or sales. **Many functional managers outrank project managers and do not value project management. They believe it adds time and cost to the process.**[9] They associate practitioners with planning, controlling, and tracking, rather than getting work done.

Thus, project managers struggle to achieve par status with these functional managers or vice presidents because these managers are entrenched in established departments that have a legacy of reporting relationships with executives, leaving them with the knowledge but not the influence to change their organizations.

## *Practitioners*

Many practitioners fuel this void, reaffirming management stereotypes by not knowing their own customers' business, isolating themselves in technical jobs, and passing up opportunities to stretch themselves. Practitioners also tend to focus more on technical project management skills rather than soft skills; a vast majority of projects are in IT, financial, or telecommunications, which lend themselves to practitioners with technical backgrounds.

When certified practitioners pursue continuing education, they focus on planning, execution, and control rather than on initiation and closure processes. Planning, executing, and controlling are important project processes of which a project manager must have a solid grasp; they are the nuts and bolts of project management. But initiation and closure are critical processes that require leadership skills: the ability to conceptualize the project vision, clearly define customer needs, and achieve measurable results.

Some practitioners view certification as the end goal of project management development rather than the starting point. Leadership training requires more commitment and control from the participant because it is personal and deepens one's understanding of the self. However, 88 percent of all project management training is still classroom-based, as opposed to being self-directed.[10] Leadership development is not as comfortable or as logical as technical training. **In 2005, 80 percent of project management training within PMI was either PMP® exam prep-based or fundamentals-based, even though the biggest training deficiencies observed by practitioners were in leadership, teamwork, communications, and negotiation.[11]**

## *Trainers*

Project management training vendors contribute to the void by promoting quick and easy classes to pass certification exams. These organizations advertise claims, such as guaranteeing you to pass the PMP exam in one week or get a full refund. These certifications accumulate huge revenues and profits for training vendors, who offer packaged materials that allow them to pass hundreds of people through their seats and never see them again. The leadership development model is different, since it requires a relationship, ongoing support and a continuous dialogue—yet 67 percent of continuing professional development for PMPs is done through training organizations as opposed to self-directed, formal academic, or volunteer service.[12]

**The dilution of the profession has become such a problem that some certified project managers have removed their designation from their business cards.** Many constituents are seriously concerned about the dilution of the profession surrounding these certifications and curative action is under way. Associations have substantially revised their advertising policy for their provider community to enforce truth in advertising, and to be representative of the integrity and credibility they desire to be associated with the certification.

## Where Do We Go from Here?

The void between service-based project leadership and project management must be defined in such a way that it can be quantified. Once it is defined and quantified, one can begin to plot a strategy to fill the leadership void. The gaps between general practitioners and service-based project leaders are:

**Relationships**—Project leaders build productive, meaningful relationships with stakeholders. Trust is the cornerstone of these relationships. Without meaningful trust-based relationships, sponsors, stakeholders, and team members have little motivation to collaborate, a project manager's foresight is impaired, and the knowledge, experience, and skill of each individual are isolated. With meaningful relationships, everyone has more at stake. The emotional investment created through trusted relationships endows the professionalism of the practitioner.

**Self-knowledge**—Project leaders thirst for self-knowledge and have a desire to continually grow in this knowledge. Project leaders renew themselves, continually changing both internally and externally to adapt to personal and professional situations. Situations that trigger visceral reactions become less intense; fears that drove unhealthy behaviors in the past are proactively managed.

**Self-directed**—Project leaders take the initiative to direct learning activities for themselves in areas of project management, leadership, and personal effectiveness. They view their jobs as a "living laboratory" and embrace experimentation that increases learning and comprehension.

**Communication**—Project leaders make a serious investment in lifelong learning of versatile communication skills. Effective project managers spend up to 90 percent of their time communicating; thus those who are not lifelong students of communication skills, including listening skills, are content with potentially doing 90 percent of their job poorly. Communication is the single most important aspect of any project. Project leaders excel at creating open, effective communication channels and actively engaging these channels. Leaders consistently find opportunities to open new channels and enhance existing ones.

**Confidence**—Project leaders must exude confidence to be given the opportunity to lead. Project leaders have confidence in their ability to lead others, even those who may be more experienced and technically knowledgeable. Project leaders translate their knowledge, skill, and experience into confidence which bolsters courage to confront the personal risks associated with leadership. They do not fear failure, but rather learn from failure and rebound with even more confidence.

**Purpose**—Project leaders, through the actions that represent their beliefs, work with a purpose. They continually internally align themselves to the purpose of their project work. When a project has significance, leaders move on. Project leaders sense the importance of their work, and are able to better handle the unpleasant or tedious work associated with projects in order to experience deeper meaning in their efforts.

**Community**—Project leaders do not isolate themselves but rather develop a community of stakeholders who become invested in their leadership growth. This community consists of social and business relationships. The members of this community support each other through good and bad times and provide comfort from the stress and chaos of project environments.

**Integrity**—Project leaders live with integrity, both personally and professionally. They are consumed with doing what is right, rather than what makes others happy. Project leaders do not seek comfort or the easy way out by compromising their own values and convictions. Instead, they set clear boundaries on what is acceptable and not acceptable for themselves, their team, and their customers, and live by them.

**Service**—Project leaders serve the best interest of others and make decisions based on reality. These leaders continually coach team members to higher levels of performance.

This is not to say that certified project managers lack these skills, or cannot attain these skills, but rather that certifications are limited in their ability to assure the development of these traits. Coupled with the dynamic environment in which a project leader must operate, measuring these traits must be done over extended periods of time. Because project situational dynamics change and resources are interchanged within and across projects, the right marriage of the situation and a project leader's traits is often happenstance and short-lived.

These leadership topics are familiar themes in projects and general management. However, in today's project management environment, the void of these traits is growing at an alarming rate. Projects are becoming more strategic, more complex, and more global, requiring greater leadership.

## Summary

Project managers aspiring to become project leaders should not overestimate the value of their certifications. Certifications in project management, while providing a beneficial harmonization of terminology and a knowledge framework among project workers, often leave a leadership void fueled by many project management constituent groups that ultimately leads to stakeholder expectations going unsatisfied. This gap can be filled by opportunistic project leaders who have the personal desire and motivation to increase their leadership competencies. Their ongoing commitment to enhance themselves and their confidence to seek leadership opportunities on projects distinguish them from certified project managers and make them project professionals.

## Endnotes

1. *Roget's II The New Thesaurus*, (Boston: Houghton Mifflin 1988).
2. *National Association of Workforce Development Professionals.* "What is a Professional?,"http://www.deed.state.mn.us/youth/conf/Chicago_11-04/E7_Mendez.pdf#search='what%20is%20a%20professional' (accessed November 8, 2006).
3. Bill L. Zwerman and Janice L. Thomas, "Exploring the Potential for Professionalization of Project Management," (Paper Presentation Proceedings of the Project Management Institute Annual Seminars and Symposium, San Antonio, 2002).
4. Ibid.
5. Ibid.
6. Ibid.
7. Michael Stanleigh, "From Crisis to Control: New Standards for Project Management," *Ivey Business Journal*, March/April 2006.
8. Joseph Zerby and others, Eds., "The Global State of Project Management Training and Education" (Paper Presentation Project Management Institute Global Congress North America, Toronto, 2005).
9. Jennifer Stanford, "What Happened to Middle Management?," (Paper Presentation Project Management Institute Global Congress North America, Anaheim, 2004).
10. Ibid., Zerby.
11. Ibid.
12. Michael Price, "Learning Preferences and Trends of Project Management Professionals (PMP): A Preliminary Report," (Paper Presentation Project Management Institute Global Congress Europe, Prague, 2004).

# Chapter 6

## Trends Favoring the Service-Based Project Leader

### Introduction

The service-based project leader has an antidote to commoditization pressures: customer focus. Customers have a sense of their needs, but do not always understand the full implications of their needs. The project team must go to great lengths to understand real customer needs.

Nothing can cripple a project more quickly than a project team or customer who does not understand the real need. A "need" emerges, is formally recognized, and then fully articulated, all prior to gathering requirements. Customer education is essential to discovering the real need. Too often this "needs life cycle" is truncated or the entire process is skipped, and the customer is assumed to know the needs and the implications of them within the context of the organization and project.[1]

Poorly defined requirements are often cited as a major cause in project failure research. Project teams now realize that poor requirements are based on a lack of understanding of customer needs, which often is a symptom of a distant relationship between project teams and customers. **Focus on the customer and the real needs is a significant value proposition for a project manager. It pushes the project manager toward the customer and provides project managers with opportunities to differentiate themselves.** The project manager taking the role of a service-based project leader can provide knowledge, insight, and experience in the needs life cycle.

She becomes an advocate for the customer, recognizing the importance of a complete needs life cycle in order to conduct further project initiation, scope, and planning activities. When customer needs are articulated properly, project planning and execution become more logical and intuitive.

As project failure rates remain unacceptably high, customers also realize they need more direct involvement in these initiatives. Customers who have tasted failure realize they can no longer blindly turn the reins over to project teams. The increased focus on the customer's real need and their increased involvement in the project are opportunities to add new value to traditional project management activities. This new value rests in the management of customer relationships. Project leaders skilled at listening, sorting, and articulating multiple customer needs can develop the project vision into a meaningful language using pictures and concepts that unite stakeholders. The subsequent conversion into workable plans is a project leader's value proposition. In fact, the trend toward a more customer-centric project manager promotes the value of the project manager, because a customer-centric project leader is recognized and valued by the customer by her alignment of services with customer's needs. She cares to understand the customer's business in detail, and aligns her actions toward customers' rational and emotional needs. She shares the view of the business opportunity. In short, she acts as a service-based project leader.[2] Table 6.1 illustrates customer-centric behavior.

Customers are keenly appreciative of a project leader whose team tailors project deliverables to their needs, rather than simply using the confines of templates or reusing previous client deliverables. They will resist if she does not show interest in their business or is motivated by forces other than their priorities. Customers embrace her when she manages the competing needs of all interested parties. Being customer-centric in project management means being stakeholder-centric!

Stakeholders perceive value when they sense the project team is working in their best interests, dedicated to creating quality outputs, and not wasting time or money. Value is perceived when customers become co-creators in the project or are at least deeply involved in decisions and review cycles. Attentiveness to the demands on their time by providing user-friendly, accessible documents makes it easier for customers to digest the relevant information and become co-creators. The necessary but often voluminous documentation of requirements, specifications, and designs rarely provides this sense of comfort and value to stakeholders. Making these artifacts meaningful is an art that creates value.

These customer-focused behaviors, though culturally influenced, are often the result of the leaders' attitudes and behaviors toward their customer. With advancements in technology, project leaders can find innovative means to increase the involvement of customers and stakeholders in projects. Project plans can be built to maximize customer involvement, address competing needs, and allow for project deliverables to be assimilated faster into their organizations.

Customers are reshaping project management because of their need for better execution strategies. Their voice is influencing the development of methodologies,

**Table 6.1  Customer-Centric or Short Sighted**

| *The Service-Based Project Leader's Customer-Centric Behaviors* | *Short Sighted Behaviors* |
| --- | --- |
| • Your entire team, not just the analysts, is interested and can articulate the customer need. | • Only business analysts or selected members understand the customer need. |
| • Your team members learn the details of the customer's business, even if not directly related to the project. | • You focus only on customer needs related to project deliverables. |
| • You create a holistic picture of past, current, and future needs of the customer. | • You focus only on the current need, with little concern for the future or historical information. |
| • You allow customer need information to be available to all team members on a need-to-know-basis. | • You promote customer need information to be held by a few with limited access to other team members. |
| • You incorporate customer education activities into project plans that enhance the definition and articulation of the customer need. | • You leave customer education up to the customer with a "buyer beware" mentality. |
| • You see all interested parties as an integrated value system. | • You focus on particular stakeholders who exert power and influence. |
| • You make decisions considering the values of the customer and their own values. | • You make decisions without regard to their own values or the customer's values. |
| • Your team looks for opportunities to provide new services to enhance the customer experience. | • You rely on replicating processes and value propositions of previous efforts. |

training, and leadership development of practitioners. You must be customer-centric, serving all interested parties, and leading your customer as cooperative creators. Are you listening?

# Projects as Strategy

Another trend driving the need for service-based project leaders is the alignment of organization strategy with projects and programs. Executives realize project portfolios have strong linkages among other projects that require constant reporting and tracking. Decisions that are made on one project often impact other projects.

A decision to unfreeze legacy software code to satisfy the needs of a new regulatory guideline may seem like a simple decision; however, other teams using that code in a test environment must be aware of these code changes and update their test plans, schedules, and resource assignments. The downstream effect of these seemingly simple decisions grows exponentially in large organizations. These organizations require leaders who can grasp the big picture and still execute tactically.

Executives are realizing the potential for gaining a competitive advantage in today's rapidly changing, chaotic environment by taking an offensive strategy and embracing an organizational project management methodology. The application of the associated knowledge, skills, tools, and techniques to organizational and project activities are then used to achieve the aims of an organization through projects.[3]

**A service-based project leader is a critical lynchpin in organizational project management maturity through her educational and advisory services.** When she embraces these services, executives will value her contributions to organizational project maturity.

## Projects Shape Strategy

Organizational project management maturity is still desperately needed in many organizations; a benchmark study published in 2003 cited that 67 percent of organizations were operating at either level 1 maturity (no established practice or standards) or level 2 maturity (existence of structured processes and standards but not considering organizational standards). Less than 20 percent reached level 3, achieving organizational standards and institutionalized processes while 7 percent indicated they were operating at level 4, in which projects are managed along defined metrics and consider past and future performance. Six point five percent operate at level 5, in which processes are in place to continually optimize project processes.[4]

One example of an organization whose strategic view of project management helped gain competitive advantage was Medco Health. As competition for prescription medications increased during the 1990s, Medco undertook a strategic initiative in 2001 to create the OMEGA facility, the world's largest automated pharmacy dispensing 780,000 prescriptions per week. Kenneth Klepper, vice president and chief operating officer, stated that, "project management is essential to our strategy for growth," and cited its importance in driving transformational change.[5]

Recognizing the strategic project's value also highlights the need for sponsors to establish an effective project leadership team. Government agencies are also recognizing the need to use project management to make government more efficient. The California Department of Transportation trained 11,000 people in project management in a two-year timeframe.[6] Many departments within the federal government are training staff in project management and have formal career paths and certifications for project managers. The Office of Management and Budget requires that managers of projects with budgets of over $5 million qualify for their positions.[7]

The list of high profile events using project management is increasing. China is expected to need 600,000 project management practitioners and 100,000 certified project managers in the coming years to pull off such events as the 2008 Summer Olympics.[8] When Salt Lake City, Utah hosted the 2002 Winter Olympics, using project management principles and tools to complete the 37,000 tasks, the 2002 games were declared the best ever.[9] Skilled practitioners with knowledge, practical experiences, and leadership skills are the driving force behind making project methodologies and practices successful in such high-profile efforts.

## Strategic Project Offices

The popularity of the project office is another trend having an impact, both positive and negative, on practitioners. Executives within organizations realize that knowledge of project management is intellectual capital and they are treating it as such. A majority of information technology projects operate within view of the PMO, which can influence the career development of the practitioner. **The intellectual capital once held and dispensed by a solo practitioner is now collected, managed, and dispensed from a central location to enable the entire enterprise to capitalize on this asset.** PMOs drive project management knowledge up the organizational ladder to senior management levels and horizontally across the organization.

Organizational behavior and project methodologies are evolving and organizations must strive to implement effective project management methodologies that can be a strategic tool to increase revenues, cut costs, and react to regulatory changes. Changes driven by new laws such as the Sarbanes–Oxley Act require organizations to disclose large investments, such as major projects, and accurately report how they impact the organization's financial performance. This concern is felt at the very top of organizations making project managers' work, decisions, and ultimately performance much more visible.

Executives are aware of these needs for project clarity; sponsors of PMOs cite sound project methodology (56 percent), clear reporting and tracking (38 percent), and the enforcement of standards and consistencies (37 percent) as best practices most important in achieving PMO success. They cite unreasonable workloads (52 percent), a lack of PMO authority to carry out objectives (43 percent), and a lack of support from business unit managers (42 percent) as the biggest barriers to a PMO's success.[10] These results confirm the awareness of the positive and negative aspects of placing practitioners in an environment that is structured, but in which they have minimal support, marginal authority, and often unreasonable workloads.

Most PMOs have been implemented within the last five to seven years and are still immature. As they mature, a greater percentage of projects become strategically aligned with organizational objectives. However, as the alignment increases, so do technical and social complexity. The number of integration points increases exponentially between the number of projects and programs aligned with organizational strategy creating a gap. This gap, between maturity and complexity, offers service-based project leaders the opportunity to add value through the integration of projects and programs across these portfolios.

For example, a new PMO has three projects under its control, Project A, Project B, and Project C, with an objective to increase revenue. Assuming the projects do have interdependent relationships, Project A is a new ordering system, Project B is the development of new products that drove the need for an ordering system, and Project C is a new marketing campaign for the new products. Since they strategically align with an organizational goal, increased sales, one change to Project A's cost, schedule, scope, or quality would need to be evaluated not just within Project A, but also in reference to the impacts on cost, schedule, scope, and quality of Projects B and C.

Maybe the technical lead from Project A, the ordering system, got recruited to another company resulting in a task on the critical path of Project A being delayed. The complexity of integration points among projects aligned with strategy will always exceed its maturity as measured in the number of projects and programs aligned with strategy. If all three projects are aligned with a strategic objective, for instance, increasing sales, then impact to Projects B and C, new products and marketing campaign, must be investigated to determine if any tangential impacts exist. Figure 6.1 shows potential tangential impacts from Project A's initial schedule change.

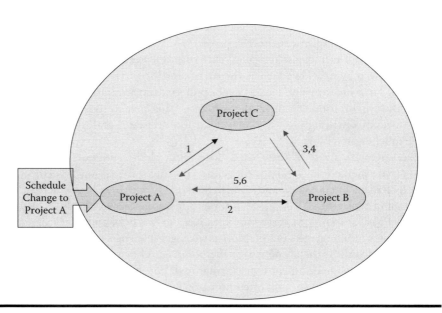

**Figure 6.1 Tangential impacts of projects aligned with strategy.**

Additionally, any impact to Projects B and C may have further impacts on Project A. In total, a strategic program or governance office attempting to align three projects that are geared to the strategic objective of increasing revenue has six potential interdependencies from just one schedule change.

These ambiguous relationships grow exponentially as projects are added to the PMO. These relationships pose significant risk to strategic programs but are also opportunities to build relationships, distill complexity, and foresee problems on the horizon.

The increased use of projects to implement organizational strategy makes project managers more visible to C-level executives, as does the elevation of the PMO out of the individual divisions (IT or R&D) to the enterprise, or strategic, level where it can most effectively oversee the enterprise portfolio of projects. The level of visibility will require making the transition from project manager to service-based project leader, performing tasks such as integrating silo organizations that do not traditionally work together but must cooperate on strategic investments. This cooperation is achieved by service-driven leadership rather than by procedures.

## Research and Education

The roots of modern project management can be traced back to World War II and the Manhattan Project, the United States government's code name for developing the atomic bomb. Imagine the application of today's formal project management processes to this highly secretive project that created the city of Oak Ridge, Tennessee practically overnight and spent $2 billion over the course of just over three years. The Manhattan Project relied on an expansive network of universities and contractors across several states, the expertise of foreign scientists, and 140,000 civilians (project team members) who worked under less than ideal conditions against unrealistic deadlines. Imagine the complexity of managing stakeholders such as the 1,000 families that were suddenly displaced from their quiet farmlands in Tennessee, aligning workers with a project vision that was held in secret, or conducting a comprehensive risk assessment of the project's handling of plutonium.[11] Was the Manhattan Project a success? It achieved its goal of developing a nuclear weapon before Nazi scientists were able to do so, but the positive and negative impacts of the project are being felt by generations in local communities such as Oak Ridge and others around the world.

Project success factors and their net social outcomes, whether at the magnitude of the Manhattan Project or an IT project, must be continually researched if we are to get better at using projects to drive positive change. Research in project management has increased dramatically as shown in Figure 6.2. Research articles have increased by over 800 percent between 1975 and 2000, and general articles about project management have increased approximately 700 percent between 1995 and 2005.[12]

These contributions are adding volumes of intellectual capital to the industry as organizations and professionals strive to understand what makes a project

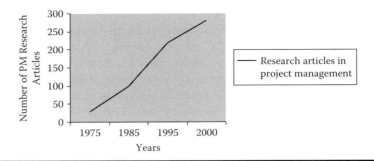

**Figure 6.2    Project management research papers.**

successful. Success is becoming more objective, and the various factors that contribute to success and failure are coming into focus thanks to scientific analysis and study. This research assists practitioners, teams, and sponsors in practice and raises the industry's stature among its customers.

The need for formal education in project management has also increased tremendously in the past 20 years and the industry has responded. The evolution of standards and the various applications of these standards across different types of projects create endless opportunities for education. Entry level education programs are now available for the average worker who finds himself assigned to project teams or even in the position of project manager. Worldwide organizations such as PMI®, International Project Management Association (IPMA), and the United Kingdom-based Association of Project Management and the Australian Institute of Project Management have certifications for the novice and serious practitioner. Many organizations offer practitioners in-house customized certifications and defined career paths for project managers.

Colleges and universities are also increasing their attention to the lucrative market for project management education. In 2005, 17 academic institutions offered master degrees in project management, 34 offered a masters of science in project management, and 51 offered a masters in business administration in project management.[13]

Worldwide, a trend is emerging to enhance the quality of these project management educational programs. The Global Accreditation Center for Project Management (GAC) is the governing body for the policies, procedures, and standards for the accreditation of university degree programs related to project management. The GAC Accreditation serves to instill quality in project management degree programs and promote professionalism in project management.[14]

Continuing adult education programs offer many programs through which practitioners can gain certificates, certifications, or general knowledge about project management. Some of these offerings are aligned with academic credits for advanced university degrees, such as masters in liberal arts, business administration, or engineering. In 2005, 70 academic institutions offered non-degree project management education in addition to the degree programs.[15] Local components of non-profit industry trade groups regularly offer members education to achieve and maintain certifications.

The growth of project management education allows customers to recognize the science behind project management. Increasing competition among training providers continues to drive costs down, opening opportunities for more stakeholders to gain exposure to project management fundamentals. The substantial growth of project management education in academia will continue to fuel project management research and legitimatize project management as a serious profession for a new generation of students already in the workforce.

## Ethics in Project Leadership

Remember Bob, the project manager who started out with some relatively straightforward projects in the systems integration business? He took over a large program and a team of software developers for a major customer who typically had three or four ongoing projects with his company. The customer was experiencing dramatic shifts in its markets, which sent its earnings and stock prices tumbling and future projects were put on hold. Bob's employer, facing their own pressures to make quarterly revenue and profit targets, realized that without Bob's customer's new projects, several billable resources would become non-billable, resulting in an unexpected loss. Bob's management decided to keep the employees working on a fictitious billable project with the confidence that Bob's customer would move forward with the new projects soon.

At month-end, his management prepared an invoice for his customer for the anticipatory work billed to the fictitious project. It was decided it was best to invoice the customer for this work, since the resources had begun working on the yet-to-be approved projects to avoid bearing the cost of these employees against the bottom lines, or releasing them and losing tacit knowledge of the customer business applications. Having no signed statement of work, Bob was faced with an ethical dilemma.

Ethics in leadership is a topic of huge interest in business and government. The topic involves more than newsworthy ethical lapses. From local politicians to university presidents to project and program managers, adherence to strict ethical guidelines is becoming critical and failure to do so is becoming very risky. Failure to align project requirements with audit and regulatory guidelines can jeopardize projects, sponsors, and a practitioner's career.

Consider the pressures to deliver new software for a financial services industry under increasingly strict customer data protection laws. The behavioral and cultural changes required to meet these regulations combined with new requirements for applications can require significant investments in programming, testing, and training that may require adjustments to scope, time frames, and cost. How does a project manager react when management either dismisses or ignores the importance of meeting these regulations?

Ethics are a systematic combination of values and morals that guide our decision-making processes and our actions.[16] To look closer, values are internal themes we possess that resonate within a practitioner's belief system. Morals are deeply held convictions that set guidelines for which behaviors practitioners deem acceptable. The marriage of values and morals creates ethical standards that guide one's decisions and actions. However, not all values and morals remain bonded or linked, and when a practitioner's values and morals are fractured, unethical behavior usually results.

**The opportunity for values and morals to fracture appears often in projects.** Practitioners who consider integrity and honesty a part of their value system sometimes do not translate them into deep moral convictions that drive their behaviors.

For example, a project manager spends three weeks with his team creating a detailed 13-month project plan to implement a new system for his sponsor. The sponsor says it is not good enough, and demands completion within six months. What is the practitioner ethically bound to do? Sponsors often cut schedules without changing scope because they feel the schedule has been padded. What if the project manager did pad the schedule and budget? Is there an ethical problem with this? Are they stealing money from other important projects?

Or, think of a project manager driving to a close-out meeting with his customer, seeking formal acceptance and final payment. Unbeknownst to his customer, the project manager gets a cell phone call and is informed by his software engineer that an undetected bug in the software is corrupting a very small percentage of the data records in their database. The project has made some money for his company, and the fix is likely to be difficult and expensive to replicate, jeopardizing his profitability-based performance bonus. What actions are ethical or unethical?

An informal survey of project managers by PMI in 1996 validated these problems. Practitioners reported pressure to alter status reports, backdate signatures, and mask the reality of project progress. Telling the truth can lead to people getting into more trouble than if they kept quiet.[17] Service-based project leaders do not hesitate to speak truth to power, but more importantly, they realize that within every communication is an opportunity to ethically succeed or fail.

Awareness of ethical dilemmas in project management is increasing rapidly. These opportunities for unethical behavior arise due to a leadership void. Leaders have convictions that align with their values and their actions—actions that consistently remind people of the leader's values.

This trend is a positive force for practitioners. Professional certifications require a knowledge of and adherence to ethical guidelines. These ethical guidelines, along with guidelines upholding the integrity of the certification testing process, are being toughened. **More responsibility is being placed on the practitioner to provide honest and accurate information to stakeholders and not knowingly make false statements or fail to disclose facts about the true status**

**of the project.** The code of professional conduct also places social responsibilities on the certified practitioner to manage relationships in a positive manner, avoid abusive behavior, and not reciprocate destructive behavior that jeopardizes project objectives.

This strengthening of ethical standards and professional codes of conduct provides a service-based project leader leverage in serving all stakeholders, credibility in the eyes of customers, and the opportunity for him to align his behaviors with professional codes of conduct by making ethical conflicts visible to stakeholders in a way that raises the level of professionalism.

## Community

Anyone attending a large project management conference will notice the commonality among all the diversity. Project management enjoys a wonderful sense of community, both locally and internationally. This community is the driving force behind the growth of project management. Not only can organizations find common skill sets around the globe, but project management practitioners can enhance their knowledge, grow both personally and professionally, and expand their perspective of the world. This global contingent of project management practitioners understands the power of project management and their ability to change the world one project at a time.

The knowledge economy has stripped organizations of their power to create their own knowledge. The traditional labor theory—workers selling their labor day by day—does not apply to a knowledge economy. **Now knowledge workers, including project managers, own their ability to create knowledge.**[18]

The internet revolution has also helped inject energy into this thriving community and has spawned specialized project management communities. Community websites allow practitioners to share knowledge, network with peers, and publish their own work. The growth of membership to these sites is increasing as white collar workers who previously would have been considered accidental project managers are now formally entering the project management profession. Project work is the future of white collar work and these workers are remaking themselves into valued change agents.

## Summary

The project management industry is growing rapidly in a world of constant change and uncertainty. White collar project workers must understand the many positive trends that are increasing the value of project management. Greater customer involvement, the use of projects to execute strategy, the growth of project offices, expanding research and education degrees, standards for ethical behavior, and global practitioner communities are positive trends for the industry.

# Endnotes

1. J. Davidson Frame, *Managing Projects in Organizations*, revised ed., (San Francisco: Jossey-Bass, 1995), chap. 4.

2. Barbara Gomolski, "Are You Really Customer-Centric?" *Computerworld*, February 21, 2005, http://www.computerworld.com/printthis/2005/0,4814,99849,00.html (assessed November 8, 2006).

3. Steve Fakrenkrog, Lisa Kruszewski, and Claudia Baca, "The Past, the Present and the Future of OPM3" (Paper Presentation Project Management Institute Global Congress North America, Anaheim CA, 2004).

4. James.S. Pennypacker and Kevin P. Grant, "Project Management Maturity: An Industry Benchmark," *Project Management Journal*, 34, no.1 (2003): 9.

5. Ross Foti, "What the Doctor Ordered," *PM Network*, September 2003.

6. Ross Foti, "Forecasting the Future of Project Management," *PM Network*, October 2001.

7. Christine M. Ford, "A growth industry: project management education programs," GCN, November 10th 2003, http://www.gcn.com/vol1_no1/daily-updates/24136-1.html (assessed November 8, 2006).

8. Project Management Institute. 2005 Annual Report. New Town Square, PA: Project Management Institute 2005.

9. Ross Foti, "The Best Winter Olympics Period," *PM Network*, January 2004.

10. Lorraine Cosgrove Ware, "Best Practices for Project Management Offices," *CIO Research Reports*, July 02, 2003, http://www2.cio.com/research/surveyreport.cfm?id=58 (accessed November 8, 2006).

11. The Manhattan Project Heritage Preservation Association, Inc., Educational Research Center, http://www.childrenofthemanhattanproject.org/HISTORY/ERC-1.htm (accessed November 8, 2006).

12. Edwin Andrews, "The Past, Present, and Future of PMI Research," (PMI Research Working Session, Project Management Institute Global Congress, Madrid, Spain, May 7, 2006).

13. Joseph Zerby and others, Eds., "The Global State of Project Management Training and Education" (Paper Presentation Project Management Institute Global Congress North America, Toronto, 2005).

14. *Project Management Institute*, s.v. "Accreditation Overview," http://www.pmi.org/prod/groups/public/documents/info/PDC_AccreditationOverview.asp?nav=0407 (accessed November 8, 2006).

15. Joseph Zerby and others, Eds., "The Global State of Project Management Training and Education" (Paper Presentation Project Management Institute Global Congress North America, Toronto, 2005).

16. Thomas Mengel, *The AMA Handbook of Project Management*. (New York: American Management Association, 2006) 227–235.

17. Jeannette Cabanis-Brewin, "A Question of Ethics—The Issues Project Managers Face and How They Resolve Them," *PM Network*, December 1996.

18. Jeannette Cabanis-Brewin, "Communities of Practice in the Projectized Organization," Interview with Etienne Wenger, *Project Management Best Practice Report* , 2, no. 4, (2001): 6.

# Chapter 7

## Discovering the New Project Leader in You

Yet every day somewhere the sun does shine,
So don't tell me it is too late,
To believe a little bit in yourself.

Nils Lofgren, "Believe"

## Introduction

A service-based project leader transforms people, systems, and ultimately organizations. To pursue this inner journey of leadership, and its accompanying risks and rewards, he must be committed in body, mind, and spirit.

### A Commitment Story

The movie, *The Cinderella Man*, tells the story of James Braddock, a former heavyweight champion whose luck runs bad during the Great Depression. Braddock seeks to provide for his family and reclaim his dignity by coming out of retirement and taking on the great German champ Max Baer, who was known for having killed two boxers in the ring with his ruthless use of power.[1]

Braddock's fall from the top was far, as he needed public assistance to provide for his family. His hard times during the Depression are marked in the movie as he struggles to meet the basic needs of his family, stripping away his dignity, but not his belief in his ability to box.

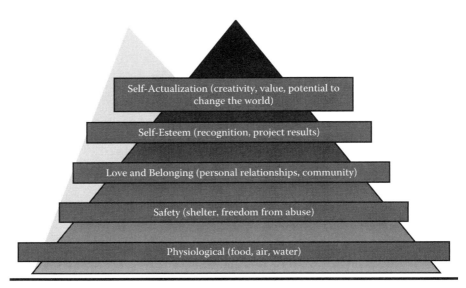

**Figure 7.1    Maslow hierarchy.**

These basic needs are the foundation of Maslow's hierarchy of human needs (See Figure 7.1).[2] The lowest level of human needs are physical needs; breathing, eating, sleeping, etc. In Braddock's case, the next level of Maslow's hierarchy—the need for safety and basic shelter—is threatened by the turmoil of the Depression. His love for his family and his needs for self-esteem and self-actualization (striving to be the best that he can with his unique abilities), are the remaining layers of the pyramid. These needs for love, belonging, status, and self-actualization are the higher-level needs that drive Braddock to get back in the boxing ring.

The lower-level needs are often referred to as "basic" needs, while the upper-level needs are referred to as "being" needs. In Braddock's case, the basic and being needs seem to have a relationship; to fulfill his basic needs, he is directed toward the fulfillment of his being needs.

Maslow's hierarchy is commonly used as a model for human needs. Viktor Frankl, a psychologist, extended Maslow's highest level (self-actualization) with "purpose" needs—the need to find meaning in one's life. Drawing on his research and personal experiences from the Nazi concentration camps in World War II, Frankl observed that prisoners in the camps who had a burning desire to live were more likely to survive. Their focus on the future, such as a vision of being reunited with loved ones, influenced their attitude toward their horrific situation.

Frankl discusses three criteria for finding meaning in life in his book, *Man's Search for Meaning*. The first is through experiential values such as love for another person. The second is creative values; finding meaning in activities such as work, projects, artistic endeavors, etc. Finally, Frankl discusses attitudinal values, critical to a healthy outlook on life, such as compassion, courage, and humor.[3] Finding meaning in life eventually results in a higher-level experience, called transcendence. Transcendence has a spiritual underpinning through which a person's meaning in life is not dependent on others, their projects, or professional life, but rather a supernatural relationship that stretches beyond human logic.[4] **Transcendence allows one to see the world differently and involves a level of integration of body, mind, and soul. It is characterized by peak performance, and removes limitations associated with people and environment.** The result is more serenity and inner peace.[5]

In the final scene of *The Cinderella Man*, Braddock has out-boxed Baer and appears to be certain to win the heavyweight title as a long shot. Braddock pursues Baer around the ring in an attempt to a knock him out, risking getting knocked out himself by the stronger Baer. Maybe Braddock's desire to knock out Baer represented an integration of body, mind, and soul and a breakthrough to a new life without the limitations of his past.

Braddock's "basic" needs appear to awaken his higher needs. The return to the boxing ring provided food and shelter for his family, but the fight with Baer is driven by the need to reclaim his lost dignity. Braddock's journey came to symbolize the common man's struggle through the Depression. He transcends himself as a representative of the people of his time and rises to a superior level of performance. James Braddock is a story of commitment and transcendence, an inspiration to millions during the Depression—and his story continues to inspire.

## Committing to Personal Change

Self-actualization and self-transcendence are important concepts in the commitment process of becoming a service-based project leader. Leadership training often produces temporary, superficial results that do not make lasting changes to individuals. The hectic pace of project life makes it difficult to focus on personal change and higher-level needs.

Project managers are paid well enough to meet physiological and safety needs, and belonging to a project organization may meet some of their higher-order needs. A project manager who is dealing with constant demands must develop a burning desire to meet his higher-level needs, even though his basic needs are satisfied. These high-level "being" and "purpose" needs cannot be ignored in this commitment process.

This poses huge challenges for practitioners. **When basic needs go unmet, it is physically and emotionally obvious to one's psyche. But when higher needs remain unfulfilled, their absence is not always obvious.** These needs are neither mandatory to sustain life, nor are they common. They must be pursued as Braddock pursued Baer.

Coupled with a desire to fulfill higher-order needs, practitioners must be aware of their natural abilities, strengths, and qualities, which when called into action bring joy and satisfaction. For Braddock, it was his boxing skills. But where did Braddock find the belief in himself to take on Max Baer even after hitting rock bottom, losing everything including his dignity, and being forced to rely on handouts to feed his family? How does a project leader come to believe in himself?

One thing that does seem to be observable in the commitment to personal change is that when lower-order needs are threatened, the shock and trauma seem to awaken higher-order needs. Often in the wake of a failed project or downsizing people ask themselves, "Why am I doing this? Is it worth it? Am I living the life I desire? What does happiness mean to me?"

## Unfulfilled Needs + Natural Abilities = Initiation of Personal Change

Here are some questions to ask yourself to determine if these higher-order needs are being fulfilled in your life and work:[6]

- Did I wake up excited about today?
- Did I laugh today?
- Did I have fun today?
- Did my relationships at work energize today?
- Do I feel optimism about the future today?

These personal questions require reflection and contemplation to determine if higher-order needs are being met. A leader serious about professional growth must evaluate who he is today, and who he really desires to be.

## Ownership: Whose Career Is It, Anyway?

A practitioner who seeks to satisfy these unmet needs must first make a conscious decision to take ownership of his career. This ownership rests in a combination of choices and decisions concerning what he desires in a career. These decisions are made with regard for the truth of his present state of being. Life choices about who he desires to be lead to continual decisions and subsequent actions to reach his ideal state of being. These decisions result in an alteration of his reality, which in turn impacts his future choices. This process is illustrated in Figure 7.2.

For example, a busy project manager may choose family life over a promotion that would require significant travel. This decision leads to an altered state

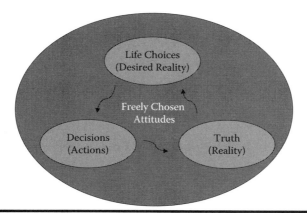

**Figure 7.2   Ownership of your choices, decisions, and outcomes.**

of being: working more conventional hours in the same office, a similar routine, and the same people. The truth may be that he misses the excitement of project work, meeting new people, and the constant challenges. This truth may lead him to conclude that there is conflict in the choice between family and work, which may lead to revisiting the initial decision. These decisions must align with who she really is. Unfortunately, many are too busy to even think about it, while others spend a lifetime trying to figure this out.

## Life Choices

A life choice commits a person to a state of being. This choice is the foundation upon which other choices are made. In order to make good life choices, he must be true to himself in thought and action, regardless of feelings and surroundings.[7] **People who have been successful in a technical career and then accidentally become a project manager often find the additional responsibilities preclude an evaluation of whether these new decisions are in tune with their desired state of being**. The new demands inherent to a project manager role include constant social interaction, dealing with ambiguity, delegating to others, and leading a team in spite of a lack of authority. These demands may not align with life choices and higher-order needs, even though more money or a new title initially created a feeling of satisfaction.

## Decisions

Decisions are actions required to fulfill the life choice of being true to himself. These decisions range from momentous ones to daily, unnoticeable ones. A decision to become a certified project manager is not a life choice, but rather a decision to fulfill a life choice. If his life choice is not clearly made, the decision to invest in a certification may be misguided. In applying the concept of life choices and decisions he might include choosing to:

- Work with people (on teams or as a liaison with management)
- Contribute to society
- Share the experience of creating new products or services

As an example of a decision made to support one of these choices, he would:

- Be a project manager
- Learn interpersonal skills
- Become a service-based project leader

### Truth

Truth can mean conformity to fact or actuality. But in the context of commitment to a service-based project leadership career, **truth is more about fidelity to an original or standard. This fidelity is measured by the discrepancy between present reality and one's desired state of being**. This fidelity is achieved through a pursuit of an inner calling, until his present career is aligned with the desired state.

Many practitioners—not just project managers, but doctors, lawyers, and others—work backwards. They make decisions about their careers before making a life choice about being true to themselves. The external journey of choosing a career or profession is too often made before the internal journey—the serious consideration of one's calling. The result is years of hard work, often producing results, but not fulfilling one's potential or higher order needs.

It is not too late to start your second career as a service-based project leader. Many successful business people reach their peak at 45 years of age. After doing very much the same kind of work for 20 years, their learning and contributions wane. Job satisfaction and challenges diminish. Yet they still have to face another 25 years of productive work.[8]

## Personal Confidence

Confidence is the bridge between expectations and performance. The leader's primary task is to build this bridge in order to attract the resources, attitudes, and discipline required for success.[9]

A service-based project leader must first instill inner confidence and belief in himself before attempting to build the bridge for others. Fear wages its battle against confidence. A constant stream of new projects, players, subject matter, and political dynamics all contribute to unknowns, which contribute to fear, which undermine confidence. **Fear has a powerful smell; like easily spooked mustangs, team members recognize a lack of confidence in their project leader**. A project leader must be sure of himself in spite of this ambiguity. A service-based project leader's confidence stems from his ability to make relationships work, more so than knowledge or processes. This ability to build confidence through the constancy of project relationships is a critical success factor to his leadership efforts.

Every organization seems to have projects that people fear. A project embroiled in controversy, continually criticized behind closed doors, and steeped in high turnover ultimately breeds a lack of confidence. Though off-site meetings and pep rallies can give some short-term elation, the root cause is a lack of self-confident project leaders, which limits the confidence of the team and customer.

## Group Confidence

Whether in sports, politics, or business, success seems to breed success. It takes a dramatic overhaul of attitudes and behaviors for losers to turn themselves around. Both visible behaviors and internal habits of thought prepare a team for success. **Confident teams share a passion for accountability, collaboration, and initiative.** They form around a worthy purpose that is attainable and objectively measurable. They demand accountability because they understand interdependence; they collaborate openly and freely because there is no time or room for blame; their relationships embody trust. They act with decisive initiative because they have purpose and time is of the essence.[10]

A leader's attitude drives his behavior and his behavior drives others' attitudes, which in turn ripple into *their* behaviors. Group moods and emotions are contagious, and projects are no exception. Establishing group confidence is a critical part of any project leader's performance appraisal.

## Psychological Barriers

Belief in oneself sounds nice, but putting it into practice can be difficult, particularly with the psychological background a leader carries forward in life.

A simple model describing how life experiences impact one's confidence, self-esteem, and ability to take risks is Eric Berne's *Transactional Analysis*. Berne's theory is that each individual has three life states (or ego states): the Adult (the only rational state), the Parent, and the Child. These states are played out in interactions with others externally, or internally within one's mind. The Parent state derives from authority figures or events that are imposed upon a person, and normally focuses on what is acceptable behavior and what is not. The Child state reflects one's feelings when exposed to external events. The brain records and stores these events and feelings and, later, the Parent and Child states play themselves out in Adult life, often without being recognized as irrational responses to the present situation.

Berne concludes when children are continually subjected to correction from parents, they form the attitude "I'm not ok, you're ok." This is not to imply that parents should not correct their children. However, Berne's research concludes that many people do not emerge from this state. As adults, they feel that they live at the mercy of others, which leads them to continually seek approval.

Some children move out of the "I'm not ok, you're ok," and into a second life position of, "I'm not ok, you're not ok." This comes about when parental correction is applied without supportive, positive reinforcement. The child develops an attitude that life is difficult, troubling, and must be survived alone and carries this into adult life.

Other children move into an attitude of "I'm ok, you're not ok," which can be carried into adult life as the feeling that life is very challenging because of the incompetence that surrounds them.

It's the fourth attitude of "I'm ok, you're ok," which represents the healthiest position. This state requires a balance of self-confidence that allows the establishment of healthy relationships and self-esteem with control of the negative, blaming responses that fuel the sense that other people are "not ok."[11]

The adult "I'm not ok" or "You're not ok" attitudes are not conducive to projects, their managers, or leaders. The project environment with its inherent demands and ambiguity can fuel these attitudes, undermining one's confidence and ability to lead, making it easier to be resigned to a less than successful outcome, or even to fail.

However, with confidence, a project manager is more likely to transition into the behaviors of a leader. These behaviors include anything from confidently strolling through the office to fostering open communication, to knowing project team members as people, not just as workers, and treating them with respect.

The service-based project leader's self-confidence leads to personal transformational experiences. By instilling confidence in the team and customer, the initiation of transformation begins. The first step is to build the bridge of confidence. This may sound overwhelming to a busy professional settled into a career and life position, but it is never too late to believe in yourself.

## Summary

Commitment begins with a desire to fulfill the higher-order needs described in the work of Maslow and Frankl, paired with an awareness of one's natural abilities, strengths, and qualities.

Practitioners who seek to satisfy these needs must first make a conscious decision to take ownership of their destiny. This ownership rests in a combination of life choices and decisions concerning what one desires in life and a career. A service-based project leader must first instill inner confidence in himself before building a bridge of confidence for others.

# Endnotes

1. James J. Braddock—The Official Website s.v. "the movie," http://www.jamesjbraddock. com/movie/ (accessed November 22, 2006).
2. Arthur G. Bedeian and William F. Gleuck, *Management 3rd ed.* (Chicago: Dreyden Press, 1983), 139.
3. Viktor E. Frankl, Man's Search For Meaning (Boston: Beacon Press 2006), 111.
4. Ibid.
5. Leland R. Kaiser, s.v. "Increasing Sense of Personal Freedom," http://www.kaiser. net/seriesindex.cfm?cat_id=29 (accessed November 22, 2006).
6. Daniel Goleman, Richard Boyatzis, and Annie McKee, *Primal Leadership: Learning to Lead with Emotional Intelligence* (Boston: Harvard Business School Press, 2004), 129.
7. Robert Fritz, *The Path of Least Resistance* (New York: Fawcett Columbine), 188.
8. Peter F. Drucker, "Managing Oneself," *Harvard Business Review*, January 2005, 108.
9. Rosabeth Moss Kanter, Confidence—*How Winning Streaks & Losing Streaks Begin & End* (New York: Crown Business, 2004), 3.
10. Ibid.
11. David Hillson and Ruth Murray-Webster, *Understanding and Managing Risk Attitude* (Hants, England: Gower Publishing, 2005), 102–103.

*Chapter 8*

# Finding Meaning in Creating, Rather Than Problem Solving

## Introduction

Project management literature often refers to the need for project managers to be good problem solvers. Unfortunately, problem solving on projects is not as binary as solving a mathematical equation, which either can or cannot be solved. In the cases when it can be solved, there is usually one way to do so. Problem solving in projects is more complex, offering a variety of solutions with a myriad of results. Those results are often temporary and result in the problem being transferred in disguise to someone else.

Project managers solve problems. Project leaders create energy. Creating involves changing the underlying structure or root cause of a problem, while at the same time bringing new realities into existence. A project leader's problem-solving focus is on the removal of barriers to allow the creative process to flourish.

When vision and creativity are lacking in projects, project teams tend to recycle previous problems or move from one version of a problem to another. Because there is no vision, they focus on solving the current problem. A strong vision is necessary to change the attitudes, behaviors, and processes associated with today's projects, particularly information technology projects. Technology can enable these changes, but too often a project team's focus on technology obscures the achievement of the vision.

An installed system is a milestone to achieving the transformation in people, systems, and organizations that are necessary to achieve strategic results. Consider the sales automation technology projects whose sales force rejects the technology because they convince themselves they are technically illiterate or because they don't believe it's their job to enter data into a computer. Other professionals such as doctors, lawyers, and even professors have resisted the adoption of new processes because of a leadership failure to transform critical attitudes and behaviors with a compelling vision.

In his book, *The Path of Least Resistance*, Robert Fritz uses a basic law of nature to help articulate how organizations function. The law is that energy will travel along the path of least resistance determined by its underlying structure. If organizations or teams are not structured properly, they will likewise take the easy, familiar path, often failing to achieve their desired results.[1] In the personal growth realm, taking charge of one's project management career and becoming a service-based project leader requires the proper structure to support this endeavor.

Fritz identifies two main structures—a conflict resolution system that tends to oscillate, producing temporary results but ultimately failing to achieve lasting results, and a tension resolution system that tends to produce success and permanent results.

Problem-solving efforts in organizations, as well as in one's personal life, often employ a conflict resolution system. The desire for change yields initial results, but because the underlying structure does not support these results, instability occurs and the structure seeks stability through resisting the change. Anyone who has tried to stop smoking or drinking realizes the potential to replace one vice with another: you give up cigarettes but wind up overeating instead. The same is true in organizations and project teams. Organizational problems may be temporarily "solved," but in reality are dispersed to other areas. A process-improvement effort to reduce the cost of operations may create customer satisfaction problems for sales and marketing, and end up costing the organization more in the long run.

Creating is important to project management because it involves more than mere problem solving that tends to lead to temporary results. The act of creating, inspired by a compelling vision, leads to permanent results. **The creative project leader and team address underlying issues and tensions to create new solutions rather than temporarily adjusting the same old situations.**

# Personal Visioning

A leader's purpose and vision—what he stands for and who he is—precedes the team purpose and vision. A service-based project leader must create a personal purpose and vision and be en route to achieving results prior to leading others. Her purpose is a statement regarding her life meaning; "Why do I exist?" The vision embodies how she is to live out this purpose.

An example of a purpose is, "to equip and motivate project managers to make the world a better place." The personal vision of how to achieve this purpose may be "by developing and delivering quality educational materials, writing articles and books, and speaking at conferences or seminars."

A purpose influences one's values, convictions, and strengths, brings enjoyment, and provides a feeling of significance, not just success. Values such as justice, peace, harmony, and recognition along with strengths such as creativity, public speaking, and analytical capabilities will impact an individual's purpose.

Some examples of a purpose and personal vision are:

Purpose—Improve public education.
Personal vision—Implement cost-effective technology infrastructure in public schools K through 12.
Purpose—Increase the availability of health care to the unemployed and homeless.
Personal vision—Provide education to the uninsured on government health care guidelines through printed materials, multi-media, and workshops.
Purpose—Create a high-performance research and development function.
Personal vision—Implement project-friendly policies that eliminate barriers to performance and increase innovation.

It is easy to imagine how these personal visions align with an individual's core values, and how each vision could translate into several projects.

A personal vision should conjure up mental images of one's ideal self. This image should be appealing to both you and to those around you: family, co-workers, friends, etc. A personal vision must be attainable and have achievable stretch goals with enough clarity that decision making toward the goals is facilitated. The vision should not be too rigid, which prohibits flexibility in the face of changing circumstances. Personal vision statements can reference self-image, health, relationships, work, personal pursuits, and community aspirations.

**A personal vision is created by two components: one's current reality (where you are) and one's personal vision (who you want to be). The discrepancy creates tension that must be resolved at a personal level.**[2] Only then can one's personal vision be aligned with the larger, more inclusive group vision, which is critical for creating the energy to achieve this vision.

A personal vision is preceded by a calling: a deep understanding of identity and purpose, or as some might say, an assignment from God. A leader's calling, personal vision, and career can be tightly connected. Though one's personal vision may be shared by others, a calling is more unique to the individual. A calling is heard uniquely through one's own perceptions of her strengths, the environment that attracts her, and the needs of humanity. When one has found her calling, it is revealed through the reinvigoration of energy, steadfast belief in oneself, and satisfaction. Callings are not easy to find, nor at times are they easy to accept.[3] One's calling can be uncomfortable, as reflected in Mother Teresa's statement, "I know God will not give me anything I can't handle. I just wish that He didn't trust me so much."[4]

## Group Visioning

Organizations, whether they are multi-national corporations or small project teams, exist for reasons beyond financial gain. Of course, they intend to prosper financially, but generally they also have a more inspiring purpose that is usually found in its mission or vision statement. A service-based project leader asks whether the organization is being true to its moral purpose.

Similar to a personal vision, a group vision should conjure up mental images of the team's ideal self-image and purpose. This image should be appealing to all individuals and interested stakeholders. A group vision must be attainable and have enough focus that enables the delegation of decision making toward its purpose. Does the team want to be a high performing team? What types of behaviors, relationships, and energy does the team want to reflect? How does this compare to what the team is today? Service-based project leaders facilitate these questions and answers, because they are accountable for the results.

An example of group vision is: "Our project team will value our customers, represent all interested parties, and provide the highest quality project deliverables; including analysis, process definition and software deliverables that meet a common good. We will listen to, comprehend, and believe in our customers' goals and objectives. We will use open, honest communications with customers, stakeholders, and other team members, do what we said we would do, value other's contributions, offer assistance without expectations, and hold our team objectives over any personal ambition."

Notice the vision focuses on quality, best efforts, and a common good but also calls out specific project deliverables. It is important to include all stakeholders in this team visioning process. For instance, customers may value speed over quality in certain situations. There are also no caveats about resource availability or scope changes. It also puts a premium on customer focus and establishes group values and norms by which behavior can be aligned.

Within the strategic vision is the tactical task, or work package, vision dealing with specific project work and outcomes. A service-based project leader encourages and facilitates team members in defining the current reality with regard to tasks and deliverables. They should define what they have now, how it is organized, what resources or components exist, and then compare this to the outcome or deliverable envisioned.

**Project leaders must be able to articulate, in a concise manner, the essence of what a team is trying to create. This tactical visioning, a collaborative process, yields a shared vision, with linkages to personal visions.** This is how service-based project leaders not only transform processes and systems, but also initiate the personal transformation of themselves and others.

Beginning with the end in mind by using pictures, graphs, and diagrams is critical to sparking imagination and achieving shared visions. The creation of mental images and shared visions creates energy and hope that precedes the physical creation. An organization that is honest with itself has a healthy tension between reality and the future. The service-based project leader, with her core team, defines the current reality of the team as truthfully as possible, and then creates a compelling vision for where it wants to go or what it wants to become.

A certified project manager should know that team development is a high priority, and she should understand the conflicts inherent in a matrix organization. In the early stages of the project, the team is often not a high-performing team. Project teams often struggle with unclear goals and undefined relationships, which can generate tremendous negative energy.

The shared vision enables a team to generate positive energy. Team members sense when critical communication needs to happen and they understand each other intimately enough to know when someone needs help. Team members contribute equally; there are no hidden agendas or turf battles, everyone is excited about the customer, not just about what is in it for them. **A project leader must define this vision and the current reality and allow the tension to resolve itself. If the underlying structure is built on mutual trust, respect, and open dialogue, energy will naturally be generated toward that vision, and a high-performing team will emerge**.

A team defined by self-interest, fear, and a lack of trust may exhibit periods of high performance when everyone's interests and moods align, but will more often fall short of being a high-performing team because the underlying structure is flawed.

A catalyst to building a shared vision is trust. Trust becomes an enabling factor that resolves the tension, allowing movement toward a vision of a high-performing team. Trust-based relationships are instrumental in resolving ambiguity, conflicts, and risks.

# The Creativity in All of Us

Creativity is often regarded as an elusive talent or gift inherent in one's makeup. Though it is true that research tells us there are differences between the neural connections of highly creative people and less creative people, creativity must be appreciated and understood by project leaders who bring forth change and transformation. Leadership success factors are becoming more situational as accelerated change in organizations drives increased competition and organizational complexity. Thus leadership, particularly in projects that destabilize traditional processes and introduce dramatic change, has no preset formula. Service-based project leadership must use the awareness of self, the environment, and followers to execute leadership on the fly. This requires creativity, both planned and unplanned.

"Creating a work or doing a deed," according to Viktor Frankl, is a vital part of finding purpose in life.[5] A service-based project leader, called to journey deep within and pursue important personal questions, illuminates these creative values when she interacts with the external environment and brings about a new order to it.

Humans are uniquely creative by nature. Not only are each of us unique in our own bodies and minds, we create events and circumstances as a result of our mere existence. Our bodies create carbon dioxide, our skin regenerates, and we procreate.

There are different kinds of creativity within people as well. Some may be more inclined to revolutionary forms of creativity that inspire lateral or out-of-the-box thinking.[6] Others may be better at evolutionary creativity, such as incremental improvement. Each has a place in project teams. **The good news is that project leaders do not have to be the sole provider of creativity, but rather they must understand its purpose, and how to leverage it in their teams.**

Even if the project leader is not highly creative, at a minimum she can become skilled at creating a climate that encourages creativity. With knowledge of how creativity works, what accelerates it and impedes it, a project leader can use her influence on the project climate to foster the right mix of elements that allows team members to be creative. This climate must embody trust and accept failure as part of a learning process.

## Creativity in Project Management

As we know, a project is a temporary undertaking to create a unique product or service, having a defined start and end point, and specific objectives that, when accomplished, signify completion.

Creators have a high tolerance for discrepancy and the greater the discrepancy, the greater the forces at work.[7] This is the heart of the creative process. This is why a project leader needs to be comfortable with ambiguity. However, as a planner, risk manager, executer, and controller, project managers are continually trying to eliminate ambiguity in order to get things done. This may be a conflict for some project leaders: how to use ambiguity to create discrepancy between the current and future states, while simultaneously minimizing ambiguity. But the reality is the greater the clarity and tension between the current (reality) and future state (vision), the more efficient the team will be in defining tasks, durations, risks, and in helping the project manager execute the plan. **Project leaders who are not comfortable with this discrepancy between current reality and future vision are often easily discouraged.**

Traditional thoughts on project visioning were confined to aligning team members, helping manage expectations, and creating common understanding. A more advanced take on project visioning is that a well-crafted, articulated vision will create positive energy to fuel creativity.

## Exploiting the Creative Process in Project Management

The creative process is filled with tension, anxiety, and doubt. These seemingly uncomfortable feelings are signs of a fertile creative environment. Service-based project leaders using the creative process to their advantage learn to apply steady pressure to their conscious efforts toward a new reality and outcome until the pressure fails to produce any new movement or insight. Then they release that pressure, relax, and wait alertly for fresh insights.[8]

When a vivid discrepancy exists between current and future states of the project, the spark of creative energy sets the project team's imagination in motion. Creating involves making specific choices about the project results that the customer and the project team want to create. At the organizational or strategic level, project managers may be left out of this process or only involved at the end of this initial creative process.

This illustrates the need for service-based project leaders to be customer focused, with strong relationships that enable them to get involved earlier on in the process. The earlier the involvement in this step, the greater the energy the service-based project leader can generate within the team.

However, at the project team and work package level (tactical), the service-based project leader has a tremendous opportunity to initiate and facilitate the germination of creativity. This would include well-facilitated brainstorming sessions, team building exercises, assessments, etc. **The more clear outcomes a leader can define and cast to enhance creative energy in the current state of the project plan, the faster the project train will pull out of the station.**

Once started, the creative process becomes a learning process through experience and assimilation of knowledge back into the project team. The project team must digest what is experienced in carrying out the work of the project and reprocess it into new knowledge.

On a tactical level, a service-based project leader recognizes the need for team members to continuously process the results of the project. Just as important as the project plan is a climate that allows project team members (creators) to experience, process, and learn in a time-compressed environment. This accelerated learning can reach an impasse, but then a breakthrough occurs after a period of feeling like no progress is being made. Astute leaders understand this process and patiently wait for breakthroughs. Their main concern is maintaining a healthy environment for the creative process to work.

A service-based project leader uses milestones, lessons learned, and communication plans to assist individuals in assimilating their efforts back into her team and deliverables into the larger organization. Project plans that allow the creative process to begin earlier and the use of simulations, prototypes, and pilots enhance the learning and assimilation curve for everyone.

A service-based project leader knows when she is finished, sensing a total accomplishment of the results the project team wanted to create. The project plans include refinement activities to touch up the final results, and include steps to verify results with customers. The keys to completion are keeping the energy alive by continually projecting the discrepancy between current reality and the project vision, verifying work product results in the project plan, and acknowledging accomplishments.

The creative process aligns very closely with the project management processes. (See Figure 8.1.) A service-based project leader considers the creative process when developing work breakdown structures, tasks, and activities. The more a project plan enhances the creative process, the more likely positive results will be achieved.

The project leader always focuses on measurable results to verify and confirm project completion. Even though the outcome may require refinement, a project leader's clear vision allows the team and customer to say in unison, "We are finished when …".

At the tail end of projects, team members are tired, and many begin to be pulled on to newer, more exciting projects. Creating tasks and activities to keep the vision alive and allow the team members to experience the results of what they have created is the ultimate recognition of their individual growth and accomplishments.

The focus on creating is an important element of leadership, and particularly project leadership, where creation and transformation are necessary to bring about lasting results.

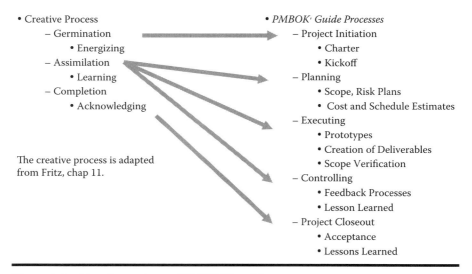

**Figure 8.1   Creative nature of PMBOK®** *guide* **process.**

# Summary

In the past, much focus has been placed on project management problem-solving skills. However, this focus tends to lead to a project team getting bogged down in viewing their project as a set of problems that have to be solved. However, when the service-based project leader is able to bring the project team and all stakeholders to a shared vision based on resolving the tension between the current reality and the desired state, she is able to turn the project process into a creative process. This creative process infuses the project with the energy needed for lasting results.

# Endnotes

1. Robert Fritz, *The Path of Least Resistance for Managers*—Designing Organizations to Succeed (San Francisco: Berrett-Koehler 1999), 3–4.
2. Robert Fritz, *The Path of Least Resistance* (New York: Fawcett Columbine 1989), 114.
3. Elizabeth Jeffries, "Work as a Calling," in *Insights on Leadership: Service, Stewardship, Spirit, and Servant-Leadership,* Larry Spears and Michele Lawrence, Eds. (New York: Wiley & Sons 1998), 29–37.
4. *Brainyquotes.com* s.v. "Mother Teresa trust" http://www.brainyquote.com/quotes/authors/m/mother_teresa.html (accessed November 25, 2006).
5. Viktor E. Frankl, *Man's Search For Meaning* (Boston: Beacon Press 2006), 111.
6. Tamyra L. Freeman, Scott G. Isaksen, and K. Brian Dorval, "Servant Leadership and Creativity," in *Focus on Leadership: Servant Leadership for the 21st Century,*. Larry Spears and Michele Lawrence, Eds., (New York: Wiley & Sons 2002), 258.
7. Robert Fritz, *The Path of Least Resistance* (New York: Fawcett Columbine 1989), 116.
8. Ibid., Freeman 262.

## Chapter 9

# Making the Commitment

Courage is the price that life exacts for granting one peace.

—Amelia Earhart

## Introduction

Why are project managers not growing into C-level management positions? The reasons may be many, including the lack of financial, marketing, or specific technical skills that may prove a project manager unworthy of C-level positions. However, a more salient reason is their unwillingness to get out of their comfort zone of schedules, tools, and templates.[1] You must be courageous to be a service-based project leader. Courage carries a price, but offers a meaningful return.

## Barriers to Commitment

### Fear of Change

Attitudes and behaviors must grow from confidence, not fear. Your attitude drives the action to start on the road to service-based project leadership. Getting started is not easy and should not be taken lightly. Many people have trouble keeping commitments to themselves and others. The commencement of an inner journey to follow a calling is impeded not just by excuses, but also by fear and stress.

Status and recognition can restrict the compelling need to stretch in new, demanding ways. **(Many have worked their way up a long difficult road to their good salary, nice benefits, predictable environment, and sense of control.) Any change—even in the direction one feels called—can be destabilizing.**

Any project manager looking to make a leap to project leadership must develop a courageous attitude that encourages decision-making based on reality and the needs of stakeholders. Staying in your comfort zone prevents you from transforming yourself and your environment.

## Stress

Getting out of one's comfort zone takes energy—energy that often does not exist. Project managers and project leaders work in an environment laden with causes of burnout. Simply put, burnout occurs whenever energy becomes deficient. One of the leading causes of burnout is stress, which has serious physiological effects on the body and diminishes psychological energy from the heart and mind. Stress is experienced when a person perceives that demands exceed the personal and social resources the individual is able to mobilize. The impact of stress on health is well researched and documented. Symptoms such as exhaustion, irritability, anger, and physical problems, headaches, or weight gain impact your health, mental ability, and emotional resilience.[2]

Stress in the workplace is reaching epidemic portions. A survey commissioned in the 1990s by the Associates for Research into the Science of Enjoyment (ARISE) found that 54 percent of office workers gave work as a current form of stress in their lives. One in three said they would not pick the same career again. Half said office stress is the result of too much work. Fifty-two percent of American workers found work to be a cause of stress and ranked second behind Hong Kong in that 27 percent said stress required them to take time off work.[3]

Stress is not only associated with work that exceeds one's capacity or skills, but with having too little work, or work that is uninspiring.

Not all stress is bad. Studies have indicated a potential positive outcome to properly regulated stress that can be very beneficial to improving performance. **The physiological arousal associated with this "eustress" can be channeled into performance energy, heightening awareness, and concentration for short periods of time.** However, over an extended period of time, this type of physiological arousal becomes harmful to the body and tends to bring about behavioral patterns that can negatively affect a team.[4]

## Impact of Stress on Your Heart and Mind

Stress, both environmental and task-induced, has always been rampant in project management. It attacks a leader's heart, the resting place of desires and goals. Environmental stress stems from relationships and organizational culture. A primary source of burnout is the inability to manage the difficult relationships that cause stress levels to escalate very quickly in a project environment. The establishment of a healthy environment minimizes environmental stress and is essential to protecting the heart and fighting the erosion of talent.

The second attack on a leader's heart is task stress, which deals with the work being attempted and the project manager's capacity to deliver or just keep up. Having too much work or work that is too difficult leaves one overwhelmed, frustrated, and laden with feelings of incompetence. Eventually, the project manager reaches the point at which he is only going through the motions, with low expectations of himself, others, and the project outcome.

Task stress also attacks the mind, the resting place of one's creative capability. A more subtle kind of task stress is that which arises from uninspiring work or work that is not connected to the project manager's core values. Uninspiring work obviates creativity and slowly deadens the mind. Job design research indicates that highly standardized, repetitive, and routine work all tend to be uninspiring, as well as any work in which one finds no value or purpose.[5] **The inability to see and experience the results of one's work can also lead to emotional numbness.** People need to be challenged, but not beyond their capability. Fatigue in the workplace can be due to too much work, or to a lack of meaningful work. Managing both environmental and task stress is a critical component of long-term professional development.

## *Durable Energy*

A project manager journeying toward service-based project leadership must be able to recharge his energy.

Consumable energy is gained through sleep, proper nutrition, exercise, and general care for the body. This kind of energy depletes relatively quickly, and must be regularly replenished. Durable energy, however, builds a connection between the mind and the heart that resists depletion. **The ability to connect to work emotionally and find a driving purpose for that work can reduce both environmental and task stress and become a force for change.** Reduced stress helps ignite the heart with passion for the tasks that must be done. This energy then moves toward the mind, where it works to inspire creativity. Simultaneously, if work is inspiring and fascinating, the mind is active and thriving, durable energy moves toward the heart, and contributes to the additional discovery of purpose. When these forces are simultaneously flowing and interacting, durable energy is created. Generating durable energy enables the project leader to sustain professional growth.

**To allow the heart and mind to remain disconnected and to continue working without growth and inspiration is to do a disservice to yourself and your profession.** Project leaders who create durable energy can more naturally exercise fundamental leadership skills associated with senior and executive level positions. This energy becomes a force for change in project work; change in people, processes, and systems. Project leaders then can witness the transformation of their community through their efforts, generating even more energy for themselves and others.

# Elements of Commitment

## *Alignment*

Commitment to self-directed leadership growth requires alignment of two important areas. The first is one's convictions, the strongly held beliefs that guide an individual's actions and decisions. These beliefs evolve over time and can strengthen or weaken, but generally stay intact over the course of a lifetime. The second is one's purpose or significance. Purpose or significance is about one's calling, which drives the self toward a personal destination of fulfilment. It answers the question, "Why am I here?" It implies a greater, even a spiritual, reason for one's existence.

When one has perfect alignment, the sum of his convictions and purpose equals expenditure of time and effort. A simple equation to illustrate strong alignment would be:

$$\frac{(\text{Convictions} + \text{Purpose})}{\text{Leader's Effort Expended}} = 1$$

In this situation, a leader's efforts are in complete alignment with what they feel strongly about and what outcomes they wish to accomplish. This alignment is evident in all aspects of a leader's life, such as work, relationships, and physical and spiritual health.

**Unintentional misalignment is found in many lives.** For instance, a project leader's convictions about drug abuse causes him to educate young people about the dangers of alcohol, yet their employer glorifies these products to the younger generations in a marketing campaign. Or a project leader with convictions about human rights may work for an organization that lobbies governments to open trade barriers despite human rights concerns.

But often, project leaders work on projects that simply have no relationship to their true beliefs and convictions. No matter how deeply they dig, they cannot find any significance to their efforts. Especially in monolithic organizations whose operations and projects have become far removed from the primary mission of the organization, project workers cannot connect their work with tangible redeeming value to customer, stakeholder, or society.

Achieving and maintaining this alignment is neither simple nor easy. As leaders apply their efforts, feedback occurs that can strengthen or weaken convictions or purpose. Readjustments are common. High-profile leaders who achieve success move on to other challenges, adjusting their efforts to more closely align with their convictions and purpose. Bill Gates moved from the CEO of Microsoft® to expending much of his time and substantial resources on philanthropic efforts. Project leaders should view their careers in a similar fashion, albeit on a smaller scale. Success on one project should encourage a project leader to recalibrate his alignment to ensure that his efforts are as closely aligned with his convictions and purpose on future projects as possible.

Without strongly held beliefs and core values, a leader has faint direction and little reason for personal change. Trying to change behavioral patterns without these will only leave one feeling frustrated, lost, and confused.

## Direction

The destination is not as important as the journey. Choosing a destination is important because it allows a project manager to orient himself for the journey. Your destination determines the direction—the types of projects, people, and the nature of the work with which you will engage in order to become a service-based project leader.

Should service-based project leadership be the destination of all project managers? Maybe not. If not, then what criteria should you use to determine if this is a proper destination for you? The criteria for service-based project leadership are few:

- A desire to transcend the past. To start over, begin fresh, experience uniqueness, creativity, achievement, unlimited potential and, of course, all its challenges.
- A desire to serve and help others. Embody an attitude of unselfish concern for the welfare of others.

These criteria may resonate at different volumes within each of us. However, evidence exists that this need for renewing oneself, being unique, expressing creativity, desiring achievement, and intending to serve is inherent in human nature.

**Our nature is to transcend the past, understand the current, and adapt to the future.** A hopeful attitude in approaching life is needed to reach beyond oneself, one's identity and circumstances, using actions that create new opportunities for life with purpose.

Altruism, unselfish concern for the welfare of others, is found in many of the world's religions as a natural way to fill the human need to love and be loved. Giving freely provides deep satisfaction and happiness. Albert Schweitzer said: "The only ones among you who will be really happy are those who have sought and found how to serve."[6]

Your direction or plan to move toward service-based project leadership should be natural but flexible to allow you to try different types of projects with different people. The journey must be feasible, have manageable steps, fit smoothly into your life, and capitalize on your strengths.

## *Authenticity*

The project manager must attempt to remain true to himself throughout the journey. It is through this process that the leader begins to discover his authentic self. Authenticity is often misunderstood, not the least by leaders or managers trying to become leaders. A definition of authentic is, "verifiably an original." The key goal behind becoming a service-based project leader is to align convictions with core values, discover those values that are focused outwardly on others, and consistently demonstrate behaviors that reinforce these values to help establish authenticity. In doing so, you are serving yourself first. A leader must enjoy the journey. If the steps are authentic, it is refreshing and invigorating.

But what if the "original," the leader, is damaged? What if being authentic means being a self that others do not appreciate? Some take pride in their combative, argumentative style, believing this is just the way they are. This **"take it or leave it" approach to being authentic**—verifiably an original—**leaves one as a verified imposter.**

Hence, the classic misunderstanding of authenticity. Being authentic is not an inate ability that one is given from above. A leader is not the judge of his own authenticity. It is not what one sees in himself, but rather what others see in a person. If authenticity is based on others' perceptions, then one can learn to manage it, control it, and disclose it on his own terms.[7]

Authentic leaders have strongly held beliefs, make these beliefs known, and act consistently with these beliefs and values. These strongly held beliefs are aligned tightly with the ethical standards and concern for the well-being for others, not oneself! Ethics and service to others are common denominators to establishing a true vision of oneself relative to others. This true vision will guide the direction of a project leader's journey toward service-based project leadership.

The journey proceeds uninhibited toward service-based project leadership when the leader does not polarize events, people, and conditions, but rather finds common ground with the team and customers without compromising personal beliefs. Expressing beliefs is reserved for the proper moments, but actions consistently display the authentic leader's service orientation, often at critical moments when progress is stopped, despair has descended, or crisis has engulfed the project. The journey is made in confidence when leaders practice what they preach, and the practice is more visible than the preaching. These beliefs are common to the masses and when carefully and thoughtfully articulated, they create unity, not division.

Often we see co-workers acting predominantly in their own self-interest. This may be considered as being true to oneself, in the vein of "survival of the fittest." For others to see his true self, a leader needs to be willing to display what he believes in. **Unfortunately, some cannot get beyond their own self-preservation to discover what they truly believe. These people often struggle or simply fail to**

**effectively lead others.** Their career growth direction becomes a crooked, self-destructive path.

The journey to project leadership is less traumatic when you engage all your senses, plus intuition and a firm foundation of values to process unconscious and conscious feedback from peers. A finely tuned antenna for feedback processes it internally, without significant biases based on emotions, fears, or delusions. When you pick up signals that sponsors, customers, and team members really appreciate a comment, behavior, attitude, or leadership style, your direction is reinforced and momentum is gained.

# Rare Opportunity

Every project leader has personal convictions about what is important in life. These convictions range from beliefs in life and work balance, education, religion, relationships, family, child-rearing, politics, ethics, etc. However, for the project manager seeking to become a service-based project leader, there are three mandatory convictions:

1. You must be fully convinced that leadership competencies are critical to project management career success.
2. You must be completely committed to the project management profession and to developing leadership competencies.
3. You must be completely open to feedback on leadership competencies.

Strongly held beliefs and core values become alive when they are combined with a purpose. Finding a purpose makes work meaningful, and if something is meaningful to the leader, it is more likely to be for the team as well. Projects leaders who have a purpose create enthusiasm that affects everyone they work with. Work with a purpose affects lives in a meaningful way.

Project leaders have a rare opportunity, and in some situations an obligation, to merge their powerful project management knowledge, skills, and experience with their convictions and purpose to change the world.

# Summary

Service-based project leadership requires serious, conscious commitment on the part of the project manager. In order to begin the commitment process, one should align core values and convictions with their purpose, which supplies energy to drive behavioral changes. The project leader must then decide the direction of his leadership journey and what types of projects and people he desires to devote himself to. Finally, he must establish a connection between his mind and heart relative to project work in order to generate durable energy.

## Endnotes

1. Sanford, Mark, email message to author. August 2005.
2. *Mindtools.com*, s.v. "Stress Management Techniques," http://www.mindtools.com/pages/article/newTCS_00.htm (accessed November 28, 2006).
3. Prime predictor of stress—Stress, Relaxation & Pleasure: A Survey among Office Workers, *Supervision*, June 1995.
4. Bronwyn Fryer, "Are You Working Too Hard? A Conversation with Mind/Body Researcher Herbert Benson," *Harvard Business Review*, November 2005.
5. Glen Bassett, "The Case against Job Satisfaction: A Satisfied Worker is not Necessarily a Productive Worker," *Business Horizons*, May–June 1994, http://www.findarticles.com/p/articles/mi_m1038/is_n3_v37/ai_15505563/print (accessed November 28, 2006).
6. Viktor Frankl, *The Unconscious God* (New York: Simon and Schuster, 1975) 85.
7. Rob Goffee and Gareth Jones, "Managing Authenticity: The Paradox of Great Leadership," *Harvard Business Review*, December 2005.

# THE MYPROJECTADVISOR® LEADERSHIP COMPETENCY FRAMEWORK

**II**

## Chapter 10

# Competence: The Foundation of Leadership

## Introduction

Committed service-based project leaders are the fuel that will ignite the project management industry, making it an indispensable profession, and enabling practitioners to fill the leadership void. Technical competence and experience will not guarantee success; it takes skills rooted within the individual's values to effectively unite and lead a group of people over whom they have minimal authority.

The art of leadership itself is undergoing changes in today's highly volatile professional environment. Someone who was an excellent leader five or ten years ago, today needs a new set of leadership skills to continue succeeding.

In the past, decisiveness, resourcefulness, and straightforwardness were the most highly valued leadership skills. But today, building, maintaining, and repairing relationships with other people are highly valued skills for leaders.[1] People skills, the ability to unite others in pursuit of a common vision, and participative management, are the future of successful project leadership. Resourcefulness and decisiveness are still important, but cooperative teams have an easier time reaching decisions than a team rife with division and self-interest.

**In project management, leadership is desperately needed; leadership that is adaptable, perceptive, timely, meaningful, authentic, and unselfish.** The success of this new type of project leadership is critical, because the impact of poor leadership on today's strategic projects and programs is too great for society to bear.

# Competence

Competence is generally referred to as the quality or condition—knowledge, attitudes, skills, and experience—to succeed in carrying out a task.[2] It is also defined by Richard Boyatzis, a prominent leadership author, as knowledge, skills, attitudes, and behaviors that are causally related to superior job performance.[3] Is competence about one's ability to perform at an above-average level or just complete the task? What about project manager competence or, for that matter, project leader competence?

Personal competence, the core to project management, integrates a practitioner's behavioral qualities (which flow outward) and attitudinal qualities (which flow inward) to affect how one works with others. Project manager competence includes project management and project context knowledge, skills, and experiences that affect how well a project manager executes project management-related activities.[4] Project leader competence encompasses both project manager and personal competence but also includes the ability to lead others in the project environment as shown in Figure 10.1.

For our purpose, let's assume the challenge of the project management environment makes the *superior performance* definition appropriate when discussing project leader competence.

# Background on Project Management Competencies

Project manager competence is not a new concept; it has been around for years with continual evolution of its definition. However, project *management* competence is not the same as project *manager* competence. Project management competence involves everyone in the project organization: the project manager, the sponsors, the customers, the team members, the project office, and key stakeholders.[5] Project management competence is associated with organizational behavior and organizational project

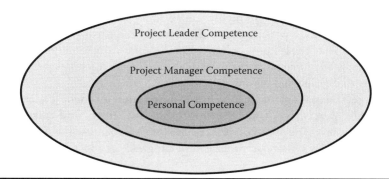

**Figure 10.1 Competency relationships of a project leader.**

management methodologies and maturity. The journey to project management competence is long and requires serious organizational commitment.

Project manager competence is specific to the individual acting in the capacity of project manager. Both project manager and organizational competence are required to achieve repeatable project management success.

Today, with increased complexity, accelerated change, and specialization of project management functions, project leadership is becoming its own competency. Because leadership is situational and dynamic, the generalist role of a project manager will become increasingly irrelevant, as specialists will compete for project management services. Not all project managers have the ability or desire to act as a leader; thus, specialized leadership competencies—though still in their infancy—are becoming an area of focus over traditional project management functions.

These leadership competencies are the most challenging to thoroughly define, develop, and improve since leadership success is hard to predict. A framework for project manager leadership competence cannot be solely dependent on an organization's project management maturity, even though organizational maturity influences the results. **Project managers can develop leadership competencies regardless of the organizational state of project management competence.** Job descriptions for senior project and program managers require proven leadership competence.

Today, project leadership competencies are embedded within project manager competence models.

PMI® has the *Project Manager Competency Development Framework*. IPMA has published Version 3 of their competency baseline. Some organizations have their own proprietary models that align with career development. Other models exist that combine the measurement of knowledge, skills, problem solving, analytical thinking, and psychometric testing. Some organizations simply rely on a certification as a measure of competence, even though most realize the limitations of this measure.

## Project Management Competency Development Framework Overview

The PMI's *Project Manager Competency Development Framework* is tightly aligned with *A Guide to the Project Management Body of Knowledge* (*PMBOK® Guide*) and its nine knowledge areas. The framework breaks down competencies as:

- Project Management Knowledge—What do individual project managers bring to a project through their knowledge and understanding of project management?
- Project Management Performance—What are individual project managers able to demonstrate in their ability to successfully manage the project or complete project-related activities?

■ Personal Competence—What are the core personality characteristics under-lying a person's capability to do a project or a project activity?

PMI's framework is focused on performing the activities associated with knowl-edge areas in the *PMBOK® Guide*. The framework emphasizes competence as a driver of performance; a competent project manager will be able to consistently achieve project goals. Emphasis is placed on traditional project performance metrics, such as cost, schedule, quality, scope, and processes associated with initiating, planning, executing, controlling, and closing projects.

The framework identifies the knowledge a project manager must have regarding each knowledge area associated with major project processes and distills them into competencies with performance criteria.

Within each knowledge area (risk, quality, scope, communication, etc.) are units of performance competence associated with the major project management processes: initiating, planning, executing, controlling, and closure. Elements of competence are broken into performance competencies, such as activity definition, performance reporting, or risk identification, and have both a criteria and evidence to illustrate the competence exists. For example, an element of competence is ensur-ing stakeholders are identified and their needs are understood. This element carries a performance criterion of identifying all stakeholders evidenced by a documented list of stakeholders.

The framework also has a personal competence section that describes the gen-eral characteristics, ideal core traits, personality, and behaviors of a project manager. They include communicating, leading, managing, cognitive ability, effectiveness, and professionalism.[6]

## IPMA ICB Standard

*The IPMA Competence Baseline Version 3*, published in 2006, is the basis for IPMA's four certification levels. It defines three components of competence; technical, behavioral, and contextual, in its "Eye of Competency."[7] The technical competence range contains 20 elements, which focus on fundamental project management ele-ments such as risk, scope, quality, time, cost, procurement, and communication. The behavioral competency range contains 15 elements, which focus on a project manager's attitudes and interpersonal skills. Leadership is a behavior competency element and is listed as one of the most important behavior competencies for indi-viduals; others include negotiation, self-control, openness, creativity, and assertive-ness. Third are 11 contextual competencies that relate to the context of the project, including managing relationships within the lines of business; understanding the business, program, and portfolio relationships to the project; and executing finan-cial, legal, and system responsibilities.

*ICB 3.0 Competence Baseline* has increased its focus on behavioral competencies in both its standard and certification process as a result of demands to define adequate professional behavior for practitioners and the recognition that these skills are becoming more critical to organizations as projects have become more numerous, complex, and varied in nature.

The weighting of the technical, behavioral, and contextual competencies varies depending on the level of certification. In general, technical competence weight is greater with the lower level certifications and weighted less in the higher level certifications. Conversely, behavioral competencies weighting increases as certification level increases.[8]

# Lack of Focus on Behavioral Leadership

These PMI® and IPMA standards, used by project management practitioners and organizations all over the world, have done much to develop and improve project manager's knowledge and process skills. Even so, less attention has been paid to improving the behavioral leadership aspect of project management competencies.

Though both organizations recognize the importance of leadership competencies, trainers, organizations, and practitioners have yet to development rigorous methods to improve these competencies and measure them uniformly. Challenges in this regard are significant for industry and practitioners alike. Any attention to behavior is usually associated with generic psychometric assessments that provide general information about one's styles or preferences. But these assessments are not tailored to the unique challenges of the project environment and the critical nature of the stakeholder relationships.

Virtually all aspects of project manager competency and organizational project management competency have been met with industry standards and tools for improvement, except the leadership aspect. The industry has responded vigorously to enhancing project management knowledge. Certifications such as PMI's PMP®, CAPM®, and IPMA's Level D certifications are all steeped in sound project management knowledge. However, as of 2006, only 6 percent of all certified practitioners in the world hold certifications that include a behavioral assessment.

Performance has also been addressed through numerous tools and templates. Project managers can quickly create schedules, charts, resource histograms, and risk plans thanks to the endless supply of software and templates available on project management sites or purchased through vendors. Every conceivable deliverable has a template or software to facilitate its creation.

On the organizational maturity side, the use of processes, people, and systems to improve organizational project management performance is also being addressed by eager consultants and professional organizations. PMI's Organizational Project Management Maturity Model (OPM3®) is an example of the industry's response to organizational project processes that enable organizational project success. Project offices and their governance policies address the management of people through the adoption of standard time-tracking against project or program tasks. Project management information systems help align projects and programs with strategy, aggregate, and report data on performance metrics.

Although IPMA's and PMI's standards include behavior constructs to define competency, the industry has failed to develop a workable framework for project leadership competencies that creates positive energy on project teams, enhances performance, and creates leadership opportunities.

Why? First, many sponsoring organizations of project management are not demanding such a framework, probably because they still believe they can achieve a high level of project management performance without measuring the behavior requirements of the project leader. They believe that continual refinement and standardization of processes and a knowledgeable, experienced project manager with a methodology are all they need to achieve project success.

Another reason why organizations are not demanding a behavioral leadership model for project managers is because they view project manager behavior as a general responsibility of the human resource department. If a project manager's behavior is detrimental to the organization, then human resource processes are initiated to formally write up performance deficiencies or assign a coach or mentor. This is rarely adequate for the behaviorally or attitudinally challenged project manager, particularly since by the time it has reached human resource's attention, significant damage has been done to the team's performance and their attitudes.

Finally, practitioners are not jumping over each other to measure their behavioral leadership competence. Though project managers cite lack of leadership, communication, and teamwork as observed deficiencies among their peers, they are not rushing to adopt a behavioral frame.[9] The obvious reason is fear associated with holding themselves accountable for their own behaviors. Now the importance of the commitment process associated with becoming a serviced-based project leader becomes clear: To be committed to leadership competencies, a project manager must first recognize the need for them—and then desire to transform herself.

## Summary

Leadership is undergoing changes in today's highly volatile professional environment. People skills, the ability to unite others in pursuit of a common vision, and participative management are the future of successful project leadership. Project leader competence is becoming its own specialized area and includes both personal competence and project management competence. Although IPMA's and PMI's standards include behavior constructs to define competencies, the industry has failed to develop a workable framework for project leadership competence that creates positive energy on project teams, enhances performance, and creates leadership opportunities.

# Endnotes

1. *The Center for Creative Leadership, s.v."changing, nature, leadership"* (by Andre Martin), http://www.ccl.org "2005 Changing Nature of Leadership Report," (accessed November 8, 2006).

2. J. Kent Crawford and Jeannette Cabanis-Brewin, *Optimizing Human Capital with a Strategic Project Office*, (Boca Raton, FL: Auerbach, 2006), 58. Just to avoid confusion of terms, even though they are increasing used interchangeably, I've more or less used Competence to mean the state of being competent, and Competency as a noun describing the specific required elements of competence, as in "There are three competencies that comprise competence: ethics, communication skills, and technical skills."

3. Project Management Institute. *Project Manager Competency Development Framework*, New Town Square, PA: Project Management Institute, 2002, 1.

4. Ibid.

5. Ibid., 2–4.

6. Ibid., Project Management Institute, 2. At the time of the writing of this chapter, the *Project Manager Competency Development Framework* standard was under going a substantial revision. The author has made an effort to review and interpreted the exposure draft of the revised standard to accurately describe the revised standard.

7. International Project Management Association, ICB IPMA *Competence Baseline Version 3.0*. The Netherlands: International Project Management Association, 2006, chap 1.

8. Ibid., Chap 3.

9. Joseph Zerby and others, Eds., "The Global State of Project Management Training and Education" (Paper Presentation Project Management Institute Global Congress North America, Toronto, 2005).

## Chapter 11

# The Customer's Perception of Your Project: Stakeholder Management

## Introduction

To succeed as a service-based project leader, it is essential to focus realistically on the project environment and stakeholders' needs. Decision-making becomes clearer when based in reality, and on the needs of others.[1] This is the basis for our leadership competency framework.

Most project management textbooks use terms or phases such as "unique," "temporary in nature," or "has not been done before" to describe project characteristics. They also describe how projects have a need or a problem statement, which is translated into project goals and measurable benefits. These project goals are the goals of sponsors, key stakeholders, end users, team members, and other interested parties. Stakeholder interest in a project is driven by success or failure's impact on their lives, careers, reputations, and other important criteria.

**All stakeholders are customers of the service-based project leader.** These customers inherently understand that the achievement of the project's goal entails risk. The more strategic the project is to the organization, the greater the risk associated with the project, and the greater the stakes are for all involved. Thus, stakeholder management is a critical success factor for a service-based project leader's project or program.

Another key characteristic of all projects is they require resources, particularly human resources, that must work together. These resources assigned to participate in and accomplish the project's goals are normally drawn from various parts of the organization. These stakeholders often have other jobs; the project is an additional responsibility.

These project characteristics subject its participants to a human condition that drives behavior—fear. Nobody likes to fail, or even worse, to be associated with a failure over which they have limited or no control. Participants worry about how uncertain outcomes may affect them personally. These project characteristics influence the customer's view of the project, particularly the paying customer.

## The Paying Customer's View

The service-based project leader has many customers, but the paying customer should be of greatest interest. Often in large organizations, the paying customer is invisible. Many times the sponsor can be considered the paying customer, particularly if the project budget is coming out of his cost center. But often projects get funds allocated from a central executing office, such as the project office or information services department. Sometimes the project costs are not easily billed back to the business units, or the allocated amount is not felt by the customers receiving the project's benefits. Large organizations struggle to make the project expenditures feel real, leaving the paying customers and project manager emotionally disconnected from each other. But when you pay for a service, you quickly get a sense whether value has been received.

It is difficult for project managers to achieve a financial relationship with customers, even though project offices are getting better at tracking and monitoring project costs. Many project managers do not desire this relationship; it adds stress, particularly in the case of under-performing project teams. **But service-based project leaders demand a financial relationship, because this relationship allows a discussion based on reality to occur.**

Service-based project leaders treat every dollar of the paying customer like it's their own. They find the paying customers and establish an emotional relationship with them. Paying customers greatly appreciate this care; if they do not, either they do not feel the real cost of the project or the project is not important to them.

## Strategic Project Characteristics

Project characteristics take on even more meaning for both the service-based project leader and its customers in strategic projects and programs. Customers do not typically have a lot of experience in managing or participating in large strategic projects, and often they do not understand the full implication of their needs. Their risk tolerances must be fully understood and managed. These strategic characteristics require the application of extraordinary leadership competencies.

## Uniqueness

Every project is unique, but the more ordinary the project, the more stakeholders are conditioned what to expect. They have a sense of the type of documentation that gets produced, what the expected results are likely to be, who must be involved, and when their participation is needed.

Strategic projects and programs are anything but ordinary. The templates and processes used on ordinary projects often break down on strategic initiatives unless the organization has reached a high level of project management maturity. Expectations vary widely in strategic projects and programs. **The enterprise nature of a program requires unprecedented and often uncharted collaboration between important constituents, both internal and external to the project.**

The uniqueness of strategic projects and programs creates a challenge to the visioning process. The ability to create a unified vision for a strategic effort that is shared by everyone is difficult due to the size and complexity of the endeavor. Most participants have not seen or experienced the intended results of the effort, and getting them to visualize, imagine, and align the practical applications of the strategic outputs to their world requires skills more common among artists than managers.

Integrating the various deliverables to suit the needs of competing interests among stakeholders often creates tension, rework, and conflicts. Getting a shared vision of program deliverables takes extra effort from the leader and team since many customers will only be able to view the result from their own vantage point. **The unique nature of strategic projects and programs creates the need for more education in managing stakeholder relationships**. It is a substantial effort to change what has existed for years—even generations in some cases—into a new state through the transformation of people, processes, and systems.

## Risk

All projects involve risk, but strategic projects and programs have more unknown risks. These risks are difficult to identify or even imagine due to the new relationships and paradigm created by the strategic effort. The magnitude of transformation in these projects is on a par with the risk magnitude. Failure of a strategic initiative has an impact on an organization similar to that of a natural disaster. Risk is difficult to quantify because organizations are not accustomed to executing transformational projects. The subjectivity of strategic project risk calculations does not accurately capture the impacts to revenue, goodwill, reputation, or market share, causing decision-making to be problematic.

The fallout from failure is nothing less than a perfect storm combining the impact of the unrealized transformation and its associated benefits with the lost opportunity cost associated with the mobilization of significant financial and human resources. This perfect storm leaves the organization in a woefully weak competitive position.

The irony is that strategic initiatives often have less tactical accountability due to the size and complexity of the temporary program organization. The necessary day-to-day accountability can be difficult to find, even though the risks are much greater than those found among ordinary projects. Ultimately, the accountability rolls up to executive levels, but by the time it has reached that level, the storm has left permanent scars on the organization's landscape.

## Temporary in Nature

Strategic projects seem to take on a life of their own, and transformation often does not have a clear end. This ambiguity causes several challenges for leaders and customers. The program tends to become operationalized. Team members begin to focus more on a constant stream of activities as opposed to focusing on clear milestones and deliverables. Urgency wanes and cynicism builds the longer the initiative goes on without visible transformation to make all customers and team members feel good about what is transpiring. Since the transformation is so monumental on strategic projects, people's careers are impacted and the political maneuvering for job security in the new transformed world begins to play out, motivating people to make the project more than a temporary endeavor. The resistance to the transition of program outcomes into operational processes impedes progress and ultimate completion.

## Playing Field

The leader's playing field increases dramatically for strategic projects and programs. The typical project may have a finite set of customers who intend to use project deliverables to achieve a particular goal related to their functional area. Strategic projects transform many aspects of the enterprise and changes to one area have ripple effects on others. The goals of one unit may conflict with the goals of another unit. Thus, the service-based project leader must work both sidelines, and on the entire area of the playing field.

Leaders and their organizations taking on strategic projects for the first time cannot see the sidelines without first exploring all perimeters of the playing field. Since strategic initiatives are aimed at accomplishing strategic goals established by executives, boards, and shareholders, the service-based project leader must also tend to their needs. Since these projects transform the inner workings of organizations and their interpersonal relationships, the human aspects of the project must also be nurtured. The behavior of everyday users and employees must be managed. This change in the management aspect of programs expands the playing field.

## Decision Making

Customers, particularly executives, must be accustomed to making fundamental decisions about the organizational change upon which they are embarking. Since conflicts become more visible in these initiatives, strategic decision-making must be facilitated by the service-based project leader, which requires both education and recommendations. Decisions on strategic projects must be made at all levels of the organization, but executives must make the fundamental choices to drive the transformation in the direction they wish to travel. The position of the service-based project leader allows them to facilitate that decision-making and align the program with those decisions.

Measuring goals on strategic initiatives is challenging. It is difficult to determine if permanent transformation has occurred in the midst of changing business conditions. Metrics can play a vital role, but often changes in market conditions or regulations must be factored out of the numbers. This makes striving for interim victories a common technique in strategic and organizational change initiatives, and an important but risky proposition for the leader's credibility.

## Diversity

Like projects, strategic initiatives require resources and most involve matrixed resources that come out of various organizations to assist the core project team to accomplish the goals. On strategic projects and programs, resources are often much more diverse and located in distant offices or foreign countries. Key team members may never even meet one another in person on one of these projects. Diversity is a huge asset for a service-based project leader, but it must be managed. These resources create their own perspectives, over which a project leader has little control compared to the project leader who has direct interaction with his team on a daily or weekly basis. The leader must find a means to disperse the realistic view of the project to these distant members.

## What Customers Really Want

A service-based project leader must understand the customer's perspective and inherent needs. The paying customer, often the sponsor, has a financial investment in the project, which creates a deep emotional commitment to the endeavor. Their career, reputation, and the overall health of their organization may be riding on its success. With minimal or no similar experiences to rely on, the customer is first looking for guidance from the service-based project leader. The customer wants to know how to get started, what critical events need to happen, and what he specifically needs to know, do, and decide. This type of information needs to be laid out in a constructive manner for them to act. Ultimately, the customer is looking for advice and recommendations from a competent individual with whom they can trust their reputation or career.

Second, the customer wants a relationship with a leader who really cares. They want the leader to have their best interests in mind when making tactical decisions or communicating to constituents. They desire a relationship that will build on mutual respect and trust. This relationship is based on needs of both the project leader and the sponsor or customer. Both must have something of value to give and both must have needs that must be satisfied. Because the position of the customer or sponsor outranks that of the project leader, the onus falls to the leader to justify both the value being offered and the needs of both parties. This is a fundamental principle of our leadership competency framework: the ability to achieve a trust-based relationship with the customer. It is only when trust is established that the ability to provide advice and recommendations emerges.

Ordinary stakeholders also want a leader to be an advocate for them. They may not have as much on the line as the paying customer, but if the strategic change is not appropriately carried out, or if the leader ignores or overlooks key parts of the business, the impact could be severe to these stakeholders. These customers may not need the same level of advice and recommendations as a sponsor, but they do need a strong, trust-based relationship to ensure that their interests and concerns are being properly voiced in a manner consistent with their needs. These trust-based relationships will often lead to customers' soliciting advice, insight, or recommendations from the service-based project leader as the project progresses.

Team members are customers to a service-based project leader as well. They want a leader who believes in them and cares for their well-being. This only occurs once a strong relationship has evolved between the leader and team members and the leader has built confidence in the eventual success of the endeavor. Team members want meaningful work and the ability to control their work to some extent, while not being micro-managed or overridden at every critical juncture. They need coaching, advice, and recommendations, but none of these are effective until this trust-based relationship first exists. Trust is the bridge connecting a project manager with becoming a service-based project leader.

When we look at the basic characteristics of a project and how they resonate in a customer's mind on strategic projects, we can conclude that a service-based project leader must be adept at three critical leadership competencies:

- Relating to stakeholders and all customers. This applies specifically to the development of trust-based relationships.
- Leading without authority. They must be able to lead through consultative skills aimed at serving the best interests of others.
- Accepting the risks associated with first two. This is courage, the courage to transform into self-directed leaders who desire internal transformation as a part of the larger transformation.

## *Leader Instead of Manager*

The term "management" is traditionally viewed as directing and controlling the resources and assets within one's span of control. Managers have budgets and resources to carry out the processes needed to run organizations. The term project "manager" implies some level of control and authority, though temporarily granted by a project charter. Project managers who use this granted authority to get things done in the same manner associated with a traditional manager find marginal success at best.

A leader accomplishes goals through other people by aligning, motivating, and setting them in the right direction. A leader is accustomed to having little or no control.[2] Thus, the title project or program manager is a self-defeating label that orders one to direct and control this temporary, unique initiative with resources over which they have little or no authority, pushing project managers into more technical administrative roles with minimal strategic recognition from executives.

The sooner practitioners exchange the title manager for leader and approach programs and projects as if they have absolutely no control or authority, the more likely they will be able to understand this framework for leadership competencies and practically apply it.

## Summary

To build leadership competencies to succeed as a service-based project leader, it is essential to focus on the realism of the program environment and stakeholders' needs. All of the stakeholders are customers of the service-based project leader. The more strategic the project is to the organization, the greater the risk associated with the project, and the greater the stakes are for all customers involved. The characteristics of strategic projects and programs subject participants to a human condition that drives behavior—fear.

Because of this fear of failure, sponsors, team members, and critical stakeholders worried about uncertain project outcomes have the need for guidance and a trust-based relationship with the program leader. This establishes the major leadership competencies for strategic project and program leaders; relating to stakeholders, leading without authority, and accepting the risks associated with these relationships and the lack of authority.

## Endnotes

1. Warren Bennis and Joan Goldsmith, *Learning to Lead* (New York: Basic Books, 2003), 3.
2. John Kotter, *Leading Change* (Boston: Harvard Business School Press, 1996), 26.

# Chapter 12

## *The Strengths of a Service-Based Project Leader: The MyProjectAdvisor® Leadership Competency Pyramid*

### Introduction

Service-based project leaders are different from project managers. Certainly not everyone may be called to this type of leadership, but for those who are disenchanted with their project careers, the service-based project leader may just be the answer. Leaders exhibit many admirable characteristics, but service-based project leaders:

> *Continually build self-awareness*—The new role of the service-based project leader demonstrates the desire to increase self-awareness, particularly regarding personal values, strengths, and failings. They continually search for the alignment of convictions with their work and feedback on leadership competencies. This allows them to pursue greater, more important challenges.

*Develop a healthy level of self-esteem*—These leaders have a strong sense of their own purpose, which translates into self-esteem. They can answer the questions, "Why am I here?" and "What am I called to do?" These answers coupled with confidence and humility provide a healthy level of self-esteem. They never take team members for granted, and recognize and value others' talents without fearing them. Their healthy self-esteem enables others to aspire to personal achievement through their increased productivity and team participation.

*Put trust in the forefront*—Trust-based relationships are the cornerstone of service-based project leaders' success. These leaders are conscious of every detail that enhances or erodes trust. They recognize that people trust other people, not institutions. Thus, they develop mutually rewarding and beneficial relationships based on honesty. Their team members and customers truly believe their leader has a shared, sincere interest in the project.

*Value open, porous borders*—A service-based project leader recognizes where project organizational structures and disciplines meet, and builds interfaces between these boundaries of responsibilities, making them stronger and more open through their genuine efforts to serve and grow others. Where project team and customer borders meet, the leader uses honesty, trust, and value-added services to create stable interfaces that are porous to allow information to flow freely back and forth.

*Prefer action over planning*—Planning is important to a service-based project leader, but only insofar as it initiates meaningful action that creates results and momentum. The effort spent on planning is carefully evaluated against the cost, benefits, and risks to all stakeholders. Service-based project leaders always have a plan at hand to initiate action at a moment's notice, when stakeholders are ready. Their plans are easily comprehended by their ability to customize complex project information into user-friendly, actionable information.

*Share leadership and decision making*—Service-based leaders understand the value of having everyone participate in the leadership of the project. Decision-making is not shunned, but appropriate decisions are made by the service-based project leaders while others are distributed naturally to customers and team members. Decision-making is collaborative and free from the fear of failure.

*Embrace change*—A service-based project leader is an advocate of change. With change comes an opportunity to grow. Whether it is embracing new technology or new processes, change is embraced, consumed, and optimized. Energy otherwise spent on resisting change is channeled into consuming and optimizing activities. Service-based project leaders seek out change, being early adopters, giving them an advantage over the resistors.

*Show humility*—Service-based project leaders know their role in the project is to serve, and they do so with humility. They are aware of the awesome responsibilities entrusted to them and take seriously the reality that they cannot do everything themselves. Instead, they humbly build the strengths of their team to increase their chances of success.

*Strive for balance*—Service-based project leaders are careful not to overextend themselves, carefully balancing their work and personal lives. They choose to produce excellence in their services, by being smarter, faster, and superior in their trade, giving them flexibility to live a well-rounded life. Their capacity to excel is directly tied to the support structure they continually maintain through relationships.

*Personalize their work*—Over time, a service-based project leader's role becomes personalized to each customer and team member, establishing a unique brand. This brand lives in an emotional connection rather than in a mere business relationship. These emotional connections make the services of the leader unique and very difficult to duplicate. The services are thereby protected from commoditization, as the uniqueness of the service is integral to the person. Individual purpose and personal touch are woven together into the fabric of these unique services.

There are many other traits of a service-based project leader that embody various leadership styles. Just like all good leaders, they are adept at combining a variety of situational factors using intuition, good judgment, and experience to make positive events occur.

Leadership voids and program failures continue to be a disease for organizations and society as a whole. The reward for customers, stakeholders, team members, and society when the leap from project manager to service-based project leader is successful is a changed world, one project at a time.

# Overview of MyProjectAdvisor® Leadership Competency Pyramid

The MyProjectAdvisor® Leadership Competency Pyramid (See Figure 12.1) is designed to enable project leaders to bring passion, compassion, patience, persistence, and new ideas into their projects, instead of just pert charts, critical paths, input milestones, or parametric estimates.

Why a pyramid? Because the size of a pyramid is dependent on its base. The height and width of a structure must be matched to the base to ensure that its structure can be supported. The pyramids of ancient Egypt are mystical and wondrous creations. People marvel at these structures and wonder how they were built. A leadership competency pyramid should create similar experiences of wonder and awe; a "wow" effect at which stakeholders, including team members, customers, and peers can marvel.

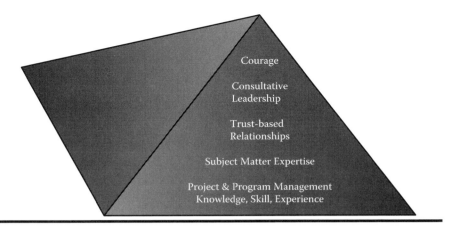

**Figure 12.1   MyProjectAdvisor® leadership competency pyramid.**

## *Knowledge, Skill, and Experience*

The base of the pyramid is a leader's project and program management knowledge, skill, and experience. This knowledge, skill, and experience exist in the form of certifications and experience on various types of projects and with various tools, methodologies, and systems. The presence of a certification is not the completion of the base—the base must continually expand if the pyramid is to grow taller. From this base, project managers can launch successful service-based project leader careers.

## *Subject Matter Expertise*

The second layer of the pyramid is subject matter expertise. Subject matter expertise is domain expertise and knowledge of particular industries, applications, or processes. There has always been a debate concerning the areas in which a project manager needs subject matter expertise. Some argue that a project manager needs to understand software technology to manage a software project. Others contend that project managers should be able to manage any project if skilled at project management; that project managers can apply the same cookie-cutter processes to any project, thus eliminating the need for subject matter expertise. This argument applies only to project managers, not strategic transformational service-based project leaders.

A service-based project leader's customer focus and transformational intent requires that he understand his customers' business—all of his customers. Customers are willing to pay for domain expertise because they are looking for insight and expertise from an objective party. If the customer is not looking for this insight, they are either getting it from somewhere else or they are not ready to create or sustain strategic change in their organization. Complexity and compressing timeframes require project leaders to gain credibility quickly; customers do not have the patience to educate a project leader on their business.

Another critical part of both foundational layers in the pyramid is a well-rounded knowledge of leadership. Expanding leadership knowledge is just as important as project and program management knowledge, skill, and experience and subject matter expertise.

## Trust-Based Relationships

The third component of the pyramid is trust-based relationships, which must be formed with all types of customers—team members, sponsors, and important stakeholders. Trust is a cornerstone for leadership; sadly, studies show that lack of trust is reaching new heights. As global competition and organizational change accelerate, it is obvious why trust is low in organizations. People tend to trust less when more is at stake; strategic projects have much at stake. Surveys of 450 executives in 30 companies found that about half of all managers don't trust their leaders.[1] The instability created by constant organizational change and ambiguity makes trust building difficult. These conditions hold for strategic initiatives and may even exacerbate the erosion of trust-building conditions.

Trust is not magic. People decide to trust. Entering into trust-based relationships takes time; they are more than relationships based on rational mutual business interests. Instead, these relationships are both rational and emotional.[2] Trust-based relationships flow from a strong base of project and program management knowledge, skill, experience and customer insight that provides a foundation for the remaining layers of the pyramid.

## Consultative Leadership

The fourth layer of the pyramid is consultative leadership. This emerges directly out of trust-based relationships. Consultative leadership is the ability to lead others without direct authority. Consultative leadership is also rooted in servant leadership. Consultative leadership combines strong advisory skills with compassion and service to enable strategic project leaders to achieve meaningful results through others. The demands of stakeholder management in strategic projects require a mixture of advisory and consultative skills to keep everyone moving of their own free will toward project objectives. Since strategic projects' results are often ambiguous and difficult to visualize and define, the service-based project leader provides consultative assistance that aligns the growth of the project organization with the desired results.

**A successful service-based project leader is one who leaves his team members more autonomous, capable, productive, and generally better off than before their interaction with him.** Consultative leadership skills are ultimately about getting people to commit to actions that drive project results and illuminate opportunities to achieve others. Service-based project leaders are dedicated to giving themselves to others in order to achieve something greater than themselves.

## Courage

Courage is the mortar that keeps the bricks of the pyramid together. The higher one works up the pyramid, the more courage is required. Trust-based relationships require the courage to know oneself better and to speak articulately and passionately about subjects in front of customers. It takes courage to develop a relationship that reaches beyond the safe rational level to the less predictable emotional one. Courage is required to serve others with no expectations of receiving anything in return. Asking, "How can I help you?" takes courage; a carefully planned day may be thrown into chaos.

Drawing the line between serving and enabling also takes courage. Many aspiring leaders do others' work to avoid having to confront them with their deficiencies. It requires courage to be honest with people but honesty without compassion is brutality. A service-based leader's behavior demonstrates honesty and sincerity through a commitment to improving the lives of others. Turning promises into actions requires courage. They need courage to simultaneously transform themselves and to create and sustain change in the environment around them.

## Balancing the Pyramid's Layers

The service-based project leader must learn to correctly balance all the pyramid's components to lead transformational projects. Most project managers have traces of each layer in their competency makeup. The challenge is to develop the proper layers of leadership competencies in order to face their unique challenges. Balancing the strengths of each layer against each other builds a stable pyramid. If certain layers are disproportionate to others, effectiveness is diminished.

For instance, a leader with a large base of knowledge, skill, experience, and customer subject matter expertise, but a minimal ability to develop trust-based relationships will struggle to be effective at consultative leadership. A project leader with many years of experience managing large complex projects, detailed industry knowledge and refined skills is likely to be a high-cost resource to the project. Without the developed layers of the competency pyramid, the leader does not create the value commensurate with his cost. Value is associated with the ability to develop positive human relationships or the ability to lead without authority. This leader will potentially become frustrated with the lack of results, or alternatively become comfortable and complacent in his role. The latter often occurs as valuable knowledge, skill, and experience go wasted due to either a desire to stay within a comfort zone or an inability to assume the risks associated with leadership competencies.

Another more hazardous imbalance in the pyramid is a leader who has tremendous courage, consultative leadership skills, and the ability to align and motivate others. Such a leader may also have the personality and people skills to quickly develop strong trust-based relationships. However, if they lack the base of knowledge, skill, and experience, the resulting imbalance weakens trust. Some leaders may be capable of overcoming these deficiencies through salesmanship and self-confidence that force direction and commitment. Nonetheless, this imbalance results in potentially excessive risks for customers and stakeholders due to the leader's lack of knowledge, skill, and experience.

Using subjective models to calculate the relative size of each layer and compare these measurements to the level of technical and social complexity of the project is possible, but not foolproof. A leader's intuition and self-knowledge are paramount in discovering the right balance of leadership competency layers for a given project. One must be careful not to skew intuition and self-knowledge with extreme risk-seeking or risk-aversion attitudes.

Building a leadership competency pyramid is not a finite task, but rather a lifelong endeavor. The following chapters focus on how to build a leadership competency pyramid that will be the framework for your service-based project leadership experiences.

When presenting these leadership competency concepts to project management practitioners on various continents, they are met with overwhelmingly positive responses. Practitioners are accustomed to developing analytical skills, but often pay less attention to the soft skills involved in dealing with people—including oneself—intelligently and effectively. It's no wonder so few projects succeed! These responses are evidence that practitioners are craving practical methods and techniques that can be practiced successfully on their projects. They desire to be a unifying influence rather than be a divisive one and recognize the need to find meaning in their project work.

So why aren't more practitioners reaching to get more out of their careers or demanding tools from training providers? Part of the reason may be the lack of a meaningful way to internalize these concepts and make them a reality. The MyProjectAdvisor® Leadership Competency Pyramid is meant to do just that.

## Summary

Service-based project leaders are different from project managers because they continually build self-awareness, develop a healthy level of self-esteem, and put trust in the forefront. They value open, porous borders, prefer action over planning, share leadership and decision making, embrace change, show humility, strive for balance, and personalize their work.

The MyProjectAdvisor® Leadership Competency Pyramid is a framework to build project leadership competencies. The base of the pyramid is a leader's project management knowledge, skill, and experience. The next layer is subject matter expertise, or contextual expertise and knowledge of particular industries, applications, or processes. The third component of the pyramid is trust-based relationships, which must be formed with customers, team members, sponsors, and important stakeholders to enable the fourth layer, consultative leadership, to emerge. Courage is the mortar that keeps the bricks of the pyramid together. The service-based project leader must learn to correctly balance all the pyramid's layers. Building a leadership competency pyramid is not a finite task, but rather a lifelong endeavor.

## Endnotes

1. Robert Hurley, "Decision to Trust," *Harvard Business Review,* September 2006.
2. David Maister, Charles H. Green, and Robert M. Galford, *The Trusted Advisor* (New York: The Free Press, 2000), p. 23.

## Chapter 13

# Building Your Base— Knowledge, Skills, Experience

## Introduction

"Knowledge is power," when integrated with skill and experience and then acted upon. However, knowledge, skill, and experience must be tightly integrated to enable leadership competencies. To have success leading a strategic project, service-based project leaders must be able to weld their knowledge, skill, and experience to create a strong value proposition for customers.

Knowledge without skill leaves the leader without the confidence to execute project strategies that may appear routine to leery customers and sponsors. Knowledge and skill without experience leaves the leader stagnating without content to build credibility. Building the base of the pyramid should be viewed holistically, with knowledge, skill, and experience each complementing the other.

## Building Project and Program Management Knowledge

Building project and program management knowledge is easier today because of the accessibility of books, websites, and training programs. But it is challenging because there is so much material available; it is difficult to know where to start.

For a newcomer to the project management environment, one with just a few years of experience working on project teams or managing smaller projects, the first step is to establish a baseline of knowledge, preferably with a formal education and certification. The value of this step is often disregarded by project managers who rush into the certification process, ignoring the skills and experiences to be gained along the way. Many certifications require a certain level of experience, but the accumulation of knowledge associated with the certification should be done in a manner that allows the project manager to apply the knowledge to his job. This makes the knowledge more meaningful, and easier to retain. The integration of knowledge and experience begins to build skills.

## A Certification Story

A project manager was unsure of whether a certification would provide any meaningful value to her career. In the meantime, she built knowledge by taking project management courses and then reevaluated the value of the certification. After a few months, she determined she was unable to use any of her newly acquired knowledge on her projects, because projects were run differently at her company. Of course, her company did care about managing costs, schedules, and risk, but she felt the knowledge and formal approaches she learned in the classroom did not fit her job. This person went on to get her certification a few years later anyway, but the real issue at hand was that she was unable to translate her knowledge of basic project management processes to her job. She failed to integrate her knowledge with experience and attempt to build new skills. Candidates for project management job positions and newcomers to project management make similar mistakes by missing the integration of the knowledge, skill, and experience and simply expecting a certification to boost their resume.

For newcomers, the recommendation is to build up a base of project management knowledge, by taking a few courses on the basics of project management, courses that introduce processes and knowledge components. Reading some books that cover project management from a broad perspective is also recommended. Suggested books for beginners include:

- *Managing Projects in Organizations,* by J. Davidson Frame. This book is a quick read and contains many valuable insights into the reality of managing projects in any organization. It provides excellent stories about real challenges project managers face. It also stresses the need to understand the real customer need.
- *Customer-Driven Project Management,* by Bruce Barkley and James Saylor. This book provides a comprehensive view of project management from the perspective of customer satisfaction. It places a strong emphasis on customer involvement in project processes and instilling quality into all project processes and deliverables.
- *Project Management Competence,* by J. Davidson Frame. This book is a good primer for someone thinking about a certification. It focuses on project manager competency.

■ *The AMA Handbook of Project Management, Second Edition,* by Paul Dinsmore and Jeannette Cabanis-Brewin. An up-to-date revision of the classic text expands on the areas covered in the PMBOK Guide, while also exploring the organizational, professional, and marketplace issues that project managers face.

At a minimum, a project manager should be able to apply basic project management concepts and begin to build skill and experience on the job. The basics of planning and executing projects using scope definition, work breakdown structures, budgets, schedules, and change control processes are necessary. Also encompassed in the basics are knowledge of risk management, quality techniques, communication skills, resource management, procurement activities, and team development that must be understood and then experienced in real projects.

For a project or program manager who is ready to supplement this basic knowledge of project management and recognizes the demand for and value of strategic change in organizations, the following organization change literature is a good starting point:

■ *Leading Change,* by John Kotter. This book outlines the essential practical steps for building lasting change in organizations.
■ *The Path of Least Resistance for Managers,* by Robert Fritz. This book takes a unique approach to creating change in organizations by focusing on structural design and consulting techniques.
■ *Conquering Organizational Change,* by Mourier and Smith. This book provides insight into successfully planning and implementing organizational change.

Senior project managers with a certification should focus on expanding their base of program management knowledge and integrating it with experience and skills. Program management requires stakeholder management, communication, benefit justification recognition, and general leadership skills that encompass project leadership skills. The challenge for many is lack of time. Making the leap from project manager to service-based project leader requires a serious commitment. A senior-level project manager may be managing a program or multiple initiatives, traveling, and trying to balance work and family obligations. A certification obligates one to participate in a certain amount of continuing education to maintain the credential, but this continuing education is not designed to fuel the leap from project manager to service-based project leader. For that, additional self-directed educational activities are required.

The senior project manager must continue to read project management literature. The project management knowledge base must be expanded to include more technical depth and specialization. Even if this technical depth is not fully utilized, it can illuminate deficiencies in current organizational or personal practices. Mastering advanced scheduling techniques, cost benefit methodologies, controlling techniques such as earned value, or advanced risk techniques is a natural progression of project management knowledge. Books, course work, and advanced degrees are available for project managers who have the desire to increase their project and program knowledge base.

As project managers broaden their base of project management knowledge, a critical component is understanding the transformation of self, others, systems, and organizations. Thus, it is appropriate to build knowledge on leadership, emotional literacy, and organizational behavior. Advanced instruction in program and portfolio project management is available as well.

Recommended books on relationship management and leadership development include:

- *Primal Leadership,* by Richard Boyatzis, Daniel Coleman and Annie McKee
- *True Professionalism,* by David Maister
- *Resonant Leadership,* by Richard Boyatzis and Annie McKee

A newer concept that is taking hold in business schools is the use of classic literature in leadership. The idea is to use classics such as Joseph Conrad's *The Secret Sharer*, or Arthur Miller's *The Death of a Salesman*, to explore the lives of the characters in these stories. These efforts help students understand the turmoil that exists inside a leader's mind and inner life so as to bring about an awareness of these challenges to future leaders. Literary conflicts are rarely black and white with clear answers; the protagonists often face moral dilemmas that must be worked through, just as today's leaders face many moral and ethical dilemmas.[1]

The senior project manager must continually seek to extract knowledge from books and journals and attempt to find areas in their work experience and social lives to implement these concepts. They should not ignore the books or research journals related to other industries, such as organizational development, psychology, or management. This information increases the opportunity for practical applications of new ideas and concepts.

Participation in research projects and authorship of articles can be translated into continuing education for certification renewals; plus, such contributions provide the industry with a dose of reality from practitioners who live and breathe project management.

Other practical suggestions for enhancing a project management knowledge base are:

- Volunteer to increase project management knowledge in your company. Hold brown bag lunches on various topics, or present a case study or lessons learned from previous experiences.
- Write an article for a journal or publication.
- Present a speech on a project management topic at a local chapter or conference.
- Apply project management principles to a nonprofit organization or community project.

In summary, your base of project management knowledge must continually grow. In order to build leadership competencies essential for service-based project leaders and transformational leadership, one must be an expert with broad, deep knowledge in project and program management.

## Building Project Management Skills

Project management skills are essential to leading a project team. These skills grow out of project management knowledge. The key to building skills is to look beyond the routine practices and treat each project as unique. Treating every project the same creates stagnation and inhibits growth, which becomes apparent to customers. Tools used to create deliverables take on a normalcy that encourages creators to gloss over details. The focus shifts the deliverable, its practical use in achieving the overall project goals to just "getting it done," faster, cheaper, or even worse, filling a spot in the governance binder. Many of these expensive project deliverables, particularly planning deliverables, sit idle in binders, project web portals, or e-mail accounts, adding minimal value to the project and becoming obsolete before the ink dries. They are the results of project managers lacking skills to make deliverables meaningful and useful to customers.

### Real Needs

A skill lacking in many project managers is the ability to find and articulate the real customer need. This skill is associated with the initiation of projects, which is often left to sponsors, but a project manager must play an important role in this process if she is expected to be a project leader.

Project managers often spend too much time studying requirements without exploring the real need, which may result in the project plan being fundamentally flawed from the beginning. Customers have a sense of their needs but often do not understand their full implication.[2] A project manager expands her skill base by seeking and validating the real customer need by first listening to the customer. **The presumption of a plan or solution does not precede the real need.** The art of questioning is a key skill that project managers should seek to continually improve. The art of questioning includes the articulation of the question, use of open-ended questioning, use of logical sequencing, reading of verbal and facial expressions, use of active listening techniques, and a tolerance for silence—the willingness to wait for others to formulate thoughtful responses.

Understanding the real need of the project and its customer is a discovery process. This discovery involves continual dialogue and collaboration, which implies that a relationship must exist between the project manager and the customer. Conducting diligent research and investigation of similar projects are practical ways of beginning this process. Articulating the need correctly is also critical. The skill of articulation takes practice, a strong command of the language, business acumen, and project management knowledge.

Validate the articulated need with team members, stakeholders, and customers to gain agreement and then create a project vision statement. Articulating the end state tells everyone when completion has been reached. Graphics can be particularly helpful in generating dialogue that leads to crystallizing the end state. Need statements should be short, precise, and bold. They should articulate what is needed and why.

## Strategic Need Statement: Example

The Operation Division of ABC Company needs to reduce per unit production cost by 25 percent, increase production capacity by 50 percent in two years and grow market share by 10 percent annually to provide satisfactory return to investors and provide employees with long-term career growth opportunities. These needs, critical to securing the future health of the organization, will require unprecedented commitment, collaboration, and innovation from employees and partners.

The statement should clearly identify a group or organization that is responsible for accomplishing the mission and it should state attainable, measurable goals. A good need statement aligns stakeholders' long-term interests rather than short-term personal goals. A need statement should acknowledge the challenges and risks associated with the undertaking and recognize the potential sacrifices people may have to make to accomplish the mission or vision. This is especially important because many people will be taking on extra duties beyond their normal jobs to accomplish it. A need statement can be more modest as well.

## Tactical Need Statement: Example

The Human Resource Department of XYZ Company needs to provide immediate access (two minutes or less) to employee records, and reduce manual filing and storage costs by 75 percent annually, starting in the first quarter of next year. By providing improved access to employee personnel records, we will better serve our valued employees by adding three staff members to recruit and train new employees.
Needs statements are essentially the same as goals and objectives, however, stating the need implies more urgency and focus. Goals and objectives often become wish lists and fade over time. A project leader who facilitates a collective needs statement that reflects the will of the people has done a tremendous feat. These needs can be translated into visions, how these critical needs will be met (i.e., new technology, distributed production operations in developing countries, new processes, etc.).

Too often, project teams have no need statement, but rather a vague vision that uses phrases such as "improve customer satisfaction," "automate processes," and "reduce costs." The "how much" and "why" are missing. Project managers, sponsors, and executives shy away from these details by not bothering to quantify them though analytics for fear of falling short, or by their inability to be honest with their employees. Six Sigma Methodology has helped overcome these obstacles, but the pace of change can be so volatile that analysis and need statements quickly become outdated.

Most importantly, a need statement creates urgency with unity that leads to a clear, compelling vision, one that invokes a mental image or picture that captivates people's imaginations. A well-constructed project vision can be explained quickly and tightly linked to the need statement.

Discovering the real need requires a project leader to pursue an open and honest dialogue with customers and sponsors. This dialogue is supported by the service-based project leader's establishment of credibility and mutual trust. The leader must justify the importance of the needs identification and articulation process. She asks such questions as:

- Why does capacity need to increase, or cost need to decrease?
- How much does it need to increase or decrease?
- How is it measured?
- What if this need is not met? What happens? Who is at risk?
- Who ultimately benefits from having these needs met?

The questions must be vigorously pursued by the service-based project leader and answered if everyone is to comprehend the vision.

## Leading with Work Breakdown Structures

Another under-utilized skill is the effective use of work breakdown structures in project planning and scope definition. The work breakdown structure (WBS) is a fundamental element of project planning but is often misunderstood and incorrectly used.

## A WBS Story

A presenter at a project management conference discussing the effective use of work breakdown structures asked a room of about 150 project certified practitioners if a WBS was created by inputting a series of tasks into a scheduling tool. Because of the way the question was asked, the audience was led to think this was a normal standard practice. Ninety percent of the audience agreed and raised their hands. This is strong evidence that practitioners do not understand the power and purpose of the WBS. Another telltale sign is whether practitioners involve the customer in creating a work breakdown structure. When workshop attendees were asked, roughly nine out of ten said no.

Project leaders must be effective in creating simple work breakdown structures—preferably graphic—that align with the real need and vision of the project. The work breakdown structure is built with and for the customer and team members.

A WBS with the appropriate level of detail for the situation is invaluable. If there is too much detail, the stakeholder will get lost; if it is too vague, it will be a waste of time. The right level of detail will generate dialogue that enhances buy-in to the project plan. Each major deliverable should have obvious value to the project or program, its processes, and ultimately its end result. Writing a short objective statement for each deliverable is recommended. The customer and team have the right to understand why valuable resources are being expended to create project deliverables. Projects that are driving change often require deliverables that help to continuously clarify the ambiguity of the change as it occurs. Writing a clear objective with each major WBS deliverable helps the team and customer understand what it is being used for and how to best manage the quality associated with the deliverable.

In technology projects that require users to adapt to change, the major deliverable from the project team may be to deliver "ready users" who are excited, knowledgeable, and trained on all aspects of the process and technology to speed the adoption and subsequent recognition of benefits. Once the project team and customers agree on this objective, the detailed deliverables, marketing materials, training deliverables, and promotional events become clearer to everyone. Now that deliverable objectives are agreed upon, acceptance criteria can be defined. What constitutes a "ready user" and how does the team measure it? Surveys, knowledge, and proficiency tests can now be discussed with the customer to define the most appropriate measurement technique that ensures success. These are questions all project leaders should be asking during the creation of their WBS. Project leaders who use the WBS to drive these discussions reduce scope creep while allowing the customer to actively participate in the creative process of planning.

Asking objective questions that produce measurable project deliverables, particularly planning deliverables, ensures the leader is spending the customer's money wisely.

## Stakeholder Management with "Simple" Project Network Diagrams

Using simple network diagrams to illustrate and highlight key dependencies and the associated decisions and risks is critical to managing customer and team expectations. As a practitioner, you understand precedence diagrams and the differences between finish-start, start-finish, start-start or finish-finish relationships or how to calculate a critical path. These are not the skills being referred to. The critical project management leadership competency is the ability to build a user-friendly logical sequence with the customer and team that brings the entire organization to an understanding of the logical flow of the project.

Consider the dependencies associated with building a golf course. Determining which tasks are dependent on each other may initially seem a like technical exercise; first develop a land use plan, then conduct environmental assessment, then develop course design, then get permits, and so on. However, it is easy to ignore the role of the sponsors and customers. The sponsors may indicate they would not expect any work beyond the environmental assessment to begin until after a membership drive has secured 100 members with cash deposits. Other customers, potential members, may demand course design prior to putting money down on a membership. This highlights the fact that the **customers must be highly involved in the sequencing of major activities and understand the risks associated with them.**

Sponsors tend to drastically cut schedules without wanting to compromise scope or quality. If a project leader has involved the customer and sponsors in the creation of the WBS at the appropriate level, the proper use of a simple network diagram allows the risks of compressing timelines to be highlighted. This art form has little to do with the technical aspects of network diagraming and everything to do with stakeholder management.

The skill of using simple network diagrams to illustrate and highlight key dependencies and their associated risks is effective in managing expectations and identifying risks.

## *Risk*

Another misunderstood skill is the articulation of risk. Project managers must understand risk management processes; risk identification, quantification, subsequent response plans, and controlling activities. But, project managers are notorious for capturing issues, assumptions, and hidden risks around projects, and aggregating them into lengthy lists that get little attention and quickly become outdated. Articulating these risks as impacts to strategic objectives that can be quantified, acted upon, and monitored is a valuable skill project managers need to lead programs.

Articulating risks with clarity makes them real and manageable. A risk statement should be a description of an event or condition and the resulting impact. If the engines fail, the airplane will crash. The event is clearly identified, which allows root causes or sources of risk to be identified and the impact quantified.

A typical software project may include an assumption that user security profiles are accurate based on business manager sign off. A project manager leaves this as an assumption, but a leader translates this assumption into a risk event:

> If user role security profiles are incorrect, the resulting changes to user profile security after user acceptance testing will create the need for additional test cycles increasing testing costs by 5 percent.

Now a discussion about the probability of the risk event, risk sources, and decisions about acceptance, mitigation, and subsequent planning activities can occur. Too often risks get documented as generic issues or assumptions or even worse, pushed under the table. By properly identifying the risk event or condition, probability, and impact, the sources can be rooted out and mitigation plans built into the project plan. Confident, rational discussions can be held with customers, sponsors, and key stakeholders allowing them to make decisions to accept or mitigate the risk. A project manager who does not aggressively pursue risk management dialogue with her customers sees her schedule and costs continually slip with no concrete evidence as to why. She is left holding the bag of project waste.

Well-developed risk statements capture the attention of customers and allow for risk quantification, mitigation, and response planning activities to be defined, thereby supporting reality-based decision-making. As with identifying real needs, open honest dialogue on risk must be pursued by the service-based project leader.

Using work breakdown structures, network diagrams, and risk statements to lead your project to a higher ground requires not just mastery of these skills, but also relationships with customers (trusted-based), their willingness to give you the authority to lead (consultative leadership), and fearless leadership (courage).

## Building Project Management Experience

The application of knowledge and skills produces experiences. Every effort to apply skills from knowledge generates experiences from which you can learn. For this reason, a project manager should seek out a variety of project management experiences. This could mean moving from one line of business to another, from information technology to more business-related projects, or into new industries. Varying experiences broadens the base by exposing the project manager to different project processes and acquiring experience with a variety of people.

It is also a good idea to participate in both large and small projects. Being a project manager on a small project is a different experience than being one of many project managers on a very large project. Building leadership competencies requires project management experience outside of one's regular job. Leading projects in your community is great soft-skill training for everyday project management.

## Summary

The base of the MyProjectAdvisor® Competency Pyramid is project management knowledge, skill, and experience. Expanding this base is critical for leadership competency development. Knowledge without skill leaves the leader without the confidence to execute project strategies. Knowledge and skill without experience leaves the leader stagnating without content to build credibility. The project manager must continually seek means to extract knowledge from books and journals and to attempt to find areas in her work experience and social life to implement these concepts. Key project management skills that help build leadership competencies are associated with real customer needs, and the proper use of work breakdown structures, project network diagrams, and risk statements. Project managers should seek a variety of project experiences, broadening the base of the pyramid by dealing with different project processes, and a variety of people.

## Endnotes

1. Joseph L. Badaracco, "Leadership in Literature," *Harvard Business Review,* March 2006.
2. J. Davidson Frame, *Managing Projects in Organizations,* revised ed., (San Francisco: Jossey-Bass, 1995) chap. 4.

## Chapter 14

# Building Subject Matter Expertise

## Introduction

Developing subject matter expertise is the most misunderstood component of the leadership competency pyramid. This does not mean a project leader must have expertise in every aspect of the project work. While it is certainly helpful to have experience with the type of work team members are doing, it is often impractical. Subject matter expertise is not about having the ability to master all aspects of the project work and tasks; rather it means understanding your customers and their business. A service-based project leader has many customers, including team members. To drive transformational change in them, you must know what they are experiencing—and what they want to experience.

Service-based project leaders are experts at project management but also need to demonstrate knowledge and familiarity with the customer's need. Customers attempting to create unprecedented strategic change desire a relationship based on mutual respect and common understanding. The risk of failure may be so great or the benefits so important to the organization that their personal association with this endeavor is irrevocable. These projects increasingly make up organizational project portfolios as the value of project management in achieving strategic objectives becomes apparent. However, sponsors, customers, and team members recognize that these projects are anything but standard. These projects can carry a legacy of failure or at least diminished expectations from previous strategic efforts and sponsors, customers, and team members approach these initiatives with trepidation.

The goal of the service-based project leader is to quickly demonstrate to the customer that one has a genuine interest in and a solid understanding of their needs.

This understanding is based on strong relationships—the kind that evolve out of mutual respect and trust.

Think about the last time you were a sponsor of a strategic project—a project that generated transformational change in your life. This might have been renovating a home, purchasing a home, settling an estate, or transitioning the lifestyle of an elderly parent. These are all transformational changes that must be dealt with in a manner that serves the best interests of numerous parties. They are strategic endeavors that involve significant risk and which, if not done properly, will likely result in a long-term problem that may prove more difficult to resolve. Would you like someone to help you who understands your situation, has knowledge and relevant experience, and has attempted similar projects? Someone who has your mutual respect and shares a common understanding?

A service-based project leader understands this customer and sponsor perspective and learns how to quickly recognize the key components of the customer's business and need, but at the same time shows a genuine interest in helping them. Customers place a premium on a leader's objectivity and recognize and appreciate his expertise in project management and his familiarity with their need, creating implicit value, which paves a path for explicit value.

Stakeholders sometimes mistakenly think project leaders must have many years of experience in the industry to be able to lead a strategic project. This is wrong. These people often make poor and ineffective project leaders because they are often too transaction-focused. They cannot see the overarching processes that are associated with creating transformational change and do not know how to create value in team members without years of similar industry experience. Almost every strategic project includes people who believe the strategic leader must have 25 years of their business experience to be credible. Savvy sponsors will not waste resources on teaching the strategic leader about the business because they have people with numerous years of experience who can fill in specific knowledge gaps. To overcome this, service-based project leaders must quickly gain subject matter expertise about the customer and demonstrate a genuine interest in the business need prior to moving up the pyramid to the next critical layer, trust-based relationships.

## Why Leaders Need Subject Matter Expertise

A service-based project leader must develop meaningful trust-based relationships with strategic stakeholders, including sponsors, influential parties, and team members. This trust begins with his credibility, which encompasses his project management expertise and its applicability to the present situation.

A sponsor's trust is crucial. She must delegate to the service-based project leader authority to act on her behalf. A lack of trust is a barrier to this delegation. A lack of knowledge of the sponsor's business is a barrier to trust. She will not delegate leadership, only managerial tasks, to someone who does not thoroughly understand her situation.

A good sponsor will initially sell the vision of the strategic initiative, particularly during its funding. But sponsors are usually very busy people and the vision must be continually communicated throughout the endeavor. Communicating the transformational change vision is often under-communicated by a factor of ten, a hundred, or even a thousand fold.[1]

**A service-based project leader must continually project the vision of the initiative to influential stakeholders, particularly those more distant or those possessing a distorted view of the initiative.** These stakeholders can generate chaos by their complacency, lack of support, or even active resistance. The projection of the vision can only be done effectively if he has a thorough understanding of the situation, its uniqueness, urgency, and hidden implications to the larger community. Through this deep knowledge of the customer situation, he becomes fully entwined in the endeavor, making it difficult to escape his leadership duty.

Finally, subject matter expertise is critical to developing credibility with team members. Team members are customers of a service-based project leader. In addition to wanting assurances that a sponsor's needs are being met, they desire a leader with knowledge of their work. He must be able to relate to the efforts of his team in a meaningful way. Through his expertise of understanding the real work his team must perform to satisfy the paying customer, his team will grant him opportunities to develop trust-based relationships that lead to consultative leadership opportunities. Does he need to be a resident expert in all aspects of project work? No. He must possess enough knowledge of his customer's business that allows him to articulate it in a manner that enhances credibility quickly.

## Mastering the Acquisition of Subject Matter Expertise

The ability to learn your sponsor's and customer's business quickly is an art. **Mastering the acquisition of subject matter expertise requires dedication to the project work, a fascination with how organizations function, tenacity, and mental toughness.** Small missteps can be devastating and require months of recovery. First impressions are often determinative, even if you have a long-standing reputation with your sponsor. You must prove yourself time and time again.

But if the initial steps are properly executed, you will have then earned the opportunity to develop deeper trust-based relationships, and authority will be subsequently delegated to execute on the initiative's vision. There are tactical methods to acquire subject knowledge expertise.

### *Follow the Money: Revenue and Cost*

The best way to understand the business and the resulting impact of a strategic initiative is to understand the basic financial processes of the organization. How does it make money and where does the money get spent? Once a project leader understands this, he can quickly see how his strategic project or program relates to the financial landscape of the organization.

Having a solid background in accounting and financial analysis is important. Leaders who have a Master of Business Administration (MBA) degree have an advantage due to the nature of the curriculum of this degree, but not having an MBA is not a limitation for a leader who is a committed lifelong learner. Community colleges offer courses that are relatively inexpensive compared to earning a master's degree, or one can acquire knowledge through the dozens of books on accounting and financial analysis available.

The revenue portion of the financial structure is usually easier to quickly figure out than the cost structure. Practically speaking, the service-based project leader should attempt to understand the revenue structure's stability or instability. If the organization is public, the certified financial statements are a start but they are often polished with good news for public consumption. The leader must dig deeper into the key metrics the organization uses to measure performance. These are often leading indicators of the ultimate revenue picture. Metrics that measure sales efficiency are important, as are the market conditions that influence these numbers.

Financial statements can identify an organization's customers who contribute to revenue, but without access to financial statements, an understanding of all of the organization's structure and basic purpose is the next best thing. By studying organizational charts, one can piece together a picture of a business unit performing income producing work and business units performing operational work.

It is necessary to understand changes in customer or market conditions that change revenue or margins as well as identifying which products or services are related to the core business and which are ancillary. Knowing how the organization recognizes revenue is important, as product and service companies often have different accounting rules for revenue recognition. Table 14.1 lists practical information to discover how revenue flows through an organization.

The cost picture of organizations is usually more difficult to discover, mainly because management protects this information. Again, public-certified financial statements are a start but are not user-friendly unless read by an auditor. Detailed

**Table 14.1   Revenue Information to be Discovered.**

- Identify which organization operating units are sources of revenue.
- Discover the organization's primary and secondary customers.
- Distinguish between revenue that is irregular versus standard operating revenue.
- Discover the characteristics of operating revenue. One-time revenue (i.e., sale of primary goods and services) or recurring revenue (i.e., maintenance or annual licenses).
- Investigate if returns or warrantees must be taken into account.
- Distinguish the actual receipt and financial recognition of revenue.
- Determine the companies' operating margins.
- Investigate revenue associated with investing activities.

**Table 14.2    Cost Information to Discover**

- Discover if the cost is associated with revenue, i.e., cost of goods sold.
- Discover if the cost is non-operating or extraordinary, i.e., write-downs.
- Distinguish investment activities and associated financing costs from other costs.
- Discover if the cost is fixed or variable.
- Determine if the cost is associated with sales, administration, or overhead.
- Determine organizational cash flow.

cost information is often buried in aggregated numbers for public consumption. The leader must dig deeper into key metrics the organization uses to measure performance. These are often leading indicators of the ultimate cost picture. Productivity metrics are very important, as are the factors that influence them.

An overlooked component of cost is charge-backs. Most organizations have charge-backs in one form or another and acquiring knowledge of them and their root causes is an important aspect of the cost structure that reflects the quality of the organization's processes. Table 14.2 lists practical questions to help understand how costs flow through an organization.

The simplest way to acquire a basic financial picture is to document each unit's primary purpose in the organization and its key performance metrics. This gives a project leader the overall view required to lead a strategic initiative. Acquiring this information is sometimes easier for outsiders than insiders. Sponsors feel compelled to give the consultants whatever information they need if it will help remove the pain that they promised to alleviate. Senior internal leaders are expected to know this information, particularly if they have been employed at the organization for several years. Others have trouble getting this information because their peers don't trust them, and still others do not have the courage to ask for it.

A leader tapped to head a strategic project makes his information needs immediately known to the sponsor, and explains the importance, and intended use of this information. The acquisition of this information is an early test of his authority. Efficient project leaders exhaust means of acquiring this information before making formal requests. Asking for information that is publicly available is equivalent to walking around the office with a blindfold on.

## Business Process Mapping

Another method of acquiring subject matter expertise quickly is the ability to mentally construct basic business processes. This mental construct precedes formal documentation of business processes and facilitates scope definition and requirements gathering. A project leader does not have the time to document an organization's business processes in their entirety, but these processes are usually documented or can be constructed at a high level that creates linkages between major processes, and identifies inputs and outputs across business units.

**Table 14.3    Business Process Information to Discover**

- Identify the major process activities of each organization and relationships between them.
- Document major inputs and outputs to each process.
- Identify the customers (internal and external) of the processes.
- Identify the suppliers of the goods or information into the process.
- Discover why certain activities are performed.
- Identify the key metrics (actual and desired) of major processes and activities.

Having a strong business process background is helpful in a similar way that having an accounting background is helpful for discovering the financial picture.

Business process knowledge is critical for a leader to understand the inner workings of an organization. The challenge is that the people involved in these processes often don't speak in business process terms but rather in transactional terms. The people are typically so close to the day-to-day work that they cannot see the bigger picture. However, an astute project leader will ask questions using terms that people understand, quickly translate responses into process terms, form a mental picture, then validate any assumptions or clarify outstanding questions. Table 14.3 lists practical questions to ask to quickly gain knowledge of a business process.

## Research and Networking

Finally, a leader acquires subject matter expertise through diligent research and the maintenance of a network of practitioners who have experience in particular industries or with particular types of projects.

A practical way to research a customer's business is to read the trade magazines the sponsor reads. These trade magazines are often sitting out on desktops or housed in corporate libraries. They can provide a quick overview of competition, industry trends, regulatory changes, and a who's who of the industry. The leader can tactically use the internet and other published sources to gain industry or process application insight. Vendors offer case studies on customers who have accomplished similar projects with their product or services.

Trade associations also offer insights into an industry. Joining the association and attending local meetings is a commitment a service-based project leader can make to gain critical subject matter expertise.

Maintaining a healthy network of practitioners allows a leader to quickly tap into experiences that can shortcut hours of research. The organization of the network is just as important as the building of it. Peers move in and out of projects, and keeping abreast of their experiences is a challenge. Ask peers for a current resume or a verbal summary of their latest project experiences and categorize them in a searchable contact database.

A customer's strategic project is serious business; the leader's ability to quickly master subject matter expertise creates value and opens the relationship to trust building. Customers are often willing to pay a premium for this expertise, thus the sooner one can acquire it, the better. A committed service-based project leader will get a head start, knowing that even if the project fails to survive, he has gained insight and subject matter expertise for future endeavors.

## Summary

Strong relationships evolve out of mutual respect and a common understanding. Customers attempting to create strategic change and transformation desire a strong relationship. The goal of the service-based project leader is to quickly demonstrate applicable knowledge and interest in the customer's business that provides the customer with a sense of understanding of his needs and a genuine interest. Gaining financial cost and revenue knowledge of customer business operations, their business processes, and conducting research on similar projects are means to acquiring subject matter expertise quickly.

## Endnotes

1. John Kotter, *Leading Change* (Boston: Harvard Business School Press, 1996), 91.

# Chapter 15

## Trust-Based Relationships

## Introduction

Developing trust is a core competency of leaders, and service-based project leaders are no exception. Failures of project leadership are normally accompanied by a breakdown of trust. Trust is an emotionally charged topic and has various interpretations. Trust has many dimensions: trust of others, trust of self, integrity, competence, and communication. Project environmental characteristics create a mutual need for a fiduciary relationship between customers and project teams, sponsors and project leaders, team members and leaders, and between team members. For this fiduciary relationship to be legitimate, it must grow into a trust-based relationship.

The absence of trust creates under-performing project teams guided by self-preservation and defense mechanisms. Perceptive stakeholders sense this dysfunction and aim their "project death bullets" at the project. Naive customers allow substantial investments to be wasted and eventually convince themselves that any output from the project is better than none at all.

Trust-based relationships must be mutual. They require active participation by both the service-based project leader and the stakeholder.[1] To engage in a trust-based relationship, the trusting party must recognize value. These relationships are sought after by many project managers but only develop for those who can demonstrate a need for the relationship. A service-based project leader must demonstrate ample reason why a team member, customer, sponsor, or critical project stakeholder should even consider entering into this relationship. Service-based project leaders demonstrate they are worthy of this relationship by bringing into play the base of the leadership competency pyramid—knowledge, skill, and experience, plus subject matter expertise about their customer.

# Obstacles

Organizational culture can impede trust-based relationships, but it should not be used as an excuse. If the culture is dysfunctional to a point that efforts to create these relationships in projects are met with resistance or even ridicule, and the leader has adequately evaluated and corrected her own failings in this process, then she should consider moving on. The best way to change organizational culture is to create leaders with a leadership mentality that embodies a healthy culture. Healthy cultures use trust as a centerpiece and service-based project leaders can play a critical role in changing cultures.

Other obstacles to trust building can be influenced by the service-based project leader. Compatibility, or the lack thereof, can be a significant hindrance to trust-based relationships. Identify behavioral styles in yourself and others, and seek to adapt your behaviors to those around you. Establishing compatibility is critical for managers and leaders. Good ones make it a tactical part of their routine, including consciously adapting their behavior to others.

Even with knowledge, skill, experience, and subject matter expertise, a lack of compatibility can be a huge barrier to developing trust and becoming a service-based project leader. Leaders who cannot adapt their behavior to the needs of others, find that conversations with stakeholders quickly fizzle. People find reasons not to engage with them. The awkwardness and discomfort of interacting with incompatible parties create tension that most prefer to avoid.

This awkwardness usually arises when people have conflicts in pace, the speed that characterizes their work, interactions, and priorities. Awkward situations arise quickly when people are unaware of their own tendencies. For instance, a task-oriented project manager trying to get a commitment from an engineer demands a completion date in front of the project team. The engineer, who has not completely assimilated all the requirements and technical nuances, feels pressured to guess and fears over-promising and under-delivering, believing his work will eventually be criticized. The inherent preferences make this relationship incompatible unless they adapt their behavior.

Someone who is more slowly paced and task oriented will need additional time to comprehend the details before committing to a date. A versatile project manager will understand this need. Style incompatibilities exist all over project organizations, creating awkward moments that impede trust building. Fast-paced "director" personalities who focus on achievements clash with personalities who prefer to put people first. Conceptually-oriented people clash with detail-oriented people, team builders clash with those who prefer to work alone, and so on.

A service-based project leader is aware of her level of compatibility with others and strives to maximize it. Those who wait for others to adapt to them often remain incompatible; service-based project leaders educate team members and stakeholders on compatibility techniques, but only after they have mastered the process for themselves. To establish compatibility quickly in project environments, service-based project leaders can take the following steps:

- Become aware of your natural relationship tendencies or social style
- Use a model with the appropriate psychometric rigor to assess your style
- Learn the characteristics of your style
- Become perceptive of others' natural relationship style
- Learn the characteristics of other styles
- Practice adapting behaviors to others to achieve compatibility

Compatibility is a steppingstone to forming a trust-based relationship.

# Building Trust on Projects

Trust-based relationships provide a project manager with an extraordinary capability to carry out the duties of the project. Trust-based relationships are not self-serving, but rather serve the project organization by generating the energy needed to drive change within change-resistant cultures. Trust can be a powerful, contagious source of emotional energy that is fueled by service to others and hope for the future.

When trust exists at this level with your sponsors and stakeholders, they begin to ask you for input and recommendations. They follow your recommendations or at least give them consideration in the decision-making progress. You become more effective in planning and executing activities. You start the transition from manager to leader.

# Building Blocks of Trust for Project Leaders

## *The Value Proposition*

Service-based project leaders recognize trust building is a mutual process and establishing a value proposition is the first step. Sponsors, stakeholders, and team members have plenty of demands on their time. To start the process, the other party must see a reason to engage with the project manager desiring to lead, not just manage, the strategic initiative. This reason is justified through a value proposition. The project manager must create the perception of his value to the critical stakeholders. This value is the sum of the stakeholder's need plus the credibility of the project manager. When a sponsor's "waking" need (a strategic project) is coupled with a project manager's compelling role to satisfy this need, a value proposition begins to emerge that can be parlayed into a trust-based relationship. Without these two elements, project managers struggle to achieve leadership stature in the eyes of their superiors.

Understanding the stakeholder's needs, including emotional and information needs, is paramount.

Team members, sponsors, and stakeholders have a variety of needs at the beginning of projects. Sponsors may want to see industry comparisons of similar projects, risk assessments, or the estimated completion date of the project. A team member may desire a certain type of work or a desire to learn a new skill set. A critical stakeholder may want to know how the project is going to impact her resources. At the beginning of any strategic project or program, the needs far outweigh the ability of any one person to satisfy them. A project manager must be selective and pick topics that maximize value by evaluating the importance of the need and strength of his credibility related to the need. Each need provides an opportunity for him to gain or lose credibility.

The strength of the need is commensurate with the power associated with a stakeholder. A common method for prioritizing these relationships is to use a stakeholder analysis, which ranks stakeholders by influence, control, concern, etc. The stakeholder analysis is an input to a leader's relationship priorities. With a clear focus on critical stakeholders, a leader can evaluate need strength with his knowledge, skill, and experience.

Trust must be earned by demonstrating competency with the proper intentions. A project manager wishing to lead must be willing to provide evidence of being trustworthy by demonstrating credibility, being reliable, being intimate with stakeholders, and showing concern for others.[2] Figure 15.1 illustrates the building blocks of trust in the MyProjectAdvisor® Leadership Competency Pyramid.

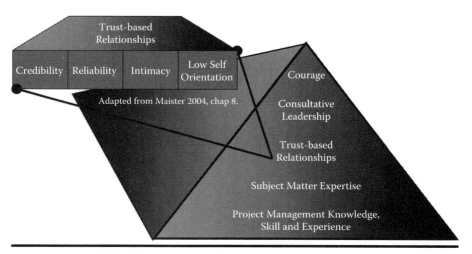

**Figure 15.1    Building blocks of trust-based relationships.**

## *Credibility*

Credibility is based on one's content knowledge and use of this content at the right moment to provide explicit value to stakeholders. Stakeholders will evaluate you on your thoroughness, how well you can articulate yourself, and the judgments you make with this knowledge.[3] The more developed the leadership competency pyramid base, the more content one has immediately available, allowing credibility to build faster on projects.

However, content knowledge, though critical, does not satisfy everyone. Strategic projects and programs often involve executive and senior level organizational leaders who put a premium on the ability to articulate content knowledge succinctly and accurately. Busy team members do not have the patience to unravel rambling, unstructured, aimless content. Good articulation of content leaves the stakeholder feeling confident about the discussion; poorly articulated content often leaves more questions than answers.

The five keys to articulation are:[4]

- Precision—the use of concise, affirmative sentences. Avoid vagueness.
- Accurate and complete information—provide information that is referenced and tell the complete story, not just the part of the story that justifies one position.
- Honesty—avoid exaggerations and admit when you don't know something. Don't guess.
- Kinesthetic experience—match emotions to the importance of the conversation, understand how and when to use social and personal space and facial expressions to convey meaning.
- Sensitivity to the listener—maximize audience's time, arrange topics in a logical order, talk in terms of risks and benefits, and create a conversation, not a lecture.

Continual practice articulating content is required since the complexity of projects and programs makes articulation difficult to master. When nervous or unsure of their content, project managers speak with extra words. When relaxed and confident, content arrives more concise and meaningful.

Timely, well articulated content about one's mastery of project management, their skills, and specific experiences in addition to knowledge of the customer's business is how a project leader creates credibility.

## *Reliability*

Reliability reinforces credibility. Reliability is driven by a project manager's actions. Making commitments and following through generates a sense of confidence and fulfillment. You are evaluated on your consistency and timeliness.[5] When successful, stakeholders view the project manager as dependable. By making promises and linking them to actions, a project manager creates a consistent track record.

Completing expected tasks, status reports, schedules, and project meetings is not the most critical aspect of reliability. The project manager must focus on what is *not* generally expected of them. A sponsor may ask for a schedule, budget, and resource requirements at the beginning of a project. Good project management practices will produce them. **A project leader, in addition, will find ambiguity, concerns, or other details of interest to stakeholders that lack clarity and resolve the ambiguity, filling emotional needs.** Ambiguity of interest to a sponsor might include risks, expert opinions, another's willingness to commit resources, or the amount of coordination required between related projects. Validated by the sponsor, the service-based project leader will make a commitment to satisfy these needs and quickly establish expectations for the outcome including timeframes and quality of work. By focusing on clarifying the ambiguity, the project leader begins to tap into the emotional needs of the stakeholder. Table 15.1 lists potential stakeholder needs that create opportunities to build reliability.

The link between credibility and reliability is strong. A conscious plan and practice will allow a project leader to quickly build them simultaneously early in the project initiation stage.

The leader must also build credibility and reliability with team members. Team members have concerns during the start-up phases of projects. No one desires to be on a poorly performing team or a project that is designed for failure. Team members can sense ambiguity and either take actions to protect themselves and their reputations or reach for additional responsibility, potentially challenging the project manager's authority. A project leader's focus on establishing credibility and reliability quickly with key team members will enhance role development and team performance. Time is limited and opportunities cannot be squandered. Below are

**Table 15.1  Stakeholder Needs That Offer Opportunities to Build Reliability.**

- Crystallizing ambiguous benefits and performance measurements
- Discovering hidden risks
- Clarifying dependencies, synergies, and impacts of related projects
- Capturing lessons learned, internally and externally
- Agreeing with customer needs and outcomes
- Clarifying user and customer expectations
- Defining who is responsible for what
- Defining major deliverables and objectives
- Defining immediate next steps
- Uncovering opposing requirements and needs

tips for creating credibility and reliability quickly with all your customers on new projects:

*Find out something about your customer they would not expect you to know.* Research and network with peers to bring forth new relevant information. If it is a new customer, read the last year's worth of press releases and an annual report. Find the CEO's latest speech to the industry on the internet. If it is an internal project, talk to managers about their biggest frustrations, take them to lunch and find out their key performance metrics and if they are meeting them and if not, why not. Find out what team members accomplished on previous projects, learn about their capabilities, and recognize previous efforts. Show a command of the customers' needs. Good team members want to make sure their efforts are going to produce results and satisfy a real need.

*Look for good opportunities to articulate content knowledge.* Timing is critical; sensing when conversations drift off track or when a lack of clarity stymies participants are the prime opportunities to inject content with commanding presence. One-on-one meetings are usually a safe place. Large meetings entail more risk, but if the timing is right, go for it.

*Make a commitment to act.* When sensing frustration or discomfort, probe with open-ended questions, such as, "Why is this unclear?" or, "Why is the answer elusive?" Seek opportunities to resolve the ambiguity and make a commitment to do so. Set clear expectations on outcomes and timeframes and follow up in a convenient manner with the stakeholder within 48 hours with an update as to its resolution or status.

*Run great meetings.* Project leaders must be able to run productive meetings, particularly early on in projects. Focusing clear objectives, setting expectations around specific outcomes, building a shared agenda with participants, defining actions to achieve specific outcomes, and organizing the meeting's content in a logical manner will increase credibility and reliability. Valuing input, encouraging participation, asking good questions, building consensus, offering to help others, and maintaining control are essential and create opportunities for the more challenging aspects of trust building.

*Let others promote you.* Avoid listing your credentials or past project successes, as they will probably already know what you have done or will find out through others. Focus on your actions in the present moment and do not rest on your reputation: it must be earned again and again.

## *Intimacy*

Intimacy is about connecting with stakeholders' inner sanctuaries where their deep beliefs and values reside, driving convictions and emotions. Intimacy is a source of private project intelligence. It is often lacking on projects and cannot be purchased on an expense account; intimacy must be genuine. Only after a clear value proposition exists for both parties, and the roots of credibility and reliability begin to take hold, should a project manager seeking to lead initiate efforts to build intimacy. Stakeholders evaluate you on your open honesty and the discretion you use with this additional information.

Maister calls intimacy "a game of mutually increasing risk," which must be initiated by the project leader.[6] The opening up of one's beliefs and values is risky; not everyone wants to participate. But there are tremendous benefits to establishing intimacy; the leader will be able to address topics usually barred from discussion, which improves decision making and builds camaraderie. Anyone leading a strategic project or program is handicapped if they cannot broach project topics that are critical to the success of the initiative, but which are kept off-limits due to politics, discomfort, or naiveté. The ability to discuss these difficult and often painful topics can give new life to an entire project organization. Most importantly, it gives a project leader more information from which to lead the initiative and make decisions based on reality and the needs of others. How the leader handles this information and what decisions are made with it will impact future efforts to develop intimacy.

Intimacy allows the project leader to influence the organization in ways others cannot. Intimacy is also a weapon against the traditional challenge of having project status modified from red to yellow to green as it moves up the management chain onto the executive's desk. As people tend to manipulate the truth about a project's status to order to protect themselves, intimacy can provide an advantage. Organizations who tolerate employees telling their superiors what they want to hear, rather than what they need to hear, is symptomatic of a sterile, unproductive culture.

## Tips for Building Intimacy on Projects

*Get to know people as individuals.* Begin by acquainting yourself with people as parents, spouses, and children instead of merely as analysts, programmers, engineers, etc. Get to know stakeholders' spouses and children by name and ask about them. Learn about their hobbies, their spiritual interests, social concerns, and show each of them respect. Learn what challenges they are facing both inside and outside the workplace. Acknowledge feelings about their successes, failures, and ongoing challenges. Empathy can be communicated by simply stating, "That situation must have been difficult for you." These simple gestures help you to connect with stakeholders as individuals. It is just as important to let them know you as an individual and not just a project manager.

*Take a personal risk.* Lead with a weakness. Often project leaders attempt to lead by demonstrating power or strength. Create intimacy by taking a personal risk. Share a personal failure and a lesson learned with an important stakeholder once you know them as an individual. This disclosure must be done with prudence. Too much information given too fast will turn people off, but sharing a failure or lesson learned on a previous project may enlighten both parties. It is critical that leaders take accountability for the failure and not place blame on others, and clearly state the lesson learned. This demonstrates a willingness to be open, honest, transparent, and a lifelong learner who can take something positive away from a failure.

*Visualize the moment.* When attempting to create intimacy, repeatedly envision the conversation, its progression, and desired outcome. Visualize facial expressions, emotions, words, and reactions before starting this process. In other words, have a plan; don't randomly begin to initiate intimacy without visualizing the process and the outcome. Take a deep breath to relax the upper body. Relaxing helps you stay within your normal behavioral spectrum. To practice, attempt this with a significant other or close friend. Initiating intimacy is risky and can produce undesirable results. But the benefits are real.

Once intimacy is seeded, project leaders will have more opportunities to bring up difficult topics that appear disguised as issues and assumptions no one is willing to challenge or deal with. When looking for difficult topics, find the project issues list, risk journals, or assumptions list. Most of these issues find dark, dusty resting places in databases, portals, or templates because no one likes to tackle them. Leaders can tactfully bring up these issues by acknowledging their difficulty, taking full responsibility for bringing them up, and then making a direct statement of the issue.[7]

Intimacy can be particularly lacking in virtual project teams. However, choosing phone conversations over e-mail and writing personal thank-you notes to others for their contributions are simple steps to start the process. It is easy to excuse yourself from getting to know remote team members or stakeholders, simply because they may live in different parts of the country or the world. The process for establishing intimacy remains the same; however, there are fewer opportunities to establish it. Planning activities to create opportunities to meet face-to-face with key stakeholders is critical. If credibility is established, chances improve that one will get these opportunities. However, without a strong foundation to the leadership competency pyramid base, and insufficient credibility, the request will more than likely be turned down, making the development of intimacy among critical virtual stakeholders difficult, if not impossible.

## Low Self-Orientation

Low self-orientation means you are more oriented towards others than yourself. Low self-orientation is not thinking less of yourself, but rather thinking about yourself less frequently. People with low self-orientation love to learn. Realizing they don't have all the answers, they are great listeners. They realize the value of others' opinions, and enjoy watching others succeed around them—realizing they can't do it all themselves. Service-based project leaders may naturally have low self-orientation or may train themselves to act with low self-orientation. Intimacy and low self-orientation reinforce each other just as credibility and reliability reinforce each other.

Today's leaders do not lead by power or fear, but rather lead by demonstrating competency and keeping their ambitions in check.[8] Therefore, low self-orientation coupled with intimacy reins in a leader's ambitions as he demonstrates competency through credibility and reliability.

Low self-orientation is aligned with good listening skills. Listening is a life skill that requires constant attention and regular feedback on how well one listens to others. Service-based project leaders engage with others not to talk, but rather to listen. Good listeners are great communicators and leaders must be great communicators.

Leaders with high self-orientation leave others with a feeling that they are in it for themselves. Service-based project leaders must communicate that they are really in it for the team member who is concerned about the demands on their time, for the sponsor whose reputation is on the line, and for the stakeholder who has little control but is highly impacted by the project results.

## Listening and Disengaging

Learning to listen takes practice and patience. Good listeners probe for more information when appropriate, listen for the story within the message, empathize, and connect with and acknowledge others' feelings.[9] Good listeners pay attention to body language and facial expressions that send emotional clues about what someone is feeling. They remove distractions such as computer screens or other visual distractions and focus solely on the conversation at hand. These are challenges for project leaders who must process massive amounts of information in short periods of time and have incredible demands on their times. The demands of getting to the next meeting often interrupt fruitful conversations just as they begin.

The art of disengaging is almost as important as that of listening. Cutting off a conversation can be awkward, leaving a stakeholder feeling empty or not worthy of the leader's time. These situations have to be evaluated quickly, but disengaging can be done tactfully by saying something like, "May we continue this at 4:00 pm?—my status meeting is going to start in two minutes." Asking permission and making a commitment to continue the conversation while giving a truthful explanation are the keys to disengaging. If the person does not grant you permission, the responsibility then falls to them to justify the importance of finishing the discussion there and then. Nine out of ten times, the stakeholder will gladly grant permission to disengage. When done properly, disengaging provides opportunities to demonstrate reliability and low self-orientation.

### Tips for Low Self-Orientation

*Practice being a great listener.* Read books on listening techniques and practice them. *How to Win Friends and Influence People* by Dale Carnegie is popular.

*Connect actions to words that demonstrate your commitment to others.* Convincing others you are in it for them requires action, not just words. Ask someone every day on your team, "How can I help?" and follow though.

*Create opportunities for informal discussions.* One-on-one time with sponsors, team members, and stakeholders is well worth the effort if a proper stakeholder analysis is done. Lunches and dinners cost money and can be worth it, but walking the halls before 8:30 a.m. and after 5:00 p.m. creates valuable informal opportunities with stakeholders. It is the service-based leader's responsibility to find them, and not wait for them to seek you out.

# Customer and Project Team Trust-Based Relationships

Service-based project leaders also must take the responsibility of creating a trust-based relationship between performing organizations. Particularly, when a strategic project changes the way a customer's business will operate, project teams must develop strong, trust-based relationships with the customer organization. The key is creating a culture in the project team that views the initiative from the perspective of the customer.

The first step toward building trust between performing organizations is clearly defining the members of the project team responsible for delivery of project deliverables and the customer team members responsible for driving the overall direction of the project. To build credibility, the project team must reach out to the customer and conduct trust-building activities. This includes creating project plans that allow the customer to easily verify the team is doing what was promised.

Building credibility and reliability can be done in planning sessions or workshops that involve the customer. Provide the outputs immediately at the end of the session so participants feel that the sessions truly accomplished something. Get the customer involved as a part of the solution by allowing customers to define the barriers and solutions thereby allowing the project team to more genuinely see the project through the eyes of the customer.

Becoming familiar with a customer's processes and terminology, dedicating serious analysis to their business metrics, providing regular status reports, responding to inquiries quickly and thoroughly, and taking inquiries seriously enhance credibility and reliability. Establishing strong quality processes assists in all aspects of trust. Survey the customer's attitude on the preparedness and meaningfulness of project team and customer meetings and working sessions. Leaders of project teams who initiate self-examination of team behaviors and conduct rehearsals of customer facing activities have more success at creating trust.

The project team builds trust by asking open-ended questions, listening effectively, and helping stakeholders define the problem before offering solutions. A project team loses trust when it presents solutions before it has convinced the customer they understand their need. A project team gains trust by showing more interest in the customer's thoughts than its own views.

## Summary

Failures of project leadership are normally preceded by a breakdown of trust. A trust-based relationship is a commitment based on emotions not to be treated carelessly. Compatibility is a steppingstone to forming a trust-based relationship. Service-based project leaders recognize trust building is a mutual process and establishing a value proposition is the first step. The building blocks of trust-based relationships are credibility, reliability, intimacy, and low self-orientation. Credibility is based on one's content knowledge and the articulation of content at the right moment to provide explicit value. Reliability is driven by a project manager's actions. Intimacy is about connecting with stakeholders' inner sanctuary, where their deep beliefs and values reside, driving convictions and emotions. Low self-orientation is convincing others of their importance. Service-based project leaders also must take on the responsibility of creating a trust-based relationship between performing organizations.

## Endnotes

1. David Maister, Charles H. Green, and Robert M. Galford, *The Trusted Advisor* (New York: The Free Press, 2000), chap 8.
2. Ibid.
3. Ibid.
4. Nick Morgan, *Give Your Speech Change the World—How to Move Your Audience to Action* (Boston: Harvard Business School Press, 2003), chap 5.
5. Ibid., David Maister et al.
6. Ibid.
7. Ibid.
8. Warren Bennis and Joan Goldsmith, *Learning to Lead* (New York: Basic Books, 2003), 2.
9. Ibid., David Maister et al.

## Chapter 16

# Consultative Leadership: Becoming a Service-Based Project Leader

## Introduction

Leadership achieves goals through others. Consultative leadership achieves shared goals through others' willing participation, for mutual benefit. A consultative leader understands and aligns the relationship between the common goal and stakeholders' personal interests. Consultative leadership helps project managers address the predicament of having substantially more responsibility for the project outcome than authority. **Consultative leadership is granted through trust-based relationships.**

Rensis Likert's presents in his book *The Human Organization: Its Management and Value*, four types of leadership behavior that will help clarify what is meant by consultative leadership in the context of this book.

The exploitive authoritative leader has no concern for people and uses fear to achieve compliance; the benevolent authoritative leader has some regard for people and uses reward systems to influence behavior but holds onto critical decision making. The consultative leader reaches out to followers and encourages an upward flow of information, but decisions are still made centrally. The participative group leader engages both followers and peers, and fosters collaboration and shared decision making.[1]

For the purpose of the MyProjectAdvisor® Leadership Competency Pyramid, consultative leadership can be defined as a leader who reaches out to followers and encourages an upward flow of information; additionally, it is a participative form of leadership that engages both followers and peers, and which fosters collaboration and shared decision making.[2] There is a strong emphasis on advising and serving stakeholders. The success of consultative leadership comes through the creation of supportive relationships based on mutual trust and respect including the recognition of the personal worth of others. Decision making incorporates the "linking pins" relationships that bind the entire group or organization.[3] Stakeholders participate freely because of the anticipated benefits.

## Advisory Nature

The term "consultative" is used as an adjective and means giving advice. "Leadership" is a noun that means guidance or direction. The project leader must use advice, not demands, to provide guidance and direction.

Advising helps to inform stakeholders of the best course of action though education and collective knowledge-sharing, but allows stakeholders, including team members, to make their own choices. Advising is not telling stakeholders what to do; it is helping them satisfy their needs including expressing why something needs to be done (aligning a stakeholder's interest with the common goal), and how to do it (educating stakeholders on the process). **A service-based project leader acts as an advisor because she seeks to serve the best interest of her stakeholders.**

Trust creates opportunities for consultative leadership. (See Figure 16.1) Customers who recognize the base strength of a project leader's leadership competency pyramid will pull project managers into a consultative leadership position requiring a conscious decision on the part of the project manager to accept this invitation to actively advise and serve others' best interests.

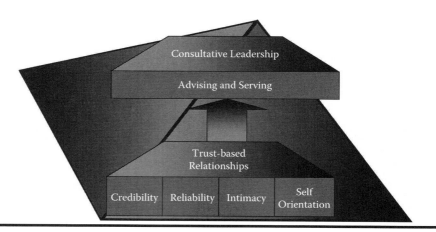

**Figure 16.1   Trust-based relationships encourage consultative leadership.**

## *Serving versus Coaching*

Service-based project leaders use advisory skills to serve the best interests of others. An important aspect of consultative leadership is servant leadership. Servant leadership starts with an inherent desire to serve others first, then a conscious choice to lead.[4]

Personal coaching is a popular trend in project management. However, a service-based project leader's use of consultative leadership is not the same as coaching. Coaching uses a process of inquiry and personal discovery to enable one's level of awareness and social responsibility. A coach provides their client with tools, structure, support, and feedback. The coaching process helps an individual define and achieve professional and personal goals faster and with more ease than would be possible otherwise.[5]

Professional coaching techniques may be valuable for project leaders, since both coaches and leaders provide advice. But coaches are not project leaders and project leaders are not professional coaches. Project leaders are accountable to deliver results to customers through a team of temporary resources. Coaches act as an independent third party helping an individual, and do not bear the burden of leadership.

# Power

As with any leadership style, consultative leadership requires power. The traditional types of project power are listed below.[6]

- Legitimate—Formal or title-based
- Reward—Incentive-based
- Coercive—Fear-based
- Expert —Knowledge-based
- Referent—Relationship-based

Consultative leadership relies heavily on expert power and referent power. In addition, consultative leadership relies on deferent power, or the power to grant power to others. Deferent power requires the courage to trust others. A service-based project leader grants power by prudently leaving it in the hands to which it belongs. This right to grant power is earned through the base of a leader's competency pyramid. Once granted, the service-based project leader uses advisory skills and serving actions to enable the power invested in others. This is consultative leadership. Figure 16.2 illustrates the use of different types of power to create consultative leadership opportunities—a critical leadership paradigm for project managers attempting to become service-based project leaders.

Every opportunity for consultative leadership must be earned by the service-based project leader, since it is not inherited. Consultative leadership is not forced upon stakeholders, but rather stakeholders grant the opportunity to project leaders to use consultative leadership. Consultative leadership opens communication,

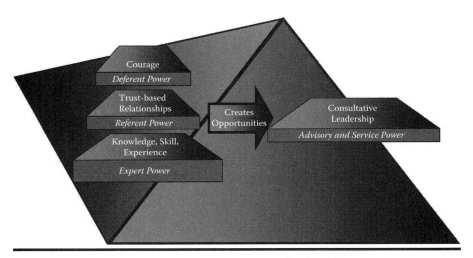

**Figure 16.2    Power associated with consultative leadership.**

enables the exchange of ideas, emboldens creativity, instills ownership of project tasks, enables leadership opportunities for others, and generates positive project team energy.

Consultative leadership distributes decision making. Team members closest to the work are entrusted with local project decisions. This allows the project leader to seek out high value proposition project work for his customers and to practice foresight, including gathering information for future decisions and improving the decision making process.

## The Need for Advising

Stakeholders are not as familiar with the project environment as the practitioner and typically have some "skin in the game"—a reputation, bonuses, or even their careers. Practitioners should never underestimate the trepidation and anxiety a person may have concerning a project, including team members, customers, and particularly the sponsors. Sponsors often have a handful of other issues, and neither need nor want another.

A practitioner will likely see additional complications and barriers to success because of her familiarity with the project environment (technical issues, lack of resources, constrained budgets, etc.). She should be careful not to unnecessarily add to the stakeholders' anxiety. Often project managers bring up issues, assumptions, and poorly stated risks that inevitably compound anxiety! From the stakeholders' perspective, they want someone who can take away anxiety, not add to it.[7]

The service-based project leader's role is to provide information and reasons as to what needs to happen and why. This can be done by providing recommendations as to how to mitigate, reduce, overcome, or eliminate threats to achieving the project's objectives. Drawing from their base of knowledge, skills, and experience, one should get the sponsor to commit to a recommended course of action, showing the project team that they have been granted consultative leadership to move the highest levels of management to action.

Education is a great temporary anxiety reliever, but education alone is not enough; an executable plan of action is required to permanently reduce anxiety. This plan of action is best developed with input from stakeholders, which provides an excellent opportunity for project managers to use consultative leadership.

## Tips for Advising

A service-based project leader works to earn the right to be a consultative leader. Once earned, team members, sponsors, and stakeholders will grant opportunities but one must listen for clues. Clues from involved stakeholders may be statements such as:

- Do you agree?
- What are you thoughts?
- Do you have experience with "_____"?
- What information are we missing?

These are clues that a service-based project leader is earning the right to begin to use consultative leadership. The key to advising is serving with good intentions coupled with the proper attitude and language.

A service-based project leader seeks input, not just acceptance. Using his pyramid base, he constructs meaningful straw models of plans and begins a dialogue with the stakeholders, allowing them to fill in the blanks. How this input is solicited is critical. Stakeholders know when they are adding value and not simply going through a tedious exercise of project planning.

Below are some methods for helping to ease stakeholder anxiety:

- Focus on deliverables and why the deliverables are important to overall plans
- Focus on educating stakeholders on the sequence and timing of events
- Allow stakeholders to make meaningful contributions to the plan
- Be positive and sincere
- Use stakeholders' time wisely, be well-prepared, have clear objectives and outcomes that can be accomplished in the timeframe allocated
- Confirm outcomes and decisions within 48 hours

A general approach to advising is allowing the stakeholders to think it was their idea with the leader assuming the role of helping them verbalize it. List the potential options and ask if any have been missed. Then discuss the benefits and drawbacks of each option, reducing the probability of misunderstandings. The desired outcome reduces stakeholders' anxiety—and therefore reduces resistance. The stakeholder should not feel he has been forced down a path. Finally, make a recommendation but let the stakeholders make the decision or make a joint decision as appropriate. The desired outcome is a shared vision and joint ownership of the actions required to complete the work assigned.

Courage plays a significant role in making recommendations. A service-based project leader leads with, "I would recommend …" and then explains his rationale. He uses consultative leadership to help invested stakeholders decide what to do, but avoids taking a stand early, thereby short-circuiting the buy-in process. Being mindful of balancing decisiveness with allowing the advising process to mature to allow stakeholder buy-in is important, but service-based project leaders who are unwilling to commit to a plan of action will quickly lose the right to use consultative leadership that they have been granted.

A challenge for some leaders is the ability to let go of some decision making. A leader with substantial experience may see more direct paths to an end result and may become frustrated with stakeholders' lack of speed or their interim steps that may seem to be waste of time. Being flexible is important; stakeholders must rationally and emotionally be ready to act and commit to a plan. Thus, they may need more time or require more interim decision-making steps. This is acceptable as long as significant delays are not accruing. If the stakeholders are comfortable with the process, they will be more forgiving of minor delays. Keep decisions in front of stakeholders and maintain a healthy sense of urgency.

Some stakeholders will never commit to a critical decision; they may ask the leader to choose for them. Ensure the information and educational needs of stakeholders have been met by asking them what information they lack to make a decision. If stakeholders choose a path that the leader cannot work with, he may withdraw. A project leader who is willing to step aside when fundamental differences exist is a true service-based project leader.

## Consultative Leadership Process

The process of consultative leadership involves aligning the actions of stakeholders with the strategy of the program or project. This process is aimed at getting customers and team members committed to the project. The process can be used at a more strategic level to align critical stakeholders such as sponsors. Figure 16.3 depicts the consultative leadership process, adapted from *The Trusted Advisor*.[8]

Five-Step Process for Consultative Leadership:

- Engage—Initiate meaningful dialogue with stakeholders based on a foundation of trust
- Listen—Earn the right to explore ideas with the stakeholder
- Frame—Crystallize and clarify complexity involved in the project

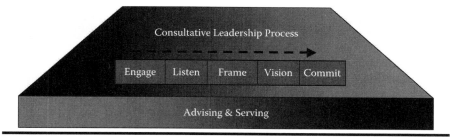

**Figure 16.3    Consultative leadership process.**

- Vision—Collaborate with team members, customers, and sponsors to define the future
- Commit—Remove barriers, including fears, to get stakeholders to commit to action

This process engages stakeholders and fosters the collaboration that reinforces existing trust-based relationships. The process recognizes stakeholders' potential for contribution and considers the intrinsic value of the work. Stakeholders, particularly team members, experience greater rewards because the service-based project leader is allowing the work to be defined in part by them. Thus, the trust-based relationship and consultative leadership layers of the pyramid work in tandem, reinforcing each other.

## *Engage*

Engaging the key stakeholders is an art service-based project leaders must master if they are to exert the proper influence on the programs they lead. Project managers fail to make the leap to project leadership when they are unable to engage with the key stakeholders, such as executives, senior managers, and even senior team members. Without a strong base to their pyramid and trust-based relationships, one is unable to create meaningful dialogue with these resources.

The challenge begins with a project leader's usually long list of issues needing attention. He must focus on a topic that has strength from a stakeholder's perspective. Successful engagement of stakeholders is tied to sharing the same vision.

Avoid jumping to the latest, hottest issue without first ranking its strength through the eyes of the stakeholder. Asking for help is fine, but the leader must demonstrate that he has pursued several courses of action and is willing to act as a catalyst to help drive the issue to closure. Transferring the issue to senior management weakens one's right to use consultative leadership. Senior management does not have time to distill all the data and facts. These are opportunities to provide recommendations and use consultative leadership.

Seeing the importance of a topic in the eyes of a stakeholder means understanding the risk to the stakeholder (not the leader) if no action is taken and understanding the amount of information available and complexity associated with the topic. The leader seeking engagement defines the reward the stakeholder will experience and the amount of relevance and influence the stakeholder claims over the topic.

When a stakeholder grants a leader time to discuss critical project topics, he should focus on a key project issue that needs their attention, add value to the discussion, research everything possible, and listen well.

## Listen

Service-based project leaders engage with stakeholders not to talk but to listen. Listening is tightly aligned with low self-orientation, a key building block of establishing trust-based relationships. Listening is a lifelong skill. The consultative leadership process requires proper preparation to ensure that the right questions are asked to get the stakeholder talking. Project managers often go into these discussions with too little information, not giving the stakeholder enough data to be able to even discuss the topic. Service-based project leaders anticipate the need for these discussions long before they occur and are able to research, document, and share the proper information with the stakeholders to allow them to begin to formulate their ideas.

## A Story about Listening

Sue, a project leader, continually presented critical decisions to the steering committee about which the committee members had little or no information to make a rational decision. Members did not have the time to sift through the information and comprehend all the implications of decisions. The more she pressed for a decision, the more uncomfortable the meetings became. Some members pushed back, others' body language showed uneasiness with the program direction, still others tuned out and responded to e-mail from their PDAs. Sue would respond with answers before members could fully express their thoughts. Sue always left unsatisfied because she did not get a decision and her project faced new delays. Steering committee members became frustrated because they felt pressured to make a decision without all the facts to reduce project slippage. Eventually Sue and others were stripped of their visible leadership role, replaced with more customer-focused leaders.

Short-cutting the consultative leadership process heightens frustration. Articulate in a compelling fashion well-documented facts to reinforce credibility, then listen to the stakeholders. Ask open-ended, probing questions to get them to expand their opinions, concerns, and feelings. Allow stakeholders to pool their institutional knowledge to create a valuable input into the decision-making process. First, listen reflectively by stating back stakeholder concerns and opinions; then listen for opportunities to follow up and resolve ambiguous issues. This reinforces the reliability and low self-orientation aspects of trust building.

## Frame

We often hear the expression, "Think outside the box." But it's hard to do that unless you recognize what box you are in! Like a picture frame, framing an issue states the parameters of either existing assumptions, or of possible new ways of thinking. Framing issues for stakeholders involves crystallizing numerous complexities and emotions into a concise opportunity statement. It provides insight and a new way of thinking about the issue or identifies the centrality of the issue that generates a host of other issues. Framing formally recognizes these new insights. For example, the following are framing statements:

> "Our falling revenue isn't a matter of poor sales performance; it's the customer perception of our lack of quality."
> "Our cost overruns are not a matter of scope creep, it's our inability to communicate effectively with our customer."
> "The book is written as though it were going to be read by practitioners. However, when you think about it, the desired audience is really executives."
> "Increasing funding for the R&D staff to shorten time to market may help in the short term, but our inability to create new innovative products instead of reacting to our customers and competitors is keeping us from being a market leader."

Each of these statements combines both facts—cost overruns, falling revenue, increased funding—with hidden, fundamental, or critical root causes that are often emotionally charged. When framing, attempt to combine the facts with these hidden, emotionally-charged issues. The goal is not solve the problem in framing, but to adjust the frame to allow others to see a new picture and then move on to creating a shared vision. Framing requires the strong trust-based relationships and underlying layers of the leadership competency pyramid. Without them, your attempts to bring new insight will feel awkward or even be outrightly dismissed. When these layers do exist, your framing will feel natural and, at a minimum, give others a reason to pause to consider the new angle. Framing occurs over a period of time, normally with multiple conversations with various stakeholders until the picture begins to crystallize.

## A Story about Framing

A company being audited by a federal oversight body was found to be out of compliance in numerous areas; management made the issue its top priority and enlisted senior managers to fix it. After several months of creating awareness programs and complex system and process changes, progress was minimal. Knowledge workers who were targeted with these changes became overwhelmed and a climate of fear began to set in.

What was lacking was a formal recognition of the impact of organizational culture. For years, the company and industry had not worried about the subtleties of these regulations. The operational culture was instinctively sales driven: "Close the deal today, and worry about the rest tomorrow."

Formal recognition of these cultural issues led to fundamental cultural changes and a new vision, which removed pressure from the operations staff. Management recognized the culture, but had to frame the emotional connection of long-standing relationships between the sales organization and management. Only then was the consultative leadership process allowed to proceed to a shared vision and the actions required to achieve it.

Framing requires alignment of stakeholders' logical and emotional perceptions. The leader must rationally explain the complexities of the issue and uncover the emotional elements. Below are some tips for framing both the logical and emotional elements of the topics requiring action.

- Use logic and content knowledge to encapsulate the issue.
- Use diagrams, charts, pictures, and logic to distill numerous complexities into a few key variables.
- Uncover the stakeholders' hidden feelings.
- Recognize the personal risks involved, for both the leader and stakeholders.
- Summarize feelings and emotions regarding an issue.

Framing takes practice. Framing reinforces all aspects of trust and gives leaders the opportunity to add explicit value. The project leader must seek out opportunities to create this value. Common places for project leaders to look for framing opportunities are issues and decisions not obvious to stakeholders, such as competing objectives of projects that are hindering performance. How a particular message is communicated, or issues that relate to the critical success factors, such as how the quality of deliverables may impact project performance and customer satisfaction may also provide a framing opportunity.

The goal of framing is not to solve the issue, but rather shed new light on it in order to create a joint vision that will create a new reality.

## Vision

Once a leader has framed the issue satisfactorily and gained formal recognition through articulating it in a concise manner, determining the essence of what is being created is the logical next step. Vision is about a destination that reflects a team's real desires.[9] Vision builds energy, and leaders skilled at this process understand the usefulness of pictures, graphics, drawings, and illustrations for creating a compelling and unifying vision. Keys to a great vision are: easy comprehension, motivation, inspiration, credibility, and demanding or stretching goals.[10]

Athletes prime their brain with mental rehearsals to improve performance, whether it's a golfer rehearsing a putt in his head, visualizing the ball's rolling off the putting face over a defined path and into the hole, or a basketball player seeing the ball float over the rim with a gentle rotation. A project leader should prime the collective brain of the team by facilitated conceptualization. Perhaps a mental rehearsal of project deliverables and detail work packages, priming their brains to create mental pictures of how the deliverable will be used, its objective, and how completion is determined. Leaders can also create mental pictures of customer experiences desired in meetings, presentations, and workshops with their team.

Conceptualization must start with a clean piece of paper to eliminate preconceptions that constrain creativity and hide unspoken differences in expectations. These preconceptions, known as assumptions and constraints, when removed unleash the power to conceptualize. Stakeholders are less likely to have the time to read thousands of words describing ideas that might otherwise be crafted into a one-page concept picture that can then generate meaningful dialogue that contributes to a shared vision. A project team that works closely with customers to conceptualize new visions is more likely to arrive at the same destination.

The next step is to translate concept to vision. Project leaders facilitate this step by asking what specific results the customer wants to achieve. Customers are more interested in specific project results, not the process of achieving them. Success metrics, critical to visioning, provide objective truth to the vision becoming reality.

Once the vision is clear and measurable, the process of defining the current state can be hindered by the implication of accountability towards incumbent management. When truth is evasive in visioning discussions, a service-based project leader uses observable experiences and documented facts rather than competing opinions to define the current reality that longs for transformation. He is not fearful in defining the current reality of a situation, because with truth comes the internal satisfaction of serving well. Trust plays a critical role in successful visioning of organizational transformation, major deliverables, work packages, and their detail tasks.

It is not until concepts have been translated to visions and current states have been defined that action can begin. The consultative leadership process makes planning intuitive and simple for stakeholders. Project managers who rush to define their plan before the consultative leadership process is complete are wasting valuable resources, are at risk of encountering considerable rework, and may leave the consultative leadership opportunity to others.

## Commit

Once the issue has been framed and a vision created, getting stakeholders to commit to action completes the consultative leadership process. Without action from invested stakeholders, the consultative leadership process has failed.

To achieve commitment to action, stakeholders must understand the details and implications of these actions. The service-based project leader explores these outcomes and gains emotional and rational commitment. Resistance to commitment is rooted in fear of the unknown, feelings about the topic or issue, past experiences, or just plain complacency. A service-based project leader removes unknowns by decomposing and reconstructing them into feasible action plans. They are obligated to do this in order to overcome resistance, and allow accountability for complacency to find its proper resting place.

Getting commitment is directly related to how much information (facts) the party has about a situation and how they feel (emotions). The combination of both of these determines how one views the predictability of the outcome of the task. The facts may show that no one has ever been fired for a bad presentation or attempting to gain support from a department head, but if the individual feels uncomfortable, he is unlikely to commit. A project leader should allow time and plan activities to help remove unknowns, generate facts to facilitate decision making, and remove the uneasiness.

The service-based project leader attempts to get the stakeholders to commit to perform certain actions that only they can do, which deepens the commitment on both sides and allows them to feel emotionally committed. In turn, the service-based project leaders commit to do something on behalf of the stakeholder. This is joint commitment, with both parties acting on behalf of one another.

Below are tips for getting joint commitment:

- Make stakeholders aware of all steps of the plan of action and all possible outcomes.
- Clearly articulate what will and will not be done.
- Articulate what the stakeholder needs to do.
- Clarify boundaries of work.
- Agree on methods and frequency of communication.
- Make clear what the end product will look like.
- Make clear how it will be delivered.
- Make clear how success will be measured.

## Summary

Consultative leadership means achieving common goals through the willing participation of others. The success of consultative leadership comes through the creation of supportive relationships based on mutual trust, freewilled stakeholder participation, and respect including the recognition of the personal worth of others. Consultative leadership puts an emphasis on advising and serving stakeholders. Advising helps to inform stakeholders of the best course of action though education and collective knowledge-sharing, but also allows stakeholders, including team members, to make their own choices.

Stakeholders are not as familiar with the project environment as the practitioner and often have some vested interest, such as a reputation, bonuses, or even their careers. Consultative leadership serves stakeholders' interests before making a conscious decision to lead.

Every opportunity for consultative leadership must be earned by the service-based project leader; it is not inherited. The process of consultative leadership is engaging in meaningful dialogue with stakeholders, exploring ideas with them, crystallizing and clarifying their complexity, collaborating with stakeholders to define the future, and gaining commitment from them to take action.

# Endnotes

1. Rensis Likert, *The Human Organization: Its Management and Value* (New York: McGraw-Hill, 1967), 14–24.
2. Rensis Likert, *The Human Organization: Its Management and Value* (New York: McGraw-Hill, 1967), 14–24.
3. Ibid, 50.
4. Robert K. Greenleaf, *The Servant as Leader*, The Robert K. Greenleaf Center, 1991, 7.
5. International Coach Federation, http://www.coachfederation.org/ICF/For+Coaching+Clients/What+is+a+Coach/ (Assessed November 28, 2006).
6. Vijay Verma P. Eng., M.B.A., *Human Resource Skills for the Project Manager* (Newtown Square, PA: Project Management Institute, 1996) 233.
7. David Maister, Charles H. Green, and Robert M. Galford, *The Trusted Advisor* (New York: The Free Press, 2000), 29.
8. Ibid. Chap 9.
9. Robert Fritz, *The Path of Least Resistance for Managers*, Design Organizations to Succeed (San Francisco: Berrett-Koehler 1999), 199.
10. Dale Christenson and Derek Walker, "Understanding the Role of "Vision" in Project Success," *Project Management Journal*. 35, no. 3 (2004): 39–51.

# Chapter 17

# Courage

Go confidently in the direction of your dreams!
— *Henry David Thoreau*

## Introduction

Courage is a state of mind that enables a project leader to face uncertainty, fear, or vicissitudes with self-possession, confidence, and resolution. The Latin root of courage is "fortitudo," meaning strength of mind that allows one to endure adversity. Building a leadership competency pyramid requires courage and fortitude. Project leaders must be passionate, mentally tenacious, morally brave, and steadfast to succeed as transforming service-based project leaders.

The top of the pyramid is the most challenging for some. In reality, courage is the mortar of the whole pyramid. It takes courage to enhance the width and depth of each pyramid layer. The course and extent of your professional growth should be consistent with your state in life and commensurate with your risk attitudes. Emotions, behaviors, and attitudes are habits learned early in life. Stepping out of your old self can be difficult, particularly when projects have their usual amount of politics and conflict.

## Environmental Impacts on Courage

One organizational barrier that impedes a project leader's progress in leadership competency development is an environment that rewards dysfunctional behavior. The project leader juggling numerous projects and the associated demands is often soured by cynical, highly political management whose philosophy is focused on short-term financial results to the exclusion of all other issues.

The organizational culture impacts emotion, attitude, and behavior. But leadership has a great influence on culture. Project workers will often conform to workplace attitudes. Professional behaviors are often learned through co-workers and the organizational environment.

A positive project environment for professionals is characterized by these statements:[1]

- Customer satisfaction is the top priority.
- Personal agendas are not permitted.
- Rewards are given to those who contribute the most to success.
- Management gets performance out of everyone.
- Employees must learn new skills.
- Investment is made in the long-term.
- Everyone respects each other.
- The quality of supervision is high.
- Professionalism is high.

In a positive environment, positive attitudes dominate and drive behaviors. Thus, a leader's attitude toward personal development, risk taking, and team development will dominate her behaviors and have a greater influence on the attitudes and behaviors of the team. The organizational environment can be unique to the entire organization or specific to the project or program organization. It is not uncommon for large programs to develop a distinct culture from the rest of the organization.

A healthy environment allows everyone to be approachable; diplomacy and courtesy are evident. Everyone's contributions are recognized. When this occurs, attitudes are more likely to be positive and those positive attitudes, coupled with a leader's strong conviction of leadership competency development, enable the intentional change process.

A hostile environment tends to neutralize one's attitudes and the environment tends to dominate behaviors. Characteristics of a hostile project environment are:[2]

- Abuse of power
- Coasting
- Disrespect
- Gossiping
- Blaming
- Hiding from accountability

Hostile environments can do serious harm to employee attitudes and morale. It is difficult to get excited about growing leadership competencies in a hostile environment where power is tightly held by a few people. Even highly motivated project team members' and leaders' convictions will wear down; personal growth will stagnate or motivated individuals will seek to leave the environment.

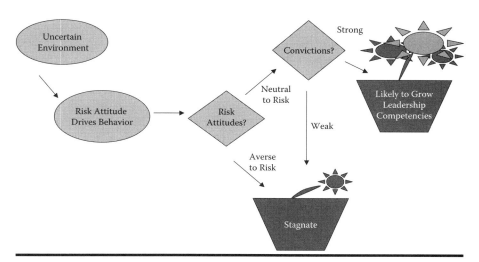

**Figure 17.1    Impact of risk attitudes in an uncertain environment.**

Project workers rarely find themselves in overtly positive or hostile project environments. Most project workers find themselves in uncertain environments. An environment that is neither overtly positive nor hostile is uncertain. This project environment is characterized by evidence of both positive and hostile characteristics, and a lack of clarity from leaders as to what is acceptable and what is not. Leadership that does not actively manifest the culture it wishes to breed creates uncertainty in the eyes of team members and project leaders as to the reception and success of their efforts to pursue a leadership growth agenda.

In this situation, a project leader's risk attitudes, in combination with her convictions toward leadership competencies, will determine whether her leadership ability stagnates or grows. A leader who is risk averse is more likely to stagnate, while a leader who is more open to risk will act on opportunities to grow. Figure 17.1 illustrates the role of risk attitudes in leadership competency development in an uncertain environment.

## Risk Attitudes

There is no broad consensus on the definition of risk.[3] The term is common and widely used in personal circumstances, business, and projects. However, the term "risk" does universally imply the characteristics of ambiguity or uncertainty. Though many situations can entail uncertainty, the term "risk" does not always come to the forefront. For example, when lying on the beach during a summer vacation without a watch, one may be uncertain of the exact time. With no pressing commitments, it probably will not matter. Thus, one's vacation can continue risk free.

When uncertainty is present and consequences are perceived, the risk becomes very relevant. Thus, risk is uncertainty that *matters*.[4]

As previously discussed, attitudes are a mental disposition, therefore representing a choice. Some attitudes are deeply rooted and tied to one's value system, while others are more temporary. But attitudes are not fixed and can be changed. Thus, a project leader's ability to manage risk attitudes is critical to intentional change and leadership competency development.

One's risk attitudes toward the leadership competency pyramid, particularly trust-based relationships and consultative leadership, must be understood. It takes courage to execute the behaviors of trust-based relationships, and there is uncertainty. Will the sponsor or stakeholder respond positively to credibility behaviors or intimacy? A negative reaction can certainly have consequences. It also takes courage to act as a consultative leader. Advising team members or sponsors on possible options involves uncertainty. Will they accept the recommendation? What if following the recommendation results in failure? This is uncertainty that matters to the project leader and potentially the project stakeholders and extended project community.

To build the leadership competency pyramid, a leader who can manage her risk attitudes has an advantage. There are four general types of risk attitudes:[5]

- Risk-Averse
- Risk-Tolerant
- Risk-Neutral
- Risk-Seeking

Like general attitudes, these risk attitudes are not fixed and can be managed. A risk-averse attitude is uncomfortable with uncertainty and has a low tolerance for ambiguity. These people seek security and resolution when facing risk. Established procedures provide comfort and every attempt will be made to minimize threats. A project leader with a risk-averse attitude is likely to take aggressive risk response actions to avoid or minimize risks.

A risk-tolerant attitude takes uncertainty in stride, seeing it as a normal part of everyday life. These leaders do not show heightened awareness or concern for risk opportunities or averse risk events, nor do they take a proactive approach to managing risks. A project leader with a risk-tolerant attitude views risk as normal and may be entrepreneurial in nature.

A risk-neutral attitude seeks plans and tactics that have high payoff and uses creativity to address unknowns. A project leader with this attitude is likely to use a mature approach to managing risk and focus on long-term goals.

Finally, a risk-seeking attitude enjoys challenges and seeks plans and tactics that have a high payoff. This leader is adaptable and not afraid to take action. She may be seeking the thrill of a challenge, but may underestimate risk's probabilities and impacts. Project leaders with this risk attitude often have a casual acceptance of risks and may pursue opportunities aggressively, sometimes at the peril of the team.

There is no wrong risk attitude; however, a risk attitude should match the type of project and its objectives. Most projects and programs would benefit from leaders that do not have extreme risk attitudes.

If a leader perceives the negative outcomes to be greater than the benefits, particularly in a hostile environment, a leader's growth will stagnate. In both hostile and positive environments, extreme attitudes become more important and the impacts of moderate risk attitudes are minimized. For instance, in a hostile environment, a risk-seeking attitude may be able to overcome the negative perceptions of leadership competency development. A positive environment may be enough to overcome one's extreme risk aversion. Uncertain environments maximize the importance of moderate risk attitudes in leadership development.

## Modifying Risk Attitudes

Risk attitudes are not hardwired into the brain, but rather are developed over a long period of time. Risk attitudes are influenced by upbringing, environment, and previous experiences. For instance, risk attitudes of those who grew up during the Great Depression (the 1930s), are influenced by those events and experiences, and they tend to distrust banks.

However, there are factors that influence one's risk attitudes that a leader has control of.[6] Specifically:

- Level of relevant skill, knowledge, or expertise
- Perception of the probability of occurrence and magnitude of impact
- Degree of personal control or choice
- Potential for personal consequences

Each of these factors can be positively impacted by the leadership competency pyramid. (See Figure 17.2)

*Level of relevant skill, knowledge, or expertise*—The level of project management knowledge, experience, skill, and subject matter expertise in a particular domain can influence a project manager's risk attitudes. When she encounters a risk, she may know, "I have done this before," or, "I understand this."

*Perception of the probability of occurrence and magnitude of impact*—The trust-based relationships a project leader is able to build with customers, stakeholders, and team members can influence her perception of how likely something is to occur and its impact. This allows a leader to delegate with confidence and distribute decision making. Because leadership competencies are people-oriented, a leader's risk is minimized through trust-based relationships that increase awareness of other's reactions to her leadership ideas and actions.

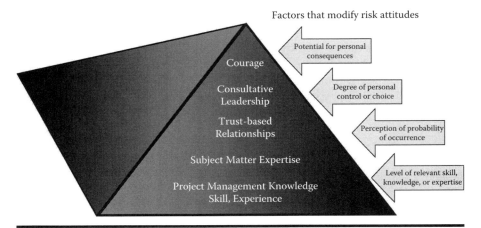

**Figure 17.2 Modifying risk attitudes.**

*Degree of personal control or choice*—The greater the depth of trust-based relationships a project manager has attained, the more control over a situation she is likely to feel. She will know that she can trust people to perform. Also, the consultative leader's ability to advise sponsors and team members enables a sense of control.

*Potential for personal consequences*—When consultative leadership is used effectively to achieve buy-in, the potential for personal consequences can be positively influenced. The team will know, "We are all in this together." The team members will feel more ownership.

## Emotional Literacy

A significant barrier to the modification of risk attitudes for some is their emotional literacy. Emotional literacy is a learned skill that involves one's ability to understand, manage, and control one's emotions in a positive manner. Emotions can have a negative impact on a leader's courage and decision-making capacity if not properly understood and managed. A project leader who has had challenging and upsetting experiences in attempting to lead a team of highly-trained technical engineers on previous projects may let her emotions lead her to disengage from them during critical phases of the project. These emotions, driven by previous experiences, can hinder decision-making and ultimately the ability to grow professionally.

Emotionally savvy leaders see through the eyes of the emotion's holder and appropriately express their emotions, allowing them to stay focused on their goal in a crisis or during conflicts. Stress management techniques, interdependent relationships, and general health help manage emotions over the long term.

For many, the perceived benefits and rewards of becoming a service-based project leader are less than the perceived risks of staying in her comfort zone, leaving her more likely to act. The leadership competency pyramid actually helps modify risk attitudes, but it takes courage to start. Below are tips for increasing courage to become a service-based project leader using the leadership competency pyramid.

- Find a more meaningful or "spiritual" purpose for your work.
- Find a neutral or non-hostile environment.
- Build a community around yourself.
- Determine your risk attitude.
- Strengthen emotional literacy.
- Recognize extreme risk attitudes.
- Build your leadership competency pyramid.

Project leaders must have courage to properly handle the uncertainties in a life of project leadership.

Courage fuels the project manager's journey to project leadership and the magnitude of it reflects a leader's conviction to initiate and sustain personal transformation for a purpose greater than oneself.

## Summary

Courage is a state of mind that enables a project leader to face uncertainty. It is the mortar of the leadership competency pyramid. In positive, healthy environments, attitudes drive behaviors. In negative, hostile environments the environment tends to drive behavior. In uncertain environments, applicable to most project managers, risk attitudes in combination with their convictions toward leadership competencies determine their leadership competency development. To build the leadership competency pyramid, a leader who can manage her risk attitudes has an advantage. There four general types of risk attitude: risk-averse, risk-tolerant, risk-neutral, and risk-seeking. The leadership competency pyramid actually helps modify risk attitudes, but it takes fortitude and courage to begin.

## Endnotes

1. David H. Maister, *Practice What You Preach* (New York: The Free Press, 2001), 63–64.
2. Ibid, chap 21.
3. David Hillson and Ruth Murray-Webster, *Understanding and Managing Risk Attitude* (Hants, England: Gower Publishing, 2005), 4–6.
4. Ibid.
5. David Hillson, *Effective Opportunity Management for Projects—Exploiting Positive Risk* (New York: Marcel Dekker, 2004) chap 9.
6. Ibid.

# SELF-DIRECTED PROJECT LEADERSHIP DEVELOPMENT

## Chapter 18

# The Conscious Leader

Follow your heart,
Yes, some must dream

—*Nils Lofgren*

## Introduction

"Consciousness precedes being."[1] Vaclav Havel spoke these words on the floor of the United States Senate in 1990. At the time, Havel was the president of Czechoslovakia, but before the Cold War ended, he had been a dissident, political prisoner, and playwright. Havel was speaking about how the economic philosophy of Communism failed because material realities are not the fundamental factor in the movement of history. Rather, *consciousness*—human awareness, thought, and spirit—is the fundamental factor that defines history.[2] Havel laid the blame for Marxist oppression not just on abusive dictators, but also on the people who, through their own passivity, allowed it to happen.

Project managers working in organizations wade against a tide of skeptics, listening to the spoken and unspoken language of "those ideas are good, but they will never work here," or "we just have to accept this is the way our organization operates." Project leaders run aground of the material realities of organizational constraints, such as resources, time, and budgets. **Organizations are full of "received wisdom" with no practical basis, such as beliefs about what information project managers can access versus what they need, the way to work and not work, what can be discussed and what cannot. These doctrines become ingrained in project managers as gospel truths that no one can question.**

Measures that can only be calculated on paper are the material realities of a practitioner's world. The heart and spirit of the endeavor are suppressed, but only to temporarily deny the reality of a leader's consciousness, thought, and spirit, which precede the material being of project costs and schedules. Caving in to the pressure to work weekends and sacrifice personal needs to serve the economic good eventually creates chaos for project leaders and their organizations.

Self-directed leadership development is a rebuke to these false realities. Self-directed development frees the practitioner of these constraints and energizes one to work on projects with meaning and to work with dignity and passion. The goal of self-directed leadership development is to dream and begin an inner journey directed by the heart that changes oneself and the world. Self-directed project leadership development has the same goal, except a leader uses projects as the trade, project management as the tool, and his consciousness as the instigator.

## Projects That Change the World

Project leaders are fully capable of changing the world. Sometimes these changes are broad and shallow, others are narrow and deep. Projects do change the world in both noticeable and unnoticeable ways. Projects can change the physical nature of the world, such as the Three River Gorge Dam in China. This controversial 1.3 mile, 610 foot dam across the Yangtze River in China will be able to be seen from space. The dam will produce energy equivalent to 15 nuclear power plants. Its original planning goes back to the early 1900s. The dam is scheduled to be completed in 2009 but requires 1.5 million people to be relocated from their homes as 13 cities and 1,300 villages will be submerged under water. In the past 2,000 years, the Yangtze River has experienced 215 catastrophic floods including the last one in 1998 that killed 4,000 people and left 14 million homeless.[3]

Other projects change the way we see the world. In 1969, three Americans—Neil Armstrong, Buzz Aldrin, Jr., and Michael Collins—traveled 238,857 miles in what many consider to be the single greatest technical achievement of mankind, setting foot on the moon. Armstrong and Collins spent 21 hours on the moon and collected 46 pounds of rocks before redocking with Aldrin in the command module and returning back to Earth. The project had political and military objectives—beating the Russians to space—but it also had a transforming effect on millions of people and on future generations. The view of Earth from the moon changed our perspective. Many could now see, along with the astronauts, the world as it truly exists, nestled in the heavens, without borders or boundaries, and with wealth beyond the governments, institutions, kings, and dictators. Perhaps humankind became more cognizant of the value of life beyond the need for petty strife.[4]

Still other projects change the way we live in the world. Dr. Gilbert Irwin started Medical Missionaries, an international humanitarian organization dedicated to providing health care, medical support, medical education, and training to the poor. Originally started by a group of doctors and nurses wanting to reach out and help those in need, Medical Missionaries has no paid employees and their projects have dispersed over $65 million worth of medicines and medical supplies around the world for an out-of-pocket expense of less than $175,000. Ninety-nine percent of these items were scheduled to be thrown away. Their largest ongoing project, the construction of a clinic in Thomassique, Haiti, will replace an inadequate one-bed clinic and bring a continuity of health care to the impoverished area. The project includes staff quarters, a 30,000-gallon water tower, and septic field.[5]

## My Story

Several years ago, my search for meaningful work led me to an off-site annual meeting with a professional services company. The speaker was a prominent writer and thought leader on professional service firms. I entered a weekend-long conference to listen to the normal pep talks and team building activities, which many companies conduct in a desperate attempt to reinvigorate and renew their employees. Listening to a creative and insightful day-long presentation in a conference room of over 200 depleted professionals energized me in a way probably unintended by my employer. The presentation message was simple; "If you don't like what you're doing, your work will be marginal at best. Find interesting, fascinating work and make it fun. If you do, your reward will much greater." Soon after, I started my own professional services and training company, got involved with large strategic programs, met many interesting and fun people, started speaking to project managers on topics such as leadership, and found an opportunity to write this book.

**Self-directed leadership development for project leaders must include work that has redeeming value.** Unfortunately, not all practitioners are working on projects that seem to be changing the world in a positive manner. Authentic, self-directed project leadership development will lead them to these projects. However, this most likely will require some change to how one lives.

A conscious desire to intentionally change self and community is the first and most important step for project managers and leaders. Project managers' lives are continually getting busier as projects and programs become enterprise-driven, increasing visibility and responsibility. **Increased complexity and endless amounts of information overwhelm a project manager's capacity, numbing the inner spirit.** Although the routine completion of tasks and resolution of problems temporarily creates a sense of fulfillment, external progress on the project does not guarantee, and may not even be related to, internal progress, the inner journey of the leader. Leaders can quickly succumb to the devastating effects of burnout, stress-induced health failures, and problematic behaviors that mask the inner problems.

To survive the continual roller-coaster project life of meetings, e-mail, airports, hotel rooms, deadlines, policing of time-tracking, internet access, and expenses requires a conscious commitment from within. Often this commitment does not truly begin until a leader has reached a nadir of despair. The saddest part of project life is witnessing people who are visibly unhappy behaving in unproductive ways and medicating to remove their pain. An unwillingness to help each other before it becomes damaging to many illuminates the selfish nature of project work. Of course, one must help oneself to truly change; self-directed project leadership is an avenue through which to grow internally through project life and with whom one works—team members, sponsors, and even customers.

## An Engineer's Story

Massimo began his career as an engineer with an Italian aerospace company. Working as a design stress engineer, he began coordinating activities of testers and validation engineers. Before long, he was accountable for resources and deliverables associated with his company's programs.

Working within matrixed project teams was new to him and the dual reporting relationships—to his engineering boss and the program manager—began to strain his effectiveness. "Everyone's approach to problem solving is not the same, our cultural differences exacerbated our inability to work effectively as a team," he recounts. "I underestimated the importance of communication, particularly the ability to adapt to others' preferences for communicating."

Massimo eventually moved and became a project manager for a leading manufacturer of heating, air conditioning, and ventilation systems. He began managing multiple technical engineering projects from inception to completion. There he is receiving some formal project management training that helps him manage costs, schedules, and functional and quality requirements, while balancing these skills with new "soft skills."

The pressure of these project timelines, coupled with demanding efficiency requirements, continues to increase. "Managing to deliverables, costs, and deadlines while being an effective communication link between my team and upper management is not easy. You have to be passionate about your work, truly believe it makes a difference. Our project work is helping make in difference by producing more energy efficient heating, air conditioning, and ventilation systems. I have concluded our most important resource is people—their opinions, values, and history of experiences."

## Overview of Self-Directed Project Leadership Development

Self-directed leadership development is a process. It is about oneself, not about others. In other words, the results of this inner journey are not contingent on others; there are no excuses. One cannot say, "Well, my boss did not give me an honest review so my leadership journey is stuck in the mud," or, "Michael missed a deadline so my project is now in the red and so my leadership experience is failing." These types of excuses have no place on this train. However, the journey is not to be taken alone.

This journey is also directed. "Direct" means to manage or conduct; to have control or take charge of an aim or goal. The self-directed journey is not solely the result of circumstances and random effects, but rather one's consciousness, actions, and decisions about the leadership affair. No one is directing this journey for the leader. It is initiated and directed by an individual with the purpose to go deep within, then outward to the world.

The journey is also about project leadership: the accomplishment of goals through others. Therefore, creating a leadership journey must involve other people, and there is no better way to learn leadership than on projects that require others' willing participation to accomplish a goal. There is no better leadership crucible than a project. The relationships with project stakeholders are the result of one's efforts to become conscious of oneself and others; the project leader becomes aware of how interdependent all human endeavors really are. This consciousness then leads to work that is not driven solely by materialistic needs, but rather a consciousness to change the world in a positive manner.

The process is developmental in the same way that a child develops into a teen and then into an adult. There are periods of continual change, such as the rapid growth of a toddler or awkward stretches as a teenager. There are periods of impaired or lapsed judgment, such as occurs with college students. There are stretches of incredible energy and brilliance, and periods of stagnation. Like all human beings, leaders develop at different rates, influenced by environmental factors, and with unique talents (or sometimes disabilities). Some discover their inner selves more quickly than others. As with any development process, it is experiential. The assimilation of data through one's senses drives the learning process, even if one is not aware of it.

Any good framework is logical, easy to understand, and practical. The MyProjectAdvisor® Leadership Competency Pyramid must be combined with a personal transformation model that enables one to grow and learn while assimilating experiences and gaining deeper self-knowledge.

Service-based project leaders stand to gain in many ways from self-directed leadership development. Taking control of one's career and defining a future as a service-based project leader makes sense given the volatile project environment. Because the self-directed leadership development model is individualized, its general structure is basic. There are important things to consider before starting on the road to being a service-based project leader. Commitment is serious business. Without commitment, no growth will occur. The goal of this section is to provide you with a guide to become a service-based project leader using self-directed leadership development. The steps are:

1. Establish direction and commitment. Be true to oneself, defining values, and establishing convictions about the benefits of service-based project leadership.
2. Acquire and assess project leadership competencies. Learn key leadership competencies as defined within the leadership competency pyramid and building personal feedback mechanisms to assess them.

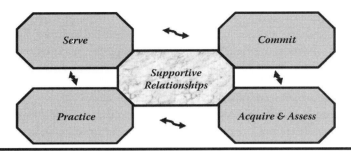

**Figure 18.1** MyProjectAdvisor® self-directed project leadership development model.

3. Practice project leadership competencies. Define and execute real leadership experiences in projects that allow regular practice and experimentation with leadership competencies; use knowledge, build trust, demonstrate consultative leadership, and bolster courage.
4. Serve a community. Lead by serving others' interests, give back to the profession, mentor others, learn from others, and experience significance.

These four steps, illustrated in Figure 18.1, revolve around supportive relationships and are the brushstrokes of building a service-based project leadership career: a career that can change the world.

Becoming a service-based project leader is a continual process, a process that evolves and grows. All steps can be occurring simultaneously as one grows more aware of a true need for self-fulfillment, learn more about what makes one tick, adjust to new seasons in life, and quietly listen to what is in one's heart.

Continual discovery is the nature of self-directed project leadership development. The model focuses on five discoveries of a project leader:[6]

■ A future self
■ A current self
■ A self-directed learning plan
■ An assimilation of project leadership experiences
■ A supportive community that provides a safe environment in which to grow

The goal of service-based project leadership development is to make these discoveries, not in a sterile learning environment, but rather in one's dynamic project environment.

The model is aligned with the five discoveries. Commitment includes discovering the project leader's real and ideal self through service-based project leadership. This would include the alignment of convictions and values with the work being performed. The commitment process includes contemplating why you may want to change and become a service-based project leader who desires to transform people, systems, and organizations. Of course, not all service-based project leaders need to be project managers, but having project or change management knowledge and expertise provides powerful opportunities to initiate transformational change.

Commitment also includes bolstering one's courage through self-confidence. The journey begins with assessments of one's strengths and talents and becoming aware of limitations or gaps. The acquisition and assessment step is a continuation of the commitment step, with more knowledge being acquired regarding the specific type of service-based project leader one desires to be. This provides the leader with an outline for personal growth, including enhancing his leadership competency pyramid. The third step is repeated practice of these leadership competencies, assimilating feedback to accelerate learning. Practicing means bringing these leadership competencies to the job and consciously executing them among sponsors, team members, and stakeholders.

Finally, the last step is service. Service is the renewal of a service-based project leader's commitment, whether serving the project community, or creating external service projects aligned to the work one truly desires. The self-directed journey to service-based project leadership is iterative, not linear. Multiple steps can be occurring simultaneously.

## New Training Methods

People learn in different ways, creating implications both for a leader's own leadership development as well as for how he interacts with his customers. Numerous books and articles have been published about learning styles and how they affect business interactions. Learning styles can be organized into simple categories: those who learn by analyzing, those who learn by doing, and those who learn by watching. Each of these styles has its own unique strengths, and the wise leader tailors tasks to an individual's learning style. For example, an analytical learner hates making mistakes; learning by trial and error is likely to cause great frustration and resentment. For those who learn by doing, voluminous reading and research will be tedious and impede learning.[7]

Thus, a leader must understand his preferred style but use a variety of learning experiences and adapt the acquisition of leadership competencies to what suits his needs. Blending learning techniques and modifying your risk attitudes through the leadership competency pyramid enables you to capitalize on individual strengths and explore new areas of learning that will enhance your experience.

As organizations embrace and utilize project management, developing new methods for turning project managers into leaders who can execute strategic projects will be crucial to organizations attributing project management to their success.

Most project management training programs are aimed at the neocortex, the part of the brain which is traditionally associated with learning and thinking. Teaching to the neocortex is appropriate, if the desired achievement is memorization of facts or passing a knowledge test. However, if the goal is to transform a project manager into a leader from the inside out, learning must occur in the limbic portion of the brain, which is associated with emotions.[8] In order to develop leaders, project managers must be ready to confront their own internal ideas, preconceptions, and thinking patterns.

The limbic part of the brain learns more slowly, requiring more commitment and persistence, since it is centered on habits and patterns ingrained early in life. The cortex learns faster, but does not retain information for as long. New neural tissue can be generated in adulthood by training the limbic portion of the brain, which leads to permanent changes in how a person thinks, acts, and reacts. This stands against the popular belief that some people are simply born leaders.[9]

Continuous practice and repetition are essential to training the limbic brain. Unlike the cortex, this part of the brain cannot learn a new pattern in the course of a seminar. While a seminar may jump-start the process of rerouting the way attitudes influence behaviors, it requires conscious repetition and evaluative feedback.

In order to bring the project management profession to the next level, industry leaders, organizations, and practitioners must find the courage to go beyond the methodology, tools, and templates and focus on the conscious inner journey required for bold leadership in a chaotic world. **Self-directed project leadership development fills the project leadership void and builds organizational leadership bench strength.**

Since these leadership skills cannot be learned strictly through traditional training methods, effort will have to be put into developing experiences (rather than courses) that will involve coaching, assessments, and "safe" communities in which to practice leadership competencies.

Achieving success in training and education has always been somewhat driven by the trainer, his material, and methods. In this new paradigm, **success will be almost exclusively determined by the individual rather than the trainer or the material.**

## Project Management and Self-Directed Project Leadership Development

The project management environment is fertile ground for self-directed project leadership development. The unique and temporary nature of projects coupled with their creative nature and matrix resource dependencies requires the projection of a strong vision and trust-based relationships. This is coupled with resources that have little to no commitment to the leader. Projects are becoming more strategic, organizational leanness requires more to be done with less, and traditional hierarchal structures are flattening. These trends create havoc for project practitioners who are accustomed to traditional project management roles and structure. These practitioners may make good salaries, but they are also reaching their breaking point due to stress and burnout. They struggle to exert their knowledge and expertise in an environment filled with change-resisting, self-preserving managers. Self-preservation stifles the organizational progress that the project manager is authorized to lead.

This lack of progress is creating a demand for service-based project leaders who create explicit value by pursuing significance and creating meaningful work for project workers. **Service-based project leaders are beacons of hope and a stabilizing force for project workers and their organizations**. They will be the leaders of a changing world.

## Summary

The goal of self-directed leadership is to dream and begin an inner journey directed by the heart that changes oneself and the world. As with any development process, it is experiential. The steps are establishing direction and commitment, acquiring and assessing project leadership competencies, practicing project leadership competencies, and serving a community.

A self-directed project leader builds on his strengths and understands his preferred learning style but uses a variety of learning experiences. In order to bring the project management profession to the next level, industry leaders, organizations, and practitioners must find the courage to go beyond the methodology, tools, and templates and focus on the conscious inner journey required for bold leadership in a chaotic world.

## Endnotes

1. Parker J. Palmer, "Leading from Within," in *Insights on Leadership: Service, Stewardship, Spirit, and Servant-Leadership*, Larry Spears and Michele Lawrence, Eds (New York: Wiley & Sons 1998) 198.
2. Ibid., 198.
3. Public Broadcasting Service, s.v. "The Great Wall Across Yangtze" http://www.pbs.org/itvs/greatwall/dam1.html (access December 11, 2006).
4. National Aeronautics and Space Administration, s.v. "Apollo 11" http://www.hq.nasa.gov/office/pao/History/apollo/apo11.html (accessed December 11, 2006).
5. Medical Missionaries s.v. "who we are" http://www.medicalmissionaries.info/index.html (accessed December 11, 2006).
6. Daniel Goleman, Richard Boyatzis, and Annie McKee, *Primal Leadership: Learning to Lead with Emotional Intelligence* (Boston: Harvard Business School Press, 2004) 109.
7. Marcus Buckingham, "What Great Managers Do," *Harvard Business Review*, March 2005.
8. Ibid., Goleman et al., 102–103.
9. Ibid.

## Chapter 19

# Commitment to Leadership: Taking Control

## Introduction

Organization-sponsored leadership development is more often aligned with the organization's goals than with the individual's goals. These programs are developed and applied in a generic fashion to teams of candidates, sometimes dozens at a time. They focus on general leadership principles such as relationships, communication, and finance. Participants are expected to promote corporate brands and learn delegation and management techniques. These programs can require candidates to take on leadership projects as a part of their learning curriculum, but these managers usually have limited project management experience and little understanding of project processes.

Project managers have limited access to these programs because they are not identified with managing large groups of employees. They usually have no broad business unit accountability next to their name. This is even though they manage matrices of resources with responsibility for project objectives aimed at improving business unit performance. The codification of formerly tacit project management knowledge and processes enables more use of temporary contractors, negating the need for project manager participation in leadership development. This paradigm of managers being asked to lead projects with limited project management knowledge, skill, or experience, and project managers being asked to lead projects with limited leadership knowledge or experience, is neither atypical nor coincidental.

The desire to control project costs constrains project managers, particularly in under-performing IT-related projects. **Project management is viewed as a necessary cost that can be managed down, removing project managers from management's consciousness as potential leaders.** Meanwhile, managers who should be standardizing processes and managing costs and margins are viewed as the future, potential leaders of the organization. These managers depend on projects to improve their performance metrics.

The traditional road of functional managers to senior management is being turned upside down by what Tom Peters calls the "Wow project." Wow projects that transform business operations and generate value are the key to white collar worker value, and project management is a key success factor to these projects.[1]

Project managers shunned by organizational leadership development programs may feel neglected, but their self-directed project leadership development is critical to a strategic project and it can carry them farther in life than any organizational program.

## Commitment

Taking command of one's journey is the first important step. A project leader must establish a destination for her journey and commitment to her profession. Being true to herself by establishing convictions about value and purpose is critical to making a breakthrough in her project management career. Before beginning the journey, she orients herself to the destination of a service-based project leader. A belief in this destination is mandatory to the transformation of a project manager into a service-based project leader. Figure 19.1 highlights the first step in the self-directed project leadership development process.

To be successful at self-directed project leadership development, a practitioner must be highly motivated. People learn what they want to learn. **Motivation is likely to be high when a practitioner sees an urgent need to change, understands the attainable benefits associated with this personal change, and feels she can influence the outcomes by following a clear road map to success.**

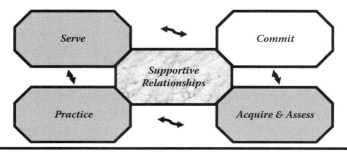

**Figure 19.1    MyProjectAdvisor® self-directed project leadership development model/commit.**

## *Human Motivation Theories and the Service-Based Project Leader*

Motivation of workers has been studied and analyzed by the likes of Douglas McGregor, Frederick Herzberg, and David McClelland, to name a few. Some build on Maslow's needs theory discussed in Section I. Maslow highlighted five needs that humans pursue incrementally after the lower level needs have been met; physiological, safety, love and belonging, self-esteem, and self-actualization. These theories and others shed light on what motivates one to commit to being a service-based project leader.

Douglas McGregor promotes the XY Theory of motivation in his 1960 book, *The Human Side of Enterprise*. The theory is simple in that it represents two fundamental ways to manage and lead people. Theory X, which relies on an authoritarian style, implies most workers do not like work, and attempt to avoid it. To get results, managers and leaders must use authority, threats, or punishment to get workers to comply. McGregor found that Theory X generally leads to poor results. Theory Y embraces the participative management style that assumes most workers find work to be rewarding and will manage themselves when they are pursuing organizational goals. Theory Y purports that people desire responsibility and willingly accept it, and that creativity and ingenuity are widely distributed in workers, not just in a select few.[2] Service-based project leaders recognize the capability of themselves and others and allow full participation in project objectives.

Herzberg, a clinical psychologist, was the first to determine that motivation varies among people and their situations. The factors that motivate one individual may not provide the same impetus to another. He distinguishes between motivating factors and hygiene factors, which relate closely to Maslow's hierarchy. He found factors that truly motivate an individual are achievement, recognition, the work itself, responsibility, advancement, and personal growth. Though these many vary by individual, these factors are more likely to result in sustained motivation. Hygiene factors or maintenance factors simply enable the motivating factors. Status, security, supervision, salary, work conditions, and relationships with subordinates, peers, and bosses provide temporary motivation that diminishes over time. Pay, a maintenance factor, often ranks lower than other factors, such as promotion opportunity and more challenging work, when workers leave one job for another. These hygiene factors must be in place to achieve the optimum motivation factors such as achievement.[3]

Service-based project leaders use achievement, the work itself, and personal growth as the primary motivating factors to change themselves. They use relationships, a hygiene factor, as a foundation for personal transformation. Through these relationships, they come to understand the motivating factors that drive those around them, factors such as recognition, advancement, or responsibility. With this knowledge, initiation of transformation within others is possible.

David McClelland's needs-based motivation, closely related to Herzberg's theory, describes a mixture of motivational needs each individual possesses. The variation or relative strength of each determines their true motivation requirements. McClelland describes three needs each worker has at some level:[4]

- Need for achievement and attainment of realistic challenging goals
- Need for power, to be influential, and have an impact on events
- Need for affiliation and cooperative relationships with others

McClelland's research led to his belief that achievement needs are the most desirable drivers for a leader. An imbalance in either the need for power or relationships produces less desirable results.[5] Service-based project leaders have a great need for achievement, but realize they need influence and cooperation to produce results in and through others. They desire to make an impact, but attaining personal power is not their primary motivation.

Charles Handy extends Maslow's hierarchy with his motivation calculus. The motivation calculus considers not just needs of workers as motivating factors but the projected results and ultimate effectiveness of their efforts. A worker has a need to measure results and determine when the results have met his needs. This ultimately determines if a worker will continue to be motivated.[6] A service-based project leader desires to see and experience the efforts of her purpose-focused work on his community.

A service-based project leader is intent on measuring results; thus, Handy's theory is very much applicable to her motivational psyche. But she does not just create equitable input and output; rather she desires to have output or reward be greater than the input or effort. This is the premise of transformational work in which service-based project leaders excel. The sum of effort released by the project organization is ultimately a fraction of the benefits resulting from transformation change. This does not mean that she does not desire to work hard. She will work hard, but leverage human effort to its greatest potential, which produces exponential benefits through ongoing transformation.

## Significance and Motivation

To achieve alignment in your projects, the level of effort should be commensurate with your intensity to achieve value-based desired outcomes (purpose). The values (what a worker truly believes in) plus purpose (the condition or outcome he desires) can be summarized as significance. Significance enhances motivation when you experience the results of your efforts. If results are lacking, motivation can diminish.

This is particularly true if the effort has become extremely great over an extended period of time and no results are measured or experienced. In this case, the significance and effort may not be grounded in reality or the service-based project leader has failed to produce the internal transformation (personal) prior to external transformation (systems and organizations).

Motivation increases dramatically when desired results are greater than the sum of significance plus effort. This is the goal of the service-based project leader, creating unparalleled results through transformation. This motivation is the energy service-based project leaders and customers use to continue to change the world.

In summary, the service-based project leader's motivation draws from familiar theories on human behavior. They motivate themselves through their higher-level needs, such as measurable achievement accomplished through relationships with customers, including sponsors and team members. This achievement is just as much a personal transformation as it is the transformation of others, their systems, and organizations. Motivation is sustained through initiating transformation and bolstered through experiencing transformation. The combination of a strong MyProjectAdvisor® Leadership competency pyramid, supportive relationships, and a motivation to achieve value-based outcomes maintains the commitment to self-directed project leadership development.

## Commitment Killers

There are several factors that often work against sustaining commitment. The initial excitement of new transformational opportunities, learning environments, or self discovery can jump-start motivation, but without commitment, motivation is likely to diminish over time as routine and daily pressures overtake the motivation to change from the inside out. Figure 19.2 shows the performance versus

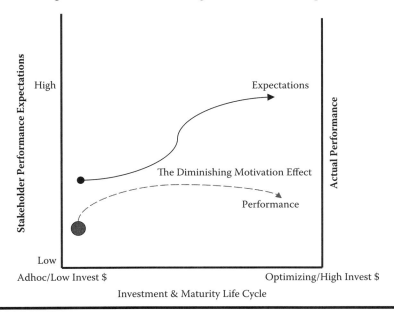

**Figure 19.2  Impact of motivation killers on the performance / expectations gap.**

expectations gap initially being closed, but over time actual performance waning due to a diminished motivation.

In today's project environment, the biggest threats to motivation are a culture of fear, fatigue, and denying failure.

## Culture of Fear

Fear itself can actually be a motivator; fear can create an urgency to act. One may realize that if she does not grow beyond her current capabilities, she may lose her job to a low-cost provider. If this fear is great enough, it can motivate her to find viable alternatives. However, when confronted with ambiguity and a sense of entitlement and comfort, the culture of fear can diminish motivation and commitment. This culture is propagated by those clinging to the status quo, and their position in the organization or sense of entitlement.

As the culture of fear metastasizes, thoughts begin to race through one's mind:

- What if I start acting like a leader and my boss rejects me?
- What if I want to start developing trust-based relationships but no one reciprocates?
- What if I advise my team, and it backfires?
- What if I challenge assumptions and I am rebuked?

These thoughts can be deafening, causing a leader to retreat, "I can do what I always do, and I will still get my paycheck at the end of the month."

There are also fears on the inner journey as well. "What if I have to confront my own personal failings? What if I do not like the person I am? What if I find out I am in the wrong profession?" These fears conjure up feelings of failure, error, and low self-esteem. The path of least resistance is often to forge ahead on the current trail, keeping busy enough to mask the real pain and fear one feels.

## Fatigue

Another motivation killer is fatigue. The constant demands of life, personal and professional, wear one down. A steady stream of obligations can emotionally drain a person. The digital age has done little to help these problems by allowing the office to follow workers everywhere they go. Personal digital assistants have become a nuisance for project managers seeking the downtime required to reenergize their bodies and minds. Fatigue is also caused by strained relationships with co-workers, peers, and customers, and by the overwhelming amount of information that must be processed in a given day.

## Denying Failure

Failure can be a traumatic experience when the focus is on oneself, a characteristic of high self-orientation. Denying failure often occurs when the real or perceived repercussions of the failure are greater than the opportunities afforded to grow and learn from the experience. Without a leader's resilience and steadfast purpose, failure can be crippling.

## The Boxer's Story

Former boxing heavyweight champion George Foreman, spoke of his loss of the heavyweight title to Muhammad Ali in Zaire, Africa, early in his career as an event that stripped him of his manhood. He admittedly said it took him months to overcome the devastating loss. After years of reflecting on the loss, Foreman says he learned an important life lesson. Even though he lost the fight, he could be proud that he was always moving forward toward his opponent, Ali, during the fight; he never backed up. In life, Foreman says, you may get knocked down, but you always have to be moving forward, not backing up. Foreman went on to remake himself not only as a boxer, but as a successful businessman and family man.[7]

When the leader focuses on learning, a characteristic of low self-orientation, the failure is much more likely to enhance motivation. Service-based project leaders embrace failure as a learning experience. Doing so allows failure to come in smaller, healthier doses. This is because failure is accepted immediately, not hidden or masked until an even bigger failure lurks. **The longer failure is denied its proper learning potential, the greater potential the failure has to demoralize project teams and leaders of personal growth through motivation and commitment.**

The culture of fear, fatigue, and denial of failure must be addressed head-on by a service-based project leader whose confidence, self-esteem, healthy lifestyles, and a genuine sense of humility pierce the fear of failure. The mortar of the leadership competency pyramid, courage, must conquer these commitment killers both internally and externally to allow the self-directed project leadership journey to continue.

# A Healthy Commitment

In Section I, we discussed important issues to be considered before one starts the commitment process. These include ownership of one's career and the pursuant choices, decisions, and truths that must be explored. Also to be considered is the basic nature of creating and bringing forth creativity in one's work. As with anything else, commitment can be misconstrued and exploited. This can be seen in cults and other dysfunctional groups. Enron's managerial staff certainly were committed to their company and its business model; but one only has to listen to the tapes of traders laughing about how they were ripping off consumers to know that this was an excited commitment that was way off-base.

The commitment to change and face the risks and personal demands inherent in this new project leadership role requires a unity of body and mind that embodies compassion and hope. Compassion for the work and its extended community and hope for the future are anchors to ensure self-directed project leadership development doesn't stray off the path.

Compassion for the work's redeeming mission as well as the community impacted by the project grounds the service-based project leader to reality. Compassion reflects the humanity of relationships. A service-based project leader's real concern for others strengthens him for the difficult leadership journey. A lack of concern creates isolation, negativity, and concern for only oneself. An individual's lack of compassion, rooted in selfishness, impedes the commitment of others.

Conversely, a healthy concern for others fuels actions with integrity. These actions create experiences and lend themselves to continual learning and self-confidence. Compassion germinates from selflessness. A project leader's desire to serve before leading allows compassion to flow more freely through the project organization. Compassion is a human quality recognized across cultures and languages. Unfortunately, so are greed, gluttony, and other selfish behaviors.

Hope is a dream that is real, attainable, and meaningful.[8] A service-based project leader maintains commitment when the dream is alive, the path to that dream is clear, and the progress down that path is filled with many positive emotional experiences. As dreams emerge, so do emotions that attract those who wish to dream. Hope has a physical impact on the body; one becomes calm, elated, energized, and optimistic. Breathing, blood pressure, and immune systems all benefit when one experiences hope. When a service-based project leader latches on to attainable dreams, and begins to navigate the path toward realizing aspects of the dreams, hope reverberates throughout the body and mind.[9]

## Summary

Practitioners leading transformational projects need leadership development. Organizations need these practitioners to experience leadership development in meaningful ways if they are to compete in dynamic, fast-paced global markets. The service-based project leader's motivation draws from familiar theories on human behavior. They use higher level needs, such as measurable achievement accomplished through relationships with customers, including sponsors and team members. This achievement is just as much a personal transformation as it is the transformation of others, their systems, and organizations. Motivation is sustained through initiating transformation and bolstered through experiencing transformation. The biggest threats to motivation are a culture of fear, fatigue, and denying failure. Compassion for work and its extended community and hope for the future are anchors that ensure self-directed project leadership development doesn't stray off the path.

# Endnotes

1. Tom Peters, "Forecasting the Future of Project Management," *PM Network,* December 2003.
2. *Businessballs.com*, s.v. "McGregor," http://www.businessballs.com/mcgregor.htm (accessed December 11, 2006).
3. *Businessballs.com*, s.v. "Herzberg," http://www.businessballs.com/herzberg.htm (accessed December 11, 2006).
4. *Businessballs.com*, s.v. "McClelland," http://www.businessballs.com/davidmcclelland.htm (accessed December 11, 2006).
5. Ibid.
6. *Businessballs.com*, s.v. "Handy," http://www.businessballs.com/charleshandy.htm (accessed December 11, 2006).
7. ESPN2 Quite Frankly, *"Stephen A. Smith interview with George Foreman*, June 28, 2006.
8. Richard Boyatzis and Annie McKee, *Resonant Leadership*, (Boston: Harvard Business School Press, 2005), 152.
9. Ibid., 154

## *Chapter 20*

# Acquiring and Assessing Project Leadership Skills

## Introduction

After committing to the process, the next iterative step in the self-directed leadership development process is to acquire and assess the leadership competencies needed to transition from project manager to service-based project leader.

Acquiring and assessing new leadership competencies is a continuous improvement process fuelled by a leader's commitment and enabled by supportive relationships. It occurs simultaneously with other steps as iterations of the cycle deepen the inner journey. (See Figure 20.1.)

## Acquisition

The primary method of acquiring service-based leadership skills is the building of the leadership competency pyramid. Most everyone has traces of each pyramid layer, which makes discovering and building the layers the primary task. The goal is to expand the pyramid and ensure uniformity among the layers. A lack of uniformity or inequity of pyramid layers can lead to problems for the service-based project leader and his customers. The size and stability of the pyramid are directly related to the base, which is made up of project management knowledge, experience, and skills. As a leader expands his leadership competency pyramid, knowledge of leadership emerges as a layer of the pyramid.

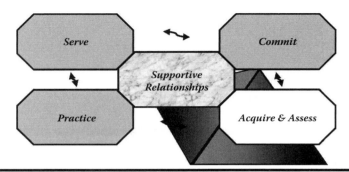

**Figure 20.1** MyProjectAdvisor® self-directed project leadership development model/A&A.

Regardless of the relationship between the pyramid layers, a service-based project leader must attempt to increase the overall size of his leadership competency pyramid. Continual growth of knowledge, skill, and experience requires him to be eager and open to new learning. The acquisition of new knowledge through reading, training, and observation must be integrated with attempts to implement new skills and assimilated through real project experiences as discussed in Chapters 13 and 14.

Trust-based relationships are acquired through a value proposition with other stakeholders and then through building credibility, reliability, intimacy, and low self-orientation. Acquiring these trust building skills involves the actions outlined in Chapter 15.

The service and advisory skills of consultative leadership are acquired through reorienting one's primal interest in oneself to interest in others. These skills are acquired through executing the consultative leadership process, enabled by trust-based relationships, and motivated by the significance of project work.

This alignment is fostered through regular listening to oneself and building a greater self-awareness. Weekly or even daily quiet time can help. This quiet time allows one to give over or release anxieties, fears, and confusion, opening a clear communication channel with oneself. This meditative state precedes the clarity and foresight needed to lead with courage. Desolation, often masked through a leader's busyness, is a poor place to make weighty decisions. When a project leader recognizes his inner voice, desolation is replaced with consolation before he moves forward with critical matters regarding his career.

Courage is acquired through the systematic building of all leadership competency layers that influence risk attitudes. Courage is emboldened when you recognize your obligation to combine your project skills with leadership competencies to change the world.

# Considerations for Assessment

## *Formal and Informal Assessments*

When assessing leadership competencies, the aspiring project leader should combine formal assessment methods with informal methods that help validate, question, or spark inquiry on his performance. Formal assessment tools (discussed by Roberta Hill in Section IV) can be employed with a specific purpose to better understand what works and what needs work. Choose a tool with a purpose. With so many assessments on the market today, it is difficult to make sense of which one is right for you and your team. Roberta provides you with a layman's guide to using the proper tool to assess leadership competencies and team dynamics.

Informal feedback is direct feedback from the pool of supportive relationships one has formed in the self-directed project leadership process. This requires open discussion and inquiry to find out what others really think and feel about specific events. Informal feedback should not be a search to satisfy one's ego, but rather a mutual exploration of specific events that can be discussed in a neutral environment. Questions such as "How did you think that meeting went?" or "How could I have communicated the vision in a more meaningful manner?" or "How could I have answered the question about the schedule in a truthful, credible manner?" encourage open dialogue. A leader should continually develop a network of relationships to collect informal, direct feedback. This feedback is accumulated for the leader to sift through and use as an input to the acquisition and refinement of his leadership competencies.

## *Internal Assessment*

Internally, it is important to assess one's own feelings. It means asking yourself, "How did I feel when the sponsor confronted me on the revised budget? Was I confident and ready for the discussion, or did I feel threatened?" Analyzing your internal feelings gives additional data points for the feedback data bank. If fear or a lack of confidence exists in certain situations, you must examine why and determine how to bolster self-confidence. The sources of fear could have arisen out of undeveloped areas of the leadership competency pyramid, such as a lack of knowledge of the subject matter, a lack of meaningful trust-based relationships, or fear of repercussions—lack of courage.

## *Style and Strengths*

Self-directed project leadership development is a personal endeavor that involves a painstaking search for one's strengths and a willingness to expose gaps or weaknesses. Strengths are emphasized while gaps are exploited by sharing leadership with another's complementary strengths. No journey is the same because it reflects individual uniqueness as well as one's working environment and life situation. The makeup of the team members, sponsors, and customers adds a complex mix of variables with which an aspiring service-based project leader must become comfortable. Thus, a leader must assess his natural abilities and preferences. Whether it is a DISC, Myers-Briggs, or Platinum Rule® assessment, these tools validate or recast his view of himself. They do not answer why one is unique but spur questions that can be explored individually, creating self-awareness, which is the intent of these tools. Everyone is unique, and each has talents that flow naturally and others that seem to need continual practice.

A strength is defined as a person's ability to consistently provide a near perfect performance in a specific activity.[1] A service-based project leader must know his natural strengths and strive to align them with his leadership role. The goal is also to understand individual stakeholder strengths—whether belief, discipline, focus, or harmony as examples from the popular book *Now, Discover Your Strengths*—and find the leadership role that maximizes them.[2] Discipline may benefit a project leader in circumstances in which structure and process provide great value to the customer, but this strength may be less important than communication or empathy in a crisis. At the same time, a strength can become a burden in the wrong situation. Strengths can go awry; for instance, the strength of belief can be construed as being too rigid and inflexible, or harmony can be viewed as impeding results due to the desire to maintain peace over achieving results. A service-based project leader understands his strengths and trusts others to bring the appropriate strengths to the table through joint leadership.

## Environment

A service-based project leader assesses the relationship with his environment with the goal of finding a fit. Project team norms and organizational cultures are often related but are not always mirrors of each other. Successful self-directed project leadership development requires an environment that is safe. This safety is constructed through supportive relationships. Culture acts as an enabler or detractor to the ability to create a safe environment.

The ideal supportive environment for the self-directed project leader is not only good for project managers seeking to grow but also for an organization's financial statements. David Maister developed a predictive package of characteristics that allows service firms to make more money.[3] Leadership competencies can transform or at least influence team environments. These predictive, money-making characteristics of service firms align with leadership competencies of a service-based project leader and influence a team environment.

Customer satisfaction is a top priority for service firms who make more money. A true goal of the service-based project leader is to serve his customers. These firms do not allow personal agendas to get ahead of customer interests. A service-based project leader's team uses low self-orientation to create a healthy, trust-based relationship with the customer. Successful service firms establish a culture that treats everyone with mutual respect, another fundamental principle of a service-based project leader.

The predictive characteristics resonating from a leader's competency pyramid infiltrate his team and positively influence project and organizational environments. You can impact your team environment, and your team can influence the organization.

## Assessing the Base of the Leadership Competency Pyramid

At the base of the leadership competency pyramid are a project leader's knowledge, skill, and experience. To assess the strength of the base, a leader should analyze the credentials such as certifications, certificates, number of years of experience, the types of projects managed, and the outcomes of those projects against peer groups. But credentials are just a start. Project management performance must be assessed against basic project management processes. This criterion emphasizes a service-based project leader's role—to serve his customers, fearlessly!

### *Initiation and Planning*

During project initiation, a service-based project leader must be fearless in identifying needs and pursue the clarification of needs through a rigorous examination of interrelated requirements and organizational processes. Fearless needs analysis addresses stakeholder politics, conflicting needs, and false needs.

The identification of all customer needs must be validated with key sponsors and stakeholders. Failure to do so is a disservice, even when the customers and sponsors are convinced they know their needs. A measure of success is the ability for customers to share and compare needs to identify and validate real needs and competing needs. Success often means facilitating difficult and uncomfortable discussions between powerful stakeholders. For instance, in software projects the need for business users to customize software often conflicts with the need for IT to support and maintain the application at minimal cost. The benefits of customization must be exposed against the cost of maintenance.

Stakeholder management requires fearless analysis to root out hidden and opposing needs in order to unify those needs before important project decisions are made. A leader uses all aspects of his leadership competency pyramid—relationships, advisory skills, content knowledge, etc.—to gain the proper level of exposure and dialogue to achieve a clear, supported direction. Structured, facilitated sessions can measure the exposure and collaboration of needs across the enterprise. Fearless needs analysis ensures the customer has a vested interest in the successful outcome of the project.

Projects benefit greatly from clearly defined scope, objectives, and baselines. Thus, a service-based project leader is held to a high standard of excellence in scope statements and work breakdown structures. The collaboration in the development of these documents and their early visibility to power sharing stakeholders is critical for the initiation of transformation. **Remaining inconspicuous—not directly interacting with customers during the critical early stages—leaves a leadership void in the customer's mind.** A project manager who emerges only to bring forth information when he is at an impasse damages his credibility.

The identification and education of stakeholders' roles is a responsibility that includes identifying the project team members who are responsible for creating project deliverables. The responsibility also includes the customer team members responsible for feedback, acceptance, and use of interim deliverables to achieve project objectives. Role ambiguity is a treatable disease, but still kills many projects. Success is measured by a stakeholder learning his role, formally accepting it, and validating the necessary skills needed to complete the tasks associated with that role. A common problem is customers being asked to review and approve project deliverables in which they have little sense of what they are really approving. Again, a service-based project leader employs surveys, outcome-based education, facilitation, and straight-talk to achieve success.

Other planning measures include clear definitions of the current state and the envisioned future by highlighting not only what is changing, but also what is not changing, and by clearly defining quality and risk plans that protect the customer's best interest. In summary, a service-based project leader's project planning performance criteria are weighted towards:

- Fearless needs analysis
- Clear and user-friendly scope definition documents
- Acceptance of agreed-upon roles and responsibilities and validation of the skills required to complete them
- Accurate depictions of the current state and the desired future state with what is changing and what is not changing
- Quality and risk plans that protect the customer, not the project team

Each of these can be measured by the quantity and quality of exposure and dialogue created with customers.

## Execution

A service-based project leader's execution skills are best shown in the management of stakeholder expectations and the building of interdependent communication channels between project stakeholders and team members. The leader does not control communication, but rather broadcasts intent to enable communication speed and accuracy. Thus, a leader is not the focal point for all project communications, but enables uninhibited communication networks that strengthen the flow of information. The effectiveness of informal, naturally forming communications networks is a key performance criterion.

A service-based project leader's execution effort is directed toward planning for the coming 30, 60, or 90 days, removing barriers and priming work for team members to execute. This constant foresight enables him to act decisively, even without complete certainty.

A signal that a project leader is under-performing is the quantity of time spent meddling in the current day's project activities. Instead, he should serve team members by removing roadblocks, and freeing workers to work. The quality of execution is measured by low turnover of project team members, because the intrinsic value of the work is carefully aligned with team members' personal and professional needs. The growth of team members can be measured through promotions or opportunities for advancement. Any surveyed project team member, when asked if he has done something new, should answer affirmatively.

A service-based project leader has procedures in place to execute acceptance decisions on project deliverables from her customer. A desired customer experience and the use of deliverables in future decisions are discovered in advance. Crisis situations concerning a customer's acceptance decision of a deliverable are rare because planning, communication, and quality processes have set accurate expectations. These services can only be accomplished through direct interaction between team members. Each can be measured by the time and resources required to gain acceptance of customer deliverables after the customer has reviewed them and the time a leader spends in the current day's project activities versus preparing for the next 30, 60, and 90 days.

In summary, the performance criteria for execution are:

- Well-managed expectations among team members and customers to ensure quick acceptance of project deliverables
- Naturally forming effective, interdependent, uninhibited communication channels
- Continuously working in advance to create unimpeded work streams for team members

## Control and Monitoring

All projects benefit from well-defined change control processes that enable good decision making. However, a service-based project leader's control is weighted toward his customers' needs. Less time is spent fiddling with budgets and schedules because he has mastered these skills and established solid processes for others to grow into managing these processes. Instead, the service-based project leader continually focuses on emerging needs, the root of change control. A performance criterion is the ability to adapt to new or hidden needs and satisfy them based on sound analysis. These emerging needs do not create havoc among team members; they create opportunities to provide more value and greater service to the customer. Changes that have low value are candidly discussed with relevant stakeholders. This criterion can be measured by the net benefits associated with emerging needs. The performance criteria for control are weighted toward:

- Frequent and open discussion with customers about developing needs
- The identification of new needs
- The captured net benefits associated with emerging needs

## *Closing*

The performance criterion for closing out a project is simple: more work is awarded. Add-on work by the customer is the most significant message a customer can provide to a service-based project leader and his team. Documenting project results and lessons learned are a project manager's responsibility. A service-based project leader gets pulled into more work because of the value proposition associated with his services.

## Assessing the Rest of the Pyramid

Appendix B, the Self-Directed Project Leadership Workbook, is provided to help you assess the rest of your leadership competency pyramid. Remember, subject matter expertise has a direct impact on building credibility, one of the four critical building blocks of trust. Also, trust must be measured by the actions resulting from a two-way relationship where both parties are acting as trustees and trustors. The trustee is the person asking for trust and the trustor is the person who must grant trust. The decision to trust by either party is a complex mix of factors that encompass the decision maker's risk attitude, a view of himself and the world, his position of authority, and situational factors such as security, or level of concern, alignment of interests, capability, integrity, and level of communication.[4]

The ultimate assessment of consultative leadership is team results. For a service-based project leader executing consultative leadership techniques, the performance criteria involve visioning, advisory skills, and his intent to serve others. A project manager can first assess the specific behaviors that should be employed to achieve results. Advisory skills such as the exploration of alternatives, education of stakeholders, instilling ownership of decisions, and framing complexity into meaningful, well-articulated statements are measured through effective decision making.

The essence of courage is the willingness of a service-based project leader to rely on others who have no obligation to him. Inner self-confidence does not breed independence but rather interdependence. This self-confidence is a reflection of his relationships with stakeholders. Courage is assessed through the willingness to lead others to action by aligning a personal stake, such as reputation or bonuses, with results. He who resists making recommendations and taking command of project execution strategy is not committed to the net social outcomes of the project and thus holds back from selfless service and participation in the development of others.

By completing the workbook in Appendix B, you will gain a sense of the strength of your pyramid.

## Summary

Acquiring and assessing new leadership competencies is a continual process fuelled by a leader's commitment and enabled by supportive relationships. The primary method of acquiring service-based leadership skills is the building of the MyProjectAdvisor® Leadership Competency Pyramid. When assessing leadership competencies, a leader should evaluate his leadership style using formal and informal methods and his environment. Leadership in project management can be assessed through customer outcomes associated with project processes and transformation of self and team members.

## Endnotes

1. Marcus Buckingham and Donald O. Clifton, *Now Discover Your Strengths*, (New York: The Free Press, 2001), 25.
2. Ibid., chap 4.
3. David H. Maister, *Practice What You Preach* (New York: The Free Press, 2001).
4. Robert F. Hurley, "The Decision to Trust," *Harvard Business Review*, September 2006.

## Chapter 21

# Practicing to Be a Service-Based Project Leader

## Introduction

Millions of dollars are spent each year on training services—most of which do little to improve employee productivity. Training is a good last step in bringing about personal change, but not a very good first step.[1] Workshops are not completely useless, but they do not replace the practice field.

Practice must be conducted in the real world where true learning can occur. Figure 21.1 depicts the practice step of the self-directed project leadership development model.

A service-based project leader must practice the conversion of knowledge and skills into meaningful experiences, while creating and maintaining supportive relationships. The practitioner has an abundance of tools to practice her leadership techniques. The work breakdown structure that aligns customer expectations with team efforts, risk registers that tap into stakeholders' fears, and project network diagrams that result in important decisions can be used to practice leadership competencies. The adaptation of these tools to meet unique customer needs is an excellent way to practice leadership.

Building symbiotic trust-based relationships requires the practice of finding project leader and customer value propositions. Increasing the aspects of trust requires conscious repetition of actions that nurture credibility, reliability, intimacy, and low self-orientation with keen observation and self-awareness. This awareness

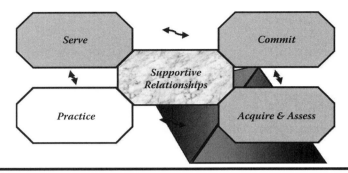

**Figure 24.1** MyProjectAdvisor® self-directed project leadership development model/practice.

allows her to tailor the trust building process to each individual's need, as stakeholders will likely require differing levels of credibility and intimacy.

Situational awareness must be practiced by increasing the level of awareness and predictability of self, team members, and interested stakeholders. A leader sees the future through a continual mental rehearsal of future events and possible outcomes that create actions or reactions and their subsequent effects.

Most training classes or leadership development programs are not conducive to practicing these competencies with consequences, and it is the consequences that allow lasting learning to occur. Benefits are minimal when efforts are disjointed, isolated, and do not coalesce. Thus, the practitioner must take it upon herself to create this opportunity for consequences if transformational learning is to begin.

A tool that allows a project leader to practice transformational work that is aligned with her core values and convictions is an Active Leadership Experience™. To be "active," the experience involves leadership experimentation on real projects. To be a "leadership" experience, it involves achieving results through others. To gain leadership "experience," she must assimilate and retain the learning through the collection of experiences and careful consideration of feedback. These experiences enable practitioners to increase individual professionalism. Leadership cannot just be practiced in a classroom or on a computer. To become an effective leader, she must learn by practicing in real-life situations.

## Active Leadership Experience™

There are five essential steps to achieving an Active Leadership Experience. The first is to internalize the vision of the project and its net social outcomes and benefits. This involves truly believing in the work's higher purpose and the linking of her core values to the work. Believing in this purpose is necessary to the second step: living the vision.

It is not enough for the leader to believe in an internal vision and purpose; she must make the vision real by linking it to her convictions. These convictions help align her behavioral patterns, decision making, ethics, and her internal attitudes. This process of living the vision of the project is the initiation of personal transformation.

Strategic objectives of project and programs cannot be accomplished alone. Building trust-based relationships is the third step in an Active Leadership Experience. Neither a project leader's alignment nor her belief in the importance of a vision is enough to carry a team to high achievement. Trustful collaboration and cooperation among team members and other participants is needed to open communication and allow her to exert power and influence. The project manager must take the first step in establishing trust through her own credibility, reliability, intimacy, and low self-orientation.[2]

The fourth step is to empower and serve others' efforts to achieve the vision. Once team members believe in the purpose of the vision and trust one another, they will demand to be empowered. Project leaders should look for opportunities to serve; a situation in which there is ambiguity, confusion, or communicational breakdown is a starting point from which to build a culture of service. Empowerment affirms the project leader's trust in her team and motivates them into more capable workers who have faith in their leader.

The final step to an Active Leadership Experience is to enable team performance through creativity. When team members trust each other and are empowered, creativity flourishes. Trust admits that failures and setbacks are a part of the creative process. Trust takes risks that would otherwise not be taken. Project teams discover unique value in each project by focusing beyond constraints and creating service experiences for customers. A leader is the face of the creative process and builds a plan and culture that embraces creativity as a means to increase team performance and customer satisfaction.

As project management maturity models make executives feel safe about their investment in project management, it is also important to ensure that practitioners feel safe enough to act on opportunities that lead to breakthrough discoveries in projects. Ignoring these opportunities leads to the practitioner being undervalued and commoditized.

Experiential project leaders fuel forward momentum for the project management industry by developing better project processes and building productive human relationships that result in rewarding experiences for all. Table 21.1 is a summary of the Active Leadership Experience process and the source of each step.

The process works like this:

1. Internalize—Write down a list of internal desired values or personal characteristics such as teamwork, achievement, comfort, winning, respect, stability, wealth, etc.
2. Externalize—Write down a list of external desired transformation changes; changes that are important to your life or job. Changes could be attitudes, processes, systems, future events, i..e., I desire to create or transform _____.

**Table 21.1   Summary of Active Leadership Experience™**

| *Active Leadership Experience™ Process* | *Source* |
| --- | --- |
| 1. Internalize the vision | Self-awareness, alignment of values and purpose (Establish significance) |
| 2. Live the vision | Model behaviors aligned with one's significance. (Initiation of personal transformation) |
| 3. Build trust-based relationships | Build credibility, reliability, intimacy, low self-orientation through the base of the leadership competency and passion about the project. (Build a team with shared values) |
| 4. Empower others to achieve the vision | Consultative leadership opportunities with advisory skills and a service attitude. (Make them successful) |
| 5. Enable creativity | Set courageous examples in leading them. (Remove fear of failure from culture and team) |

3. Connect—Look for alignment between 1 & 2. Examples:
   a. Because I personally value respect, I will create an active leadership experience by starting a diversity program in my organization.
   b. Because I personally value teamwork, I will create an active leadership experience by implementing collaboration tools for remote team members.
   c. Because I personally value stability, I will create an active leadership experience by gaining management approval for project managers to get leadership training.
4. Initiation—Identify behaviors one can exhibit to reflect these beliefs.
5. Build—Find the people who need to be involved to make this happen and build trust-based relationships with them.
6. Vision—Get others on board by using consultative leadership process to gain commitment of others to act.
7. Enable—Remove their fear of failure.

Following this process, project leaders can find transforming work that aligns with their convictions and use consultative leadership to accomplish it. In workshops, people discuss transforming the attitudes of organization-sponsored programs because of the personal characteristic or desired value of respect and equality for other human beings. Others seek to change a broken process or transform customer systems that serve a greater purpose. Active Leadership Experience™ is not about personal gain, such as more vacation time. For some, it is about transforming team members by providing an opportunity to shoot for the stars. Still others seek to transform relationships that have gone bad because of their conviction for peace and salvation. All of these transformations require willing participation that is achieved through a leader's ability to first internalize her vision, and then externalize it through her own transformation and initiation of transformation in others. Trust-based relationships and the consultative leadership process are what make this possible.

## Practicing Mental Skills

As with many professionals, notably athletes, the need to have a strong "mental game" is critical. Mental skills training is working its way from playing fields into conference rooms. Mental skills do not happen in isolation either; they are part of a dynamic environment that includes individual values, core beliefs, and brain chemistry.

It is beneficial for a service-based project leader to consider herself not just a worker, but rather a performer. A worker's mentality is doing what needs to be done. A performer's mentality is doing what she has prepared herself to do. A worker relies on experience, skills, and instincts to react to the present. Performers rely on an envisioned outcome to create the present. Performers rehearse endlessly to build sound fundamentals that can adapt with graceful instinct to rapidly changing situations. Great performers learn how to muster the determination, poise, positive mental outlook, concentration, and resilience to perform consistently at superior levels.

"There is power, genius and magic in boldness." —Goethe

Leaders must practice mental skills training to enhance their performance. Much like athletes, they can focus on the present, and use imagery, relaxation, and self-talk to improve the performance.[3]

Imagery is the process of generating kinesthetic images in one's mind of how an action is to occur. These images are kinesthetic because they focus on the feeling rather than how it appears. For an athlete, this is feeling the action of shooting a free throw or hitting a baseball. For a project leader, this is the feeling of speaking the truth about a sensitive matter, or the feeling of running a productive, high-energy meeting. When the images become too visual, it is easy for them to become negative if one has low self-esteem, and envisions a clumsy attempt to swing a bat or an awkward attempt to express a concern. Using kinesthetic imagery can help leaders overcome fear though replacing negative visual images with images of positive feelings. The focus and release technique accepts the negative image floating in and around one's mental consciousness, embraces it, and then releases it in exchange for positive kinesthetic—how it *feels*—images. These are common mental skill challenges for leaders entering events that cause anxiety such as high-powered meetings, confrontations, presentations, and intense problem solving. Kinesthetic imagery primes the regions of the brain responsible for doing the action by initiating neural connection, thereby making the brain more efficient.[4]

Leaders must stay focused on the present task and situation. Many people struggle with letting past events or future events preoccupy their mind when executing leadership competencies such as articulating content knowledge to establish credibility. Athletes use a reset signal to bring them back into the present. Leaders can do the same. Simple things such as making a simple letter or figure with a pen, standing up and stretching, or touching a finger between the eyes at the top of the nose can trigger the brain to reset and get out of the past and future and into the present.

Leaders must also practice relaxation techniques when in the middle of a leadership performance. Relaxing is not the same as being aloof. Relaxation is brought on by action and thoughts of the performer. Athletes use triggers, breathing patterns, and specific thoughts to quell nervousness that inhibits performance. The process of relaxation involves intense imagery associated with an outcome or goal, then releasing the accumulated tension and anxiety while actually pursuing the goal to trigger a breakthrough performance. A leader can use signals, such as deep breathing, closing her eyes for a few seconds to eliminate distractions, or allowing her mind to wander aimlessly for a few moments before taking action.

Self-talk is the ongoing relationship and discussion between a leader's inner voice and her actual self. Some refer to this as the "committee," which often creates a negative relationship with herself. Negative self-talk results from low self-esteem. However, performers who master self-talk can turn the committee from a tormenter into a consoler, healer, and advocate. When self-talk is negative, performance normally diminishes. When self-talk is healthy, it is not judgmental, but promising. Negative self-talk divides the two selves, creating isolation, while positive self-talk unifies, heals, and motivates performers. Using positive phrases that acknowledge grief or bad judgments but quickly refocus on hope and compassion will enhance a leader's performance.

## Summary

A service-based project leader must practice the conversion of knowledge and skills into meaningful experiences, while consciously repeating the actions that increase credibility, reliability, intimacy, and low self orientation. These exercises create opportunities to practice the consultative leadership process. A leader's situational awareness must be practiced by increasing the level of awareness and predictability of self, team members, and interested stakeholders, including taking it upon herself to create an opportunity for consequences for real learning to occur.

A tool that allows a project leader to practice transformational work that is aligned with core values and convictions is Active Leadership Experiences™. While practicing these leadership competencies, a leader can use mental skills training to enhance performance. Much like an athlete, a leader can focus on the present, and use imagery, relaxation, and self-talk to improve performance.

## Endnotes

1. David Maister, "*Why (Most) Training is Useless*," 2006, http://davidmaister.com/articles/4/96/1/.
2. David Maister, Charles H. Green, and Robert M. Galford, *The Trusted Advisor* (New York: The Free Press, 2000), chap 8.
3. Dr. Richard Keefe, *On the Sweet Spot—Stalking the Effortless Present* (New York: Simon & Schuster, 2003), chap 5.
4. Ibid.

# Chapter 22

## Serving Your Community as Teacher and Student

### Introduction

In 1830, philosopher Auguste Comte defined the term "altruism" as the act of self-lessly caring for others without a concern for self. All of the major world religions promote altruism as a very important moral value. Altruism was central to the teachings of Jesus found in the Gospel. "For even the Son of Man did not come to be served, but to serve, and to give his life as a ransom for many" (Mark 10:45). One of the duties of a Muslim is care for the needy. The Buddist's Dharma teaches that the path to enlightenment is simple—stop cherishing yourself and learn to cherish others.

Without opening a theological discussion, the act of selfless service in self-directed leadership development is ultimately aimed at *meaningfulness*. When a leader has meaningful work, his work is likely to produce greater results, leading to increased satisfaction and perhaps even happiness.

Viktor Frankl, in *A Man's Search for Meaning*, concludes that a search for personal meaning requires one to transcend subjective pleasure by doing something that "points, and is directed, to something, or someone, other than oneself … by giving himself a cause to serve or another person to love." Frankl also quotes Albert Schweitzer, "The only ones among you who will be really happy are those who have sought and found how to serve."

Serving others selflessly through project leadership can fulfill one's higher-level needs. But, many project managers work in a vacuum of meaningfulness, leaving their true talents and capabilities in limbo.

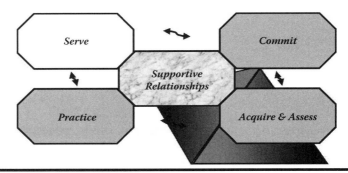

**Figure 22.1** MyProjectAdvisor® self-directed project leadership development model/serve.

Figure 22.1 depicts the service step in self-directed leadership development.

The act of serving others is not simply about a project leader serving his sponsor. A service-based project leader is called to be a citizen of service to his project team, customer, stakeholders, and community. This approach validates his self-directed mission—**by strengthening others through service, the project leader serves himself by becoming a more capable leader.**

Project teams can become overly dependent on the need for leaders. It is much easier for a team member to stand on the sidelines and wait for direction. It is often less risky for a project manager to idle in his cubicle and wait for direction from sponsors. A service-based project leader serves her community by initiating the leadership that lies dormant in project teams and organizations. These communities bring forth new life in organizations and in society.

## Three Calls to Serve

Project leaders are called to serve in three ways: through obedience, inquiry, and action. The first and most critical is a leader's obedience to serve himself by obeying his inner calling. The leader has a responsibility to serve himself through alignment of his values with his efforts. This service to self is ultimately a gift to others found in the durable energy that it emancipates. This obedience allows the inquiry and action to be a natural progression that is free of expectations for personal gain.

The second way is to inquire and validate the interests of another. A service-based project leader must do more than just give a stakeholder what he wants; he must serve him by first inquiring and validating his interest in the strategic initiative. This service is a courageous call for truthful dialogue and spurs the initiation of the transformation of individuals that is required to transform larger human systems. Whether it is a team member's desire for more training or a stakeholder desiring a scope change, the leader integrates the interest of the individual for a greater good and instills accountability that will produce measurable results. Once validated as beneficial to all, the leader is prepared to consciously promote the interest of the individual at his own risk, trusting he has tightly aligned his interest with the initiative.

The third is to serve through action. He acts on behalf of another's interest. This service is not tainted with the familiar legalist contractual mindset of "The customer is paying me to do this, nothing more, nothing less." Instead, he understands and balances all of his customers' interests in the net social outcomes of the endeavour. He is granted authority to act through his relationships and competence and his calling justifies his actions when questioned by detractors.

Project standardization and methodology can dilute direct interaction—or calls to serve—between project leaders and customers for the simple reason this direct interaction is very difficult to standardize, but these standardization efforts must not detract from a service-based project leader's call to visibly work for all stakeholders.

## The Teacher Becomes a Student ... and Vice Versa

Serving benefits self-directed education through a leader's actions and mindfulness and allows life-changing learning to begin when the student becomes the teacher. In this case, the student of self-directed project leadership development becomes the teacher by serving his community of stakeholders. People learn by reading, observing, and doing, but teaching allows life-changing learning to occur.

Practitioners, when adopting self-directed learning, become not just students, but also teachers, linking the learning concepts being acquired to their own desired actions. He who teaches himself the techniques of adapting his behaviors to achieve compatibility with team members will be more likely to use these techniques if he also teaches and encourages his team members. He will also get more out of the techniques if he becomes a student and learns from pupils.

The service-based project leader first must be student and teacher of himself and then a teacher and student of others. He who learns leadership competencies but fails to bring forth his knowledge into workable behavioral competencies creates a shield to his own hypocrisy. As a source of hypocrisy, his leadership tenure is short. When a leader becomes a teacher and student of others, the shield to hypocrisy is removed, allowing more light to shine on his consciousness, accelerating his growth.

## Giving to Receive

Service-based project leaders are not magical healers or therapists with special powers. Instead, they focus first on an inclination to serve others, listen for leadership opportunities, and then follow their desire to lead. By placing oneself in the true capacity of servant first, one will arrive as a more capable leader. By giving first, a leader does receive.

Opportunities to serve confront a project manager every day, requiring a conscious effort not to rely solely on his institutional knowledge for career success. By giving, a leader learns not only through his actions but also receives information about his calling. Because projects are universal in nature, they provide a common platform from which to learn by serving. Projects serve humanity as new beginnings that remove decay and enhance the spirit—a road to change both for the leader and stakeholders.

As the world struggles with huge resource inequities around the globe, conflicts, natural disasters, and the hatreds that exacerbate these situations, you truly can change the world by starting with yourself and your organization.

## Model for Advancement

As for the future, the project management industry must consider adding criteria to professional certification requirements that measure project leadership, specifically service-based project leaders. The criteria should be focused on advancing the profession, increasing the value of service, and creating future leaders for organizations. Requirements for achieving the higher level of certification would include participation in a self-directed leadership plan. Four components can be measured and recorded that align with the self-directed leadership process:

- ◾ Aligning professionalism in project management with core values, convictions, or a personal mission
- ◾ Continual use of assessments and objective feedback tools for one's leadership competencies
- ◾ Practicing leadership through Active Leadership Experiences™ with measurable results
- ◾ Serving a community that can benefit from project management

The practitioner can define his personal mission for his project management career. This is evidence of a commitment process, in which values and convictions are purposely considered and aligned with the work a practitioner undertakes. Using a community of practitioners and technology, he could collect input on his mission and be aligned with a community of interest that can be a source of supportive relationships. His mission could evolve and even change over time, but the conscious effort to apply project management to what he really cares about is what matters.

The practitioner who aspires to achieve project leadership credentials can participate in feedback mechanisms independent of traditional job performance reviews. These feedback mechanisms would be complementary to traditional performance appraisals, but provide more detail regarding how his project and program management leadership activities are being received.

Active Leadership Experience™ results can demonstrate the magnitude of his ability to change the world. These results measure his practice of leadership competencies: his ability to internalize, live his passion, and realize the transformation that could not be achieved alone. His Active Leadership Experience™ is a service not only to his community of stakeholders but also indirectly to a community of practitioners around the world who can potentially learn from him.

This leadership credential would require commitment to the service of others' interests without expectations of any payback. This step involves his service hours linked to his personal leadership vision. He may have a strong passion about project management and its potential to change the world, so he serves associations linking a purpose to increase project management to his core values. Or he may serve other non-profit, religious, or charity organizations by using his valuable project leadership skills. Measuring service ensures his commitment to a service-based project leadership.

Project management certifications are evolving rapidly. The real value of these certifications will arrive when lifelong learning intersects with a practitioner's meaningful work that can be shared with a community of practitioners around the world. Other professions are familiar with the practice of sharing breakthrough procedures in technology or medicine because they are focused on the common good.

## Measuring the Service-Based Project Leader

Measuring these subtle and often ambiguous service capabilities can be difficult. A holistic measurement is needed to reflect the value of the individual project leader, insulated from environmental factors, and his ability to serve the project organization.

The industry puts much focus on selling project management to executives on the grounds that it is critical to business results. Yet the bottom line is that great companies, products, and services do not need to be sold. People find out about them and word spreads like wildfire. These successful organizations or services are concerned with one thing and one thing only: creating a memorable experience for customers. This experience starts and ends with people. Measuring memorable experiences is just as difficult as measuring how indispensable project management is to organizations. Studies abound, trying to objectively prove the value of project management as being indispensable to organizations. You should not wait for others to justify your existence. Rather you should look inward, and ask, "Am I aiding the growth of my own profession?" One way to measure the growth is to ask this very simple question:

> How likely is it that you would recommend [a product or service] to a friend or colleague?

This one question, often referred to as the Net Promoter® question, cuts straight to the core of what every customer satisfaction survey seeks to determine; namely, the percentage of customers who are actively helping a business grow. By posing this question to your sponsors, customers, team members, and stakeholders, you can obtain a fairly accurate snapshot of customer loyalty to your project leadership capabilities.

This question operates on the premise that when customers recommend a service or business to someone else, they are putting their personal reputation on the line. Therefore, they must be more than passively satisfied with the service they have received—they must be enthusiastic about it. This prevents a customer satisfaction rating from being unrealistically boosted by the "passively satisfied" group. Organizations that score high on this question have higher growth rates.[2]

When viewing project management as a service, and your profession as a service provider, you can adapt the Net Promoter® question to become your PMPromoter process. Select a group of customers, team members, and stakeholders to ask, "How likely is it that you would recommend [my project leadership services] to a friend or colleague?" They will respond on a scale of 0–10. "Promoters" answer with a 9 or a 10, the "passively satisfied" with 7 or 8, and "detractors" with 0–6. Your PMPromoter score is tabulated by subtracting the percentage of detractors from the percentage of promoters, ignoring the passively satisfied group, as they have little or no effect on your professional growth.

Your final PMPromoter score indicates what percentage of your customers are actively helping you enhance your project leadership profession. You simply pose this question to your team members, customers, stakeholders, and the users of your project's product or service. The higher your score, the greater the growth of your project management profession.

Use PMPromoter at the beginning, middle, and the end of projects to identify trends to yield a complete picture of your service-based project leadership performance. This quick and simple method measures how much your customers truly value your services, a measure that can springboard you to professional growth. PMPromoter is certainly not the only way to measure project leadership effectiveness. In the end, the underpinning idea is that you must take the initiative to measure your service, even if it requires non-traditional methods. The more you can objectively measure your service value, the more project management becomes indispensable to your stakeholders!

## Summary

Serving others selflessly through service-based project leadership can fulfill one's need to give of himself. But, many project managers work in a vacuum of meaningfulness, leaving their true talents and capabilities in limbo. Project leaders are called to serve in three ways, through obedience, inquiry, and action. The service-based project leaders are students and teachers of themselves and then teachers and students of others, removing the shield of hypocrisy. By giving, a leader learns not only through his actions but also receives information about his calling.

Adding credentials to measure project leaders is critical to our industry. A service-based project leader should be measured by the alignment of his profession with his core values, the continual use of objective feedback on leadership competencies, by practicing leadership through Active Leadership Experiences, and by serving a community that can benefit from project management. He should not wait for others to justify his existence through the benefits of project management as a whole, but rather adopt direct feedback from customers regarding his service value, using the PMPromoter question, "How likely are you to recommend my project leadership services to a friend or colleague?"

# Endnotes

1. Viktor E. Frankl, *Man's Search For Meaning* (Boston: Beacon Press 2006), 110.
2. Frederick Reichheld, "The One Number You Need to Grow," *Harvard Business Review*, December 2003.

## Chapter 23

# Communities of Practice

## Introduction

Project management services compete on a global basis. While competition is good for the project management profession, it can also inhibit project leaders from learning from each other. Learning long-term, valued leadership skills can be compromised when organizations are understaffed, impacting deadlines while expecting project workers to carry the extra burden, as they so often do. Many CIOs desire short-term relationship agreements with skilled IT workers instead of long-term relationships—consuming mass amounts of resources to build a bigger fire that quickly burns out. A third of new hires in some industries are temporary workers.[1]

Thus, in today's business environment, cutthroat competition among project practitioners is the name of the game. Unfortunately, merely striving to outperform one another isn't always the road to achieving personal growth. Whether it is political maneuvering or throwing others under the bus, project environments often grow into battlefields where only the politically savvy survive.

These dynamics lead to organizations losing knowledge and expertise that must be relearned by workers—often without the proper time or tools—instead of creating new knowledge that advances their cause. Project leaders have much to learn from each other and the knowledge they can potentially gain by communicating with one another would serve to advance those individuals as well as the entire profession.

This is why the path to a role as service-based project leader should, if possible, include involvement in one or more "communities of practice."

A Community of Practice (CoP) is a group of people who share a concern, a set of problems, or a passion to deepen their knowledge and expertise by collaborating.[2] The concept was developed as part of a movement aimed at reframing the process of learning as something that occurs in conjunction with others—not in solitary study.

Communities of Practice exist everywhere that people interact with each other within a common plane of activity—in schools, at home, within hobbies, etc. Being alive as human beings means engaging in the pursuit of purpose and achievement in which interaction with each other and the world creates learning opportunities. Over time, this collective learning results in practices that reflect both the pursuit of one's purpose and achievement and the attendant social relations. These practices are the property of a community created over time by the sustained pursuit of a shared purpose.

Some communities are formally acknowledged, others are not, but regardless learning still occurs. The Community of Practice changes learning from something that is pursued as individual for the good of the individual, and turns it into a shared social practice with a common good. This concept, when applied to organizational learning, presents itself as a useful tool for the advancement of groups.

A project team is a community of practice; so is a professional association, especially at the level of chapters or special interest groups. Not only do project management communities spur professional growth, but communities designed around your industry or personal interests can as well. For example, a project manager participating in a local advocacy group for sustainable development practices will both add expertise to the group and learn leadership lessons.

## Communities of Practice: Role in Self-Directed Learning

A CoP gives a project manager company along his self-directed development journey toward project leadership. If engaged with a CoP, a project leader is no longer an isolated individual embarking on a strange journey. He has like-minded people with whom he can share his experiences and learning. When tacit knowledge is shared, new knowledge is created.[3] This new knowledge can then be shared leading to more knowledge. A CoP is a living organism whose existence breeds new knowledge. A practitioner's ability to reach his full potential is related to his ability to participate in an exciting community that breeds new knowledge.

A CoP provides a safe space, particularly when it connects him with other project leaders outside of his organizational boundaries, which eliminates biases, fears, and politics from the community. Leaders within the network serve each other by asking questions, sharing lessons learned, or even anxieties they may have about their leadership experience. While a workshop or training class provides an environment for questions, a CoP is more strongly tied to self-directed learning because a project leader's involvement in it is entirely under her control. An individual may participate in a CoP to the extent, regularity, and depth that she desires. She gets out of the CoP what she puts into it. Since tacit knowledge is shared among individuals, learning is highly individualized. It can be tailored to meet the goals of a service-based project leader's self-directed leadership plan.

# CoPs Reinforce Self-Directed Project Leadership Development

CoPs fit well into all aspects of self-directed learning for a service-based project leader, including establishing commitment and direction, acquisition and assessment of a leadership agenda, practicing leadership competencies, and serving a community. A leader's commitment to the CoP is a visible sign of the commitment to grow and learn. Participation can solidify and clarify his intention and direction for becoming a service-based project leader.

Group discussions, sharing of information, and subsequent feedback expose new skills, techniques, and capabilities to the participants. In addition, the presence of the group itself requires some structure and leadership to foster effective communication, which presents real leadership opportunities for practitioners similar to that of the project environment. In the knowledge economy, no one owns all the knowledge needed to complete a project. A project leader's ability to elicit tacit knowledge from experts to create new knowledge parallels the aims of a CoP.

Finally, serving others in the group connects him back to the commitment process. These groups often provide the opportunity to change the focus from one's current challenges and problems to focusing on others' challenges and problems, providing new insights, changing negative attitudes to positive attitudes, and rewarding one's natural inclination to serve others.

At the center of the model lie supportive relationships that enable all of the steps to provide maximal benefits to the project manager seeking to transform herself into a service-based project leader. A CoP is a good place in which to start constructing these supportive relationships. These relationships, which exist on a common plane, provide relevant feedback.

# Benefits of a Community of Practice

The establishment of a CoP can have countless benefits for project managers seeking to serve and lead. A CoP is an ideal environment to acknowledge and face project leadership challenges. A community of project leaders from different organizations and industries bring experiences providing members with diverse viewpoints. Combining these viewpoints, a leader can create new, distinct knowledge.

Access to needed expertise can help a service-based project leader build the foundational layer of a leadership competency pyramid. A CoP can provide access to quickly build subject matter expertise, which is critical to the credibility process of trust building. A community can increase her confidence through the affirmation that comes from the communal sharing of learning experiences. CoPs spawn new relationships and activities that flow out of mutually shared interests that build confidence. Shared interests in hobbies or literature can initiate the gathering of peers in activities on the perimeter of the community. In addition to these activities being fun, relaxing, and rewarding, they can actually be opportunities for leaders to build to intimacy, a key component of trust.

A project leadership community can develop resources that can be a source of personal development. Facilitating book clubs, presenting to groups, or writing articles for the community can help a member develop professionally. Regular communication with peers builds her professional identity as a member of the project leadership community by connecting with other virtual leaders.

There are also broad benefits for the project management industry. A CoP increases the speed at which knowledge is acquired and disseminated through the industry. The distribution and adoption of new standards and best practices can be substantially increased and passed along with greater meaning and retention.

## Starting a Community of Practice

When first establishing the domain of the CoP, in this case, project leadership, the domain must be meaningful and valuable to members. Sponsoring representatives must be convinced of the strategic business value and aligned with an organization's core values. If the rapid commoditization of project management or the leadership void crippling strategic project execution does not resonate with constituents, we're in trouble! Second, the members and their relationship must be defined; a CoP dedicated to project leadership can be geared toward project managers, business analysts, certified practitioners, program managers, and change managers. The sponsoring representatives are project officers, chief project officers, and senior executives.

The third pre-developmental step is the establishment of the boundaries of the learning areas—the body of knowledge and its accompanying tools, methods, and sources. For project leadership this includes leadership theories, case studies, leadership competency development, and sources of specialized subject matter, such as organizational development and psychology. The aim of the CoP is to create new knowledge through sharing tacit knowledge; members must be excited about the subject and its contents and reap benefits. Involving experts legitimatizes the community and helps mitigate the risk of apathy.

Figure 23.1 provides a summary of the steps to starting a community of practice.[4]

Start spreading the word to potential members and educating them on the benefits of community learning. Conduct workshops to educate management and potential members. Doubts can be assuaged by demonstrating how CoPs are inherently self-defined and self-managed.[5]

While CoPs are not complex in their structure, it is common to focus too much on technology as the solution to community learning. The most important aspect of design is the social design, allowing members to connect and contribute content easily. Supporting many file media types, logical grouping of topics, and integrating the technology with commonly used applications to keep the community in the forefront of the members' minds is critical.

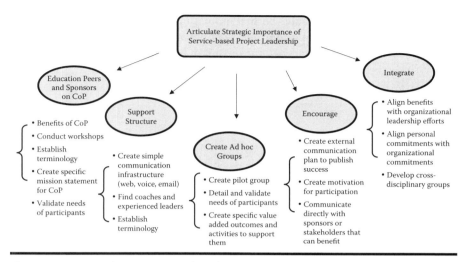

**Figure 23.1    Starting a community of practice.**

Get your community going as early as possible and generate results quickly; people will learn by doing and word spreads quickly. Interview potential members to find out what issues they would like to see addressed and identify potential leaders. Focus on cutting-edge issues that pose a stretch for members to solve but also offer benefits that can be felt. As these early members gain confidence, encourage them to reach for more ownership.

As the young CoP grows, practitioners will usually be able to see its value. Keeping it aligned with organizational goals can be done by finding new sponsors with leadership problems. Promote successes and discoveries that advance the organization and others will likely buy in.

The CoP does not have to integrate into a formal organization. As long as there are members who thirst for new knowledge on the subject and receive benefits from it, informal communities can flourish outside of corporate sponsorship. There must be processes and structure in place to preserve the community that simultaneously leaves room for natural self-development. CoPs should fit the formality or informality structure in which they operate. Understand your constituent's information protection and anonymity requirements prior to launching a community.

## Summary

Communities of Practice are rapidly shaping how people learn and manage knowledge. While they are not the only method for providing continuing education to project managers and project leaders, it is beneficial to recognize the benefits of learning through teamwork and normal human interaction. Giving these interactions the formal structure of a community of practice harnesses these benefits and directs them toward a specific goal, the pursuit of becoming a service-based project leader through self-directed project leadership development. Start or join a CoP now!

# Endnotes

1. J. Kent Crawford and Jeannette Cabanis-Brewin, *Optimizing Human Capital with a Strategic Project Office*, (Boca Raton, FL: Auerbach, 2006), xxi.
2. Etienne Wenger, Richard McDermott, and William M. Snyder, *Cultivating Communities of Practice*, (Boston: Harvard Business School Press, 2002), 4.
3. Jeannette Cabanis-Brewin, "Communities of Practice in the Projectized Organization," Interview with Etienne Wenger, *Project Management Best Practice Report*, 2, no. 4, (2001).
4. Ibid., Wenger, chap 4.
5. Ibid.

## Chapter 24

# Developing Your Action Plan

## Introduction

Now, it's up to you to develop and execute a plan! Using the MyProjectAdvisor® leadership competency pyramid as a model, and following the transformational steps associated with self-directed leadership development, you are well on the way. This chapter outlines broad timeframes and discusses specific actions and tools for you to begin your journey. The timeframes are general and may be shorter or longer depending on the individual. Actions are outlined for each of the four steps—commit, acquire and assess, practice, and serve. Table 24.1 is a summary of the recommended timeframes, steps, and actions to follow over the first year. Use this model to create a custom plan that is right for you. Appendix B contains several exercises and tools to guide you through the process.

## Thirty Days to Sixty Days

### Commit

Though commitment has to be continuously renewed, during the first 30 to 60 days, a practitioner should identify his core convictions, value system, and beliefs. This is the beginning of an intense inner journey, probing the consciousness of a future leader prior to making any hasty decisions.

You must consider not just what success means but also what significance means. Success may be having a new sports car or a vacation beach house, but

**Table 24.1  Summary of Self-Directed Project Leadership Plan.**

| | Commitment and Direction | Acquire and Assess | Practice | Serve |
|---|---|---|---|---|
| 30–60 days | ◼ Commitment Exercises (Part One) <br> ◼ Draft Personal Leadership Vision (Part One) | ◼ Leadership competencies self assessment (Part Two) <br> ◼ Desired supportive relationships (Part Three) <br> ◼ Complete Leadership Competency Development Acquisition Plan (Part Four) <br> ◼ Platinum Rule® Assessment <br> ◼ PMPromoter Assessment | ◼ Increase compatibility—identifying and adapting to situations and coworker preferences (use Platinum Rule Report) <br> ◼ Develop trust-based relationships using reliability (Part Four) | |
| 2–6 months | ◼ Updated Personal Leadership Vision statement (Part One) <br> ◼ Discuss vision with supportive relationships <br> ◼ Identify Active Leadership Experience (Part Five) | ◼ Assess Risk Attitudes (Part Six) <br> ◼ Additional Formal assessment (style, preference, strengths) <br> ◼ MyProjectAdvisor® 360-degree self assessment only (Part Seven) <br> ◼ Leadership Competency Development Acquisition Plan (Acquire Knowledge, SME) (Part Four) <br> ◼ PMPromoter Assessment | ◼ Increase compatibility—with trust-based relationship <br> ◼ Develop trust-based relationship action plan using credibility, reliability (Part Four) <br> ◼ Initiate Active Leadership Experience (Part Five) | |

| 6–12 months | | | | |
|---|---|---|---|---|
| ■ Final Person Vision Statement<br>■ Update Leadership Competency Development Acquisition Plan | ■ Leadership competencies self assessments (Part Two)<br>■ Leadership Competency Development Acquisition Plan (Acquire Knowledge, SME and Trust-based relationships) (Part Four)<br>■ PMPromoter assessment<br>■ Assess Risk Attitudes (Part Six)<br>■ MyProjectAdvisor® 360 Stakeholder Assessment (Part Seven) | ■ Execute trust-based relationship action plan (credibility, reliability, intimacy, low self orientation) (Part Four)<br>■ Identify consultative leadership opportunities (Part Four)<br>■ Use consultative leadership process (service and advisory skills) (Part Four)<br>■ Monitor Active Leadership Experience (Part Eight) | ■ Complete service questionnaire (Part Nine)<br>■ Identify opportunities for service<br>■ Begin Service leadership project |

significance is achieving a positive, lasting transformation of yourself, through a project, extending to your community.

At a minimum, begin pursuing the development of your Personal Leadership Vision. A purpose is an outcome linked to values, for example, "to equip and motivate project managers to make the world a better place." The personal leadership vision is how to achieve this purpose, i.e., "by developing and delivering quality, educational materials, writing articles, books and speaking at conferences or seminars." These exercises should be not be completed in one sitting but rather considered over a period of 30–60 days with serious reflection. Use Appendix B, Part One, to begin the commitment process.

## *Acquire and Assess Leadership Behaviors*

The self-directed leadership model is not linear; multiple steps can be occurring simultaneously. So, during the first 30 to 60 days, begin to assess the strength of your leadership competency pyramid. Each layer of the leadership competency pyramid must be assessed independently before the layers can be compared. A low level of trust may be related to deficiencies in other pyramid layers such as knowledge, skill, experience, or courage. The checklists in Appendix B, Part Two, can help provide an initial assessment of each layer.

A practitioner should also begin to identify candidates for a strong network of supportive relationships. These will provide a safe environment and the accountability required to proceed through each step of the self-directed project leadership process. These must include a number of people with whom you work on a daily basis—project managers, team members, sponsors, or even customers. They can also include people outside of work, such as peers, a spouse, a friend, or spiritual advisor. Use Appendix B, Part Three, to help identify your supportive relationships.

Once you have considered a Personal Leadership Vision and desired supportive relationships, and have begun to evaluate the relative strength of your leadership competency pyramid, begin developing a plan to enhance your leadership competency pyramid. First, develop a written plan to acquire additional project management knowledge and subject matter expertise regarding your customer. Focus on the needs of your project.

Remember that strong trust-based relationships should naturally lead to opportunities to execute consultative leadership. Jumping straight into a leadership role or executing the consultative leadership process prematurely is a mistake. The groundwork must be laid to provide a stable base upon which to build leadership competencies. Complete the questions in Appendix B, Part Four with the help of one of your new supportive relationships. The leadership competency pyramid acquisition plan is used to guide you in building a robust pyramid. Starting with the base, assess yourself and document specific actions you can initiate to acquire these competencies.

The Platinum Rule® Behavioral Style Assessment is an inexpensive tool (*http://www.platinumrule.com*) that provides leaders with a quick means to self assess their compatibility style. It includes a detailed report on how to increase compatibility with your project stakeholders. The Platinum Rule offers unlimited observer feedback opportunity by sending it out to others and asking them to complete it on you anonymously. This assessment may be one of the most important self-improvement steps you will ever take. The tool is excellent for project kickoff meetings. It's online distribution and reporting capability allow virtual teams to establish compatibility.

The Platinum Rule® is a powerful tool that can help you optimize your business and personal relationships. With its unique personal and observer assessments, it is designed to give you a **complete** view of how you interact in everyday situations. The 18-question self-assessment has been validated and takes only three to five minutes to complete. **Your results will be plotted on your personal eGraph, accompanied by a comprehensive, personalized report.** The report explains your behavioral style, how to identify someone else's style, and how to adapt to other styles to professionally and personally improve communications and overall effectiveness. When you are finished, you will have a chance to invite an unlimited number of people to assess you, as they see you. Be sure to include people from your social life as well as your work life, because we are frequently perceived differently in different environments.

Today's fast-paced project environment requires you to build trust-based relationships with team members, customers, and stakeholders quickly. These trust-based relationships are critical to your leadership development process. Understanding your own and others' behavior styles will make it faster and easier to develop trust and positive energy on project teams.

Use the PMPromoter tool from www.myprojectadvisor.com to evaluate how well you are growing in your profession. Send the PMPromoter question to 15 or 20 people who have worked with you. This will allow you to ask your customers (team members, critical stakeholders, and sponsors) if they are willing to recommend your services to a peer. The tool will calculate your promoters and detractors and provide you with a real time PMPromoter rating. This rating will be a baseline for future PMPromoter assessments.

During the course of a day, project managers can experience a variety of situations that allow them to monitor their internal feelings and perceptions. Begin conducting some informal assessments, such as querying stakeholders regarding their perceptions and seeking feedback about your actions and behaviors in project situations. Constructive, relevant dialogue is good for self-directed learning. Isolation, often the result of fear, is a barrier. The act of keeping a simple journal can help connect the events, conditions, and activities occurring during the day along with the feelings and the resulting attitudes and behaviors associated with them.

## *Practice*

Once you have taken the Platinum Rule® assessment and reviewed your eGraph and report, it is time to begin practicing compatibility with your project team. Practice identifying others' preferred behavioral styles and consciously adapting your behavior to get positive results.

Now that you have comprehended the building blocks of trust and your project stakeholder analysis is up-to-date, begin working on developing trust-based relationships with the most important stakeholders. Use Appendix B, Part Four, the leadership competency pyramid acquisition plan, and first focus on building reliability. Reliability is action-driven and can be built quickly by removing ambiguity and making specific commitments to generate a sense of repeated fulfillment of expectations.

## *Outcomes*

At the end of the first 60 days, a practitioner should have:

- A draft of a Personal Leadership Vision
- Identified desired supportive relationships
- A leadership competency pyramid acquisition plan
- A completed Platinum Rule® assessment
- A PMPromoter baseline

# Two to Six Months

## *Commit*

The commitment process continues! Update your Personal Leadership Vision and begin discussing it with the supportive relationships you identified. Complete Appendix B, Part Five, to develop an Active Leadership Experience that aligns with your Personal Leadership Vision. The purpose of an Active Leadership Experience is to provide you with an opportunity to lead. Often projects do not offer this opportunity due to organizational structure, politics, or your experience. If you are in a leadership position on your project, you should still define an Active Leadership Experience by reinforcing your Personal Leadership Vision, facilitating growth and experiential learning while testing your level of commitment.

## *Acquire and Assess Leadership Behaviors*

Assess your risk attitudes as they relate to the leadership competency pyramid and your Active Leadership Experience. A risk-seeking attitude may lead a practitioner to move quickly into the risk-bearing roles associated with leadership. Conversely, a risk adverse attitude is likely to delay a prominent leadership role on projects. When analyzing your risk attitude, it is important to focus on both the facts of the situation as well as your feelings. Facts relate to how well you can calculate the outcome of a risk event or condition. Feelings relate to how you feel about a risk event or condition. The two can influence each other. Appendix B, Part Six, is designed to help you understand both risk elements.

Feel free to create your own questions that are applicable to your work life. If these questions leave you with a high level of uncertainty and discomfort, a risk-seeking attitude is required to promote growth of your leadership competency pyramid. Modifications to the pyramid base, such as greater levels of trust, may be needed to reduce the level of discomfort and uncertainty to achieve a more comfortable risk level.

Once you have articulated your Personal Leadership Vision, consider additional formal assessments to gain a more distinct picture of your natural preferences and strengths. Section IV has a review of several tools that can be useful.

Once the results are reviewed, preferably with a coach or person trained in providing the assessment, absorb this self-knowledge and identify your natural abilities. Don't be surprised if this leads you to modify your project management career to fit strengths and natural aptitudes.

Next, review the service-based project leader 360-degree questions and assess yourself to identify where you meet or do not meet expectations. Over a period of time, attempt to improve on this performance criterion and have others assess you. Review Appendix B, Part Seven, to start the self-assessment portion of the service-based project leader's 360-degree survey.

During the early stages of this two- to six-month timeframe, you should be accelerating the growth of your leadership competency pyramid, particularly the conversion of knowledge into skills and new experiences. Refer to Appendix B, completed in the first 30–60 days, and begin to acquire the new knowledge, skill, and experience that will benefit your stakeholders. The growth of subject matter expertise, or business context, must be significant. You should be more confident with introducing new project management knowledge and converting that knowledge into project skills and experiences. Whether one has acquired knowledge through formal training or reading a book, acting quickly on it while it is fresh will enhance retention and facilitate additional learning.

Don't forget to take another snapshot of your PMPromoter rating during this timeframe.

## *Practice*

You should now be practicing compatibility with more team members, sponsors, and stakeholders to increase the speed of trust-building. Use the results from your Platinum Rule® assessment to achieve greater compatibility with not just peers and co-workers, but also the critical stakeholders that deserve a trust-based relationship.

Trust is a two-way street; you must provide a value proposition for a stakeholder to enter into this relationship. This value proposition starts with credibility—the careful articulation of content knowledge that adds values. As a practitioner, you should have been able to acquire the specific knowledge identified in Appendix B, convert it to new skills, and articulate it in a manner that builds credibility. You should now be building trust-based relationships with stakeholders through credibility and reliability and based on a clear value proposition.

Also, practice building trust-based relationships with the key stakeholders involved in your Active Leadership Experience. Then initiate it.

## Outcomes

The self-directed outcomes of this timeframe are:

- An updated Personal Leadership Vision
- An identified Active Leadership Experience
- An additional formal style or strengths assessment
- An assessment of risk attitudes
- A self-assessed project leadership 360 degree
- Acquired knowledge, skills, and experiences
- Updated PMPromoter rating
- Establishment of trust-based relationships using credibility and reliability
- An initiated Active Leadership Experience

# Six months to One year

## Commit

It is now time to finalize your Personal Leadership Vision. It may be helpful to review your commitment exercises again from Appendix B, Part One, and update your leadership competency pyramid acquisition plan (Part Four) against your current project, particularly if your project has changed. The first six months may not be marked with dramatic external changes, but rather with meaningful internal progress.

## Acquire and Assess

If you have been seriously pursuing self-directed leadership development, a reassessment of your leadership competencies using the checklists in Appendix B, Part Two, should show an improvement from your initial assessment in the first 30–60 days. Acquiring leadership competencies—beginning with new knowledge—should become a regular part of your routine. Reading four to six books a year on the subject should be the minimum goal, supplemented by trade journals, and other relevant materials. Trust-based relationships with important stakeholders should be growing as your base grows. You should be more efficient at quickly mastering relevant customer subject matter and creating value propositions to build more trust-based relationships.

Reassessing with PMPromoter is also recommended during this timeframe. A practitioner's promoter percentage should be increasing as the competency pyramid grows and the self-directed project leadership process matures. Continue practicing all forms of assessments and requesting feedback from your supportive relationships.

Toward the end of the six- to twelve-month timeframe, reassess your risk attitudes using Appendix B, Part Six. This should show a shift in your risk attitudes if your leadership competency pyramid is growing. Also, consider initiating a formal project leadership 360-degree assessment using a mixture of team members, critical stakeholders, and sponsors. The on-line assessment can be accessed at www.myprojectadvisor.com.

## Practice

Now that credibility and reliability have been built with your critical stakeholders, you should begin to move forward with attempts to build intimacy and low self-orientation. Intimacy is risk driven and low self-orientation is values driven. You may be able to accelerate this process but be cautious not to initiate intimacy prematurely without the presence of a value proposition and credibility and reliability. Some stakeholders, depending on their preferences, will either want more or less intimacy. Use the Platinum Rule® assessment results to determine stakeholder preferences.

By now, you should be presented with opportunities to demonstrate consultative leadership. Pay careful attention to your stakeholders as they will begin ask you to take on roles atypical for traditional project managers. Identify these opportunities and begin to use the consultative leadership process—engage, listen, frame, vision, and commit.

Since your Active Leadership Experience may be tangential to your project, continue to check its progress by using the checklist in Appendix B, Part Eight. These experiences should not be multi-year efforts, but shorter-term with measurable results and noticeable transformation beginning to occur. Create new ALEs if existing ones fail to fully materialize or if you feel you can handle more than one. Be fearless, others are counting on you to lead.

## Serve

The focus of the first six months of self-directed project leadership is commitment, assessment of leadership competencies, and your Active Leadership Experience. Now the service step can be initiated to accelerate your learning experience. The service step is a link back to the commitment process. The drive to transform yourself, other people, systems, and organizations can now be used to generate change and transform your community. Complete the questionnaire in Appendix B, Part Nine, to help align and identify service projects with your values.

This service can take many forms. The goal is to ensure that the practitioner has the correct intentions. These intentions are validated by these three points:

- The transformation is aligned with your core values.
- You have no expectation of receiving anything in return with the exception of experiencing meaningfulness.
- The transformation will require you to stretch your project leadership competencies.

If your intention is to first serve and not control, opportunities will quickly appear to apply these project leadership skills. Basic project management skills are vital elements to any service initiative. As a service-based project leader, you can validate your commitment step particularly if you are willing to become a student first and then earn the opportunity to become a teacher.

The renewal of your commitment to self-directed project leadership is initiated by your acts of service. These opportunities for service can be found on the internet or in a leader's community. The number of opportunities to serve is limitless and the need for strong project management and leadership skills is great.

## *Outcome*

The outcome of this time period should be:

- Stable Personal Leadership Vision
- Noticeable transformation in your Active Leadership Experience
- Established trust-based relationships based on credibility, reliability, intimacy, and low self-orientation
- Reassessment of PMPromoter; leadership competencies and risk attitudes showing progress
- Opportunities to practice consultative leadership
- Initiation of a service project and renewal of your commitment step

## Summary

This chapter has outlined a one-year plan for the project manager's self-directed project leadership development journey. The first 30–60 days should be spent drafting a Personal Leadership Vision, identifying desired supportive relationships, and developing a plan to grow leadership competencies. Months two through six are spent on assessments, acquiring leadership competencies, and initiating Active Leadership Experience. In months six through twelve, continue to acquire and assess your leadership competencies and initiate service projects to validate your commitment to self-directed project leadership development.

# UNDERSTANDING  ASSESSMENTS

by
Roberta F. Hill, MBA, MCC

# Chapter 25

---

# Introduction to Assessments for Project Leaders

---

## Introduction

With all the pressure on the technical aspects of getting the project done on time, within budget, and to specification, why would a project leader invest effort in assessments? Just as time spent on gathering the right tools for project planning pays off in the long run, good tools on the people side of the project also benefit both people and projects. Unfortunately, project leaders and teams rarely get valid, honest, open feedback, nor do they know how to go about getting that important information.

As a project leader, you play a critical role in improving team performance. Consider how assessments can improve your team's performance and help each member to grow as a leader. The proper use of these tools can improve decisions, speed up the process of implementation, and leverage overall results. Assessments are both an early warning system when the project has the potential of getting off track, as well as a method of creating synergy among team members.

To use assessments wisely, first educate yourself about them. Assessments can be misused, so use caution. But once you understand the theories behind the assessments, their practicality, and how to use them, you will be prepared to implement them to improve performance.

## Windows of a Leader

There are things that we know about ourselves that we choose to share with only a few intimate others. But each individual also has traits of which he is completely unaware: blind spots. The Johari Window was created by Joseph Luft and Harrington Ingham in the 1950s as a model for mapping personality awareness.[1] Like many other behavioral models, the Johari Window is based on four quadrants and is often described as a window with four panes. While different terms are sometimes used, the most common labels used for the four awareness windows are the Arena, also known as open or public pane; the Façade or hidden pane; the Blindspot and Unknown panes.

The application of the Johari Window as shown in Figure 25.1, comes in expanding the Arena, thereby making the other three areas as small as is appropriate. This can be achieved through two methods. The first method is asking for and receiving feedback, which reduces the blind area. The second is through disclosure, which reduces the hidden area. Disclosure is accomplished through a regular and honest exchange of feedback and a willingness to disclose personal feelings. The outcome is increased trust and support.

The Johari Window is a communication model that can be used to improve self-understanding as well as understanding between individuals within a team or in a group setting. Productive project teams show a willingness among members to open up the public arena to improve relationships and understanding. By explaining the idea of the Johari Window to the project team, a project leader can help

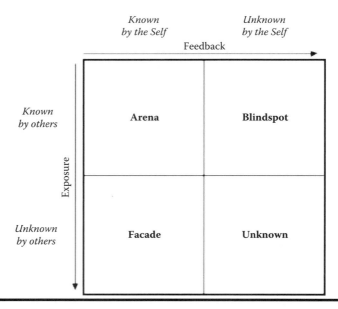

**Figure 25.1   Johari window.**

team members understand the value of self-disclosure, and gently encourage people to give and accept feedback. When done appropriately, more trusting relationships develop, issues are more quickly resolved, and a project's effectiveness is increased. Based on self-disclosure and feedback, the Johari Window can be used to improve a group's relationship with other groups or project teams.

No matter how enlightened a person may be, each one of us will have a subjective and biased view of our skills, abilities, and style. When someone takes a self-assessment, it is based on his own opinions. Does that mean all of these self-assessment instruments are useless? No. On the contrary, they are an excellent starting point for further examination. It is not the answers that are important; it is how an individual goes about verifying and expanding on the data and information.

There are numerous other leadership assessments available from reputable organizations. Diligent research should be done in all instances before selecting any tool.

## When to Use Assessments

Assessments are not toys or games to be used as fillers in team-building activities. They are serious tools; badly implemented, they can even cause legal problems for organizations. Everyone involved in using assessments must be diligent in determining that the process is not used in a way that is harmful. So before offering or administering an assessment, the following questions need to be addressed:

What outcomes are to be achieved?
How will results be used?
Is this the right timing?
What is the attitude towards assessments?
Have others completed like assessments?

After these questions have been answered, it can help determine if using any assessment is the right approach. Once it has been decided that an assessment could add value to the process, determining the right one is the next important step. Before a final decision is made, at least one or two people should take the instrument as part of the evaluation to see if it will resonate with the team as a whole.

## Types of Assessments

There are three categories of formal assessments that should be considered when improving team and individual performance.

■ General behavioral assessments—These are assessments to assist teams to understand the interpersonal dynamics and communication patterns among individual members.

- Leadership 360-degree feedback—These instruments bring to light areas for the project leader to address in his expertise as a leader and areas in which to develop key competencies.
- Team effectiveness surveys—These assessments highlight areas where teams can enhance and leverage their performance as a whole entity.

Before choosing a formal assessment tool, it is important to put into perspective what they really are. Assessments are feedback mechanisms that provide data and information on a particular aspect of an individual's "personality." The overall purpose of an assessment should be to measure some aspect of you—your traits, competencies, personality, etc. It is not exact nor is it etched in stone. The person completing an assessment can be influenced by events or feelings on the day when the instrument is taken and it can influence the output. It is only a snapshot in time, and while it may remain consistent over time it is open to change. The output from an assessment enables individuals to self-evaluate. Assessments can contain biases and must be used with reservations. No assessment or instrument is 100 percent accurate.

Assessments operate from theories or working hypotheses to help us explain how the world operates. There are some people who like to argue that the world is flat. Consequently, one needs to be wary of the underlying theory upon which the assessment is based, the organizational culture, and the person who administers the tool.

Assessment instruments, like other tools, are helpful when used properly but can be useless, harmful, or illegal when used inappropriately. Often, inappropriate use results from not having a clear understanding of what you want to measure and why you want to measure it. Only use tests that are appropriate for your particular purpose.

For proper meaning to be derived, good supervision from a properly trained and accredited person is necessary. High-performing project teams may be able to use many team assessment checklists without outside intervention, but facilitative advice is recommended for or project teams experiencing conflict.

## Steve's Story

Steve started his career as an engineer working in his home town of Dallas for one of the multi-national telecommunications companies headquartered there. Within four years, he had been promoted to team leader. By his late twenties, he was heading up large national projects responsible for the introduction of new products within the United States. The company appreciated Steve's outgoing and persuasive style, which was often missing in engineers. Other functional heads and suppliers found Steve to be friendly, approachable, and knowledgeable. Three years later, at the age of thirty and identified by the company as having high potential, Steve was being groomed to move into a director role. He had been assigned three virtual teams, all working on designing new products for the mobile division. Each project team consisted of about eight people and focused on different design elements. The U.S. based team was in New York City, and the European team, primarily Germanic, was located in Oslo. The third team representing the Pacific Rim was in Tokyo. While some of these members were Korean, two-thirds were Japanese.

Steve had visited and spent time with the New York team but had not been able to personally meet with the other team members. Within three months, it was clear that Steve was experiencing trouble with one team in particular. Despite all of his efforts to make a personal connection through conference and web calls, he was finding that one team continued to bypass him and keep him out of the loop.

A trip was planned to visit the other two teams and Steve needed to determine a strategy immediately. A coach suggested a communications survey called *The Platinum Rule® Behavioral Style Assessment* to help Steve improve his and the entire team's communicative effectiveness.

Steve discovered some interesting things about himself. After debriefing with his coach, Steve was able to better understand how his various team members might perceive his style based on cultural differences. This particular assessment also had a multi-rater component and Steve was able to ask others to assess him. The feedback only confirmed what he suspected. See Figure 25.2.

As you can see, Steve's results show that most people see him as relatively open and direct, which places him in the quadrant of Socializers. However, a few evaluated him as being more guarded and less fast paced than others. This raised questions in Steve's mind.

Steve was so excited about the assessment that he offered it to his team members. First, he shared his results, what he had learned, and how he was planning to modify his behavior. Three-quarters of his team took him up on his offer. The various team graphs—without names—were sent out to everyone to allow remote teams to understand other teams' behavioral preferences.

## What Steve Discovered—and His Team Already Knew

Steve identified himself in this particular model as a Socializer, which briefly meant that he was highly relationship-oriented and direct in his communication style. Generally speaking, this expressiveness fit well with his North American team which understood this to be the primary "operating style of the business." When team members completed this on Steve, all the off-shore members of the team saw Steve's style as being even more strongly entrenched in the expressive behavior. The Asian team was more accepting of Steve's approach. The Koreans adopted the American style and while most of the Japanese team members were more indirect and reserved in their communicating (Relaters), they respected Steve's value of relationships. The European team (mostly made up of Thinkers), again in general terms, saw Steve as evidencing a bit of bravado and not as focused on the details and

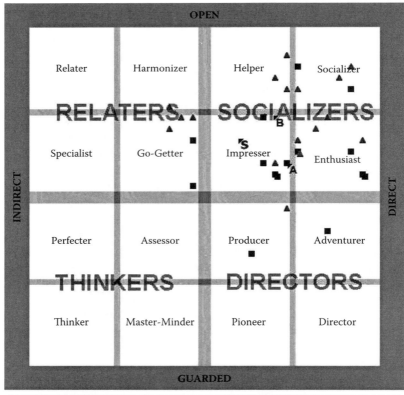

| Symbol | Description |
|--------|-------------|
| ʳS | Self-assessment |
| ʳA | Observers who know you in this setting: Work (North American team) |
| ■ | Average of observers in this setting: Work (North America team) |
| ʳB | Observers who know you in this setting: Work (Other teams) |
| ▲ | Average of observers in this setting: Work (Other teams) |

**Figure 25.2   Steve's results.**

due dates as they preferred. They were also more likely to express their disagreement if they did not agree with the established goals.

## *Outcome*

All three teams report that communication has improved dramatically, conflict situations have decreased, and they are likely to give their colleagues the benefit of the doubt. Steve received a rating in the top 10 percent of his company last year.

He has made a concerted effort to tone down his unbridled enthusiasm with all of his teams and take the time to listen to the in-depth analysis that some team members liked to present. Members are more comfortable telling him that what they are saying is important. The American team, European team, and Korean team tell him rather forcefully while the Japanese wait patiently and begin again. One North American team member said it best, "Steve means well. Before we just thought he was unfocused. Now we understand that he likes to brainstorm and come up with lots of options. He is young, ambitious, and tries hard. Since seeing Steve's profile, we understand him a lot better. I know that I am more comfortable with him and he seems to be more compatible with diverse team members."

# The Platinum Rule® Model

*The Platinum Rule® Behavioral Style Assessment can help project leaders and teams discover their relationship and communication strengths.[2] The Platinum Rule® Behavioral Style Assessment focuses on four primary behavioral styles, each with a very distinct and predictable pattern of observable behavior. Once you understand these patterns, you have the key to unlock your ability to get along with nearly anyone.[3] It also demystifies those lesser known, but scientifically proven, internal forces that are the motivating clues behind behaviors. In other words, this assessment helps individuals understand why they do what they do. It draws directly from the work of Marston and Merrill and Reid's Social Styles. Unlike most of the instruments around observed behaviors, this 18-question instrument also offers a full multi-rater system where users can have social acquaintances, project team members, and customers or clients give neutral feedback on how they see the person's style. Project team charts are easily created, that can asses the styles of various team members and can be recreated when membership changes.*

The Platinum Rule® divides behavioral preferences into four basic styles using the behavior continuums of direct and indirect, open and guarded. The four resulting quadrants are known as: Director, Socializer, Relater, and Thinker. While everyone possesses the qualities of each style to various degrees, each person has a dominant style. Below is a brief description of the dominant behaviors for each quadrant.

## *Directors*

Directors are driven by two governing needs: control and achievement. Directors are goal-oriented go-getters who are most comfortable when they are in charge of people and situations. They want to accomplish many things; they focus on no-nonsense approaches to bottom-line results.

Directors seek expedience and are not afraid to bend the rules. They figure it is easier to beg forgiveness than to ask permission. Directors accept challenges, take authority, and plunge headfirst into solving problems. They are fast-paced, task-oriented, and work quickly and impressively by themselves, which means they become annoyed with delays.

Directors are driven and dominating, which can make them stubborn, impatient, and insensitive to others. Directors are so focused that they forget to take the time to smell the roses.

## Socializers

Socializers are friendly, enthusiastic "party-animals" who like to be where the action is. They thrive on the admiration, acknowledgment, and compliments that come with being in the limelight. The Socializer's primary strengths are enthusiasm, charm, persuasiveness, and warmth. They are idea-people and dreamers who excel at getting others excited about their vision. They are eternal optimists with an abundance of charisma. These qualities help them influence people and build alliances to accomplish their goals.

Socializers do have their weaknesses: impatience, an aversion to being alone, and a short attention span. They are risk-takers who base many of their decisions on intuition, which is not inherently bad. Socializers are not inclined to verify information; they are more likely to assume someone else will do it.

## Thinkers

Thinkers are analytical, persistent, systematic people who enjoy problem-solving. Thinkers are detail-oriented, which makes them more concerned with content than style. Thinkers are task-oriented people who enjoy perfecting processes and working toward tangible results. They're always in control of their emotions and may become uncomfortable around people who are very outgoing, e.g., Socializers.

Thinkers have high expectations for themselves and others, which can make them overly critical. Their tendency toward perfectionism, when taken to an extreme, can cause "paralysis by over-analysis." Thinkers are slow and deliberate decision-makers. They do research, make comparisons, determine risks, calculate margins of error, and then take action. Thinkers become irritated by surprises and glitches; hence their cautious decision-making. Thinkers are also skeptical, so they like to see promises in writing.

## Relaters

Relaters are warm and nurturing individuals. They are the most people-oriented of the four styles. Relaters are excellent listeners, devoted friends, and loyal employees. Their relaxed disposition makes them approachable and warm. They develop strong networks of people who are willing to be mutually supportive and reliable. Relaters are excellent team players.

Relaters are risk-aversive. In fact, Relaters may tolerate unpleasant environments rather than risk change. They like the status quo and become distressed when disruptions are severe. When faced with change, they think it through, plan, and accept it into their world. Relaters—more than the other types—strive to maintain personal composure, stability, and balance.

In the office, Relaters are courteous, friendly, and willing to share responsibilities. They are good planners, persistent workers, and good with follow-through. Relaters go along with others even when they do not agree because they do not want to rock the boat.

# Other Tools

## *MBTI*®

The Myers-Briggs Type Indicator® (MBTI®) was first developed in the 1940s and refined during the 1950s. Over the years, various forms and versions have been created emerging from paper and pencil, self-scored to online versions. Consultants, counselors, coaches, therapists, and many other people with interests or training in psychology, human development, and social interaction may be qualified to administer the MBTI® instrument, verify MBTI® type, and discuss personality results one on one or in a group. The MBTI® is designed to help individuals become aware of their particular gifts as well as pointing out areas in need of developing. Through this process, individuals gain an understanding and appreciation of the ways in which people are different. The MBTI® assessment has been one of the most consistent personality assessments of choice for over 50 years and is taken by more than two million people each year.[4]

Giving an in-depth, personalized account of an individual's personality preferences, the MBTI® provides a report of personality type and, secondly, gives an indication of the unique way individuals express their preferences. Differences in people's behavior are actually a result of each person having preferences for particular ways of perceiving and judging. This report has been employed by a variety of users in small businesses and large corporations, service industries and manufacturing concerns, consulting and training services, government agencies, and educational and health institutions.

The four preferences are as follows. Where does the individual prefer to focus his attention (Extraversion or Introversion)? How does the individual prefer to take in information (Sensing or Intuition)? Which way does the individual prefer to make decisions (Thinking or Feeling)? How does the individual orient himself to the external world (Judging or Perceiving)? The forced choices will arrive at one of sixteen types based on the combination of the various preferences. It is the conversation that ensues that uncovers the real motivation and purpose and also reveals the foundation for one's personal aspirations.

## DISC-Based Instruments

All DISC type assessments look at the observed behavior and attempts to identify "surface traits" or characteristic ways of behaving in a particular environment. (This starts with the emotional response and then relates this back to the behavior.) DISC instruments provide information about one's natural strengths and weaknesses as well as highlighting those environments in which the individual would be most likely to excel. Like many assessments, an important aspect of this instrument is that it helps increase appreciation of different behavior profiles. This increased awareness allows an individual to anticipate and minimize potential conflicts with others.

DISC based assessments look at personality on four dimensions of behavior and the associated emotion:

- Dominance (anger)—the way one deals with problems
- Influence (trust and optimism)—the way one deals with people
- Steadiness (expressiveness)—the way one deals with pace
- Conscientiousness or Compliance (risk and fear)—the way one deals with procedures and processes

The majority of DISC instruments consist of 28 groups of adjectives. Each group consists of four words and requires the individual to pick the word that most describes him and the word that least describes him.

## The Kolbe Indexes

The Kolbe System is the latest in a series of successful psychological systems developed by the well-known and highly honored author and theorist, Kathy Kolbe. The Kolbe System has grown out of Kathy's scientific studies of learning differences among children that began in 1970. The Kolbe "Indexes/Instinct" are brief questionnaires that can be completed online in less than 20 minutes. Backed by more than 20 years of research and practical applications, they give an accurate map of natural instincts in a format that is perhaps the most positive format available. This is what Kolbe calls the modus operandi, or MO.[5]

## Strengths

Over the past few years, there has been a significant trend to move away from trying to develop one's weaknesses but rather leverage one's strengths. The principles have been well researched by the Gallop organization and compiled into a book, *Now, Discover Your Strengths*.[6] As part of the purchase of this book, one receives a unique identification number that allows access to the Clifton StrengthsFinder Profile on the Internet. This Web-based assessment analyzes instinctive reactions and immediately presents the user with their five most powerful signature themes.

# Endnotes

1. Joseph Luft and Harry Ingham, "The Johari Window: A Graphic Model of Interpersonal Awareness," (Proceedings of the Western Training Laboratory in Group Development, Los Angeles, CA, 1955).
2. Tony Alessandra and Michael J. O'Connor, *The Platinum Rule: Discover the Four Basic Business Personalities and How They Can Lead You to Success*, (New York: Warner Books, 1996).
3. Roberta Hill, s.v. "predictable," http://www.assessmentsnow.com/assessmentorder.asp (accessed January 4, 2007).
4. CPP, Inc., s.v. "2 million," http://www.cpp.com/products/mbti/index.asp (accessed January 4, 2007).
5. Kolbe Corporation, s.v. "MO," http://www.kolbe.com/the_kolbe_concept/the_kolbe_concept.cfm (accessed January 4, 2007).
6. Marcus Buckingham and Donald O. Clifton, *Now, Discover Your Strengths* (New York: Free Press, 2001).

## Chapter 26

# What?! My Boss Wants Me to Take a 360-Degree: What You Need to Know

## Introduction

Many organizations use a 360-degree multi-rater assessment to help determine who has leadership potential. The term 360-degree feedback has become synonymous with obtaining feedback from multiple sources. Other names include multi-source, full-circle, group performance review, 180-degree, and more recently, the 720-degree. The tools combine input from supervisors, peers, and direct reports to provide a broad perspective of an employee's strengths and developmental needs. It has also been used extensively as part of an organization's performance appraisal system. In addition, the aggregate data (cumulative results for a group) provide an organization with crucial information for effective strategic planning, succession planning, overall training needs, improved team building, and customer service.

## Debbie's Story

Debbie had been leading various projects and teams in her organization for over 20 years. Her responsibilities had grown in looking for major investments or recommending mergers. She often oversaw teams of up to 20 people from various backgrounds and disciplines. She knew how to put a good team together. However, half of the key resources requested to be on her projects and the other half avoided her projects. She viewed her high standards and expectations of herself and others as positive. Over time, Debbie began to notice that her performance reviews were leveling out and she was no longer seen as a key player by management. Younger people were coming in and Debbie wanted more challenging projects. She approached Human Resources to see what development might be useful. They suggested a coaching program that included a 360-degree feedback process.

A generic but extensive leadership assessment looking at 10 areas was selected. Debbie sent out a memo to her direct superior, the managing partner, her current and previous team members, and five other project team leaders with whom she had worked over the past few years. She explained what she was doing and asked for their honest and sincere feedback. Everyone except the managing partner completed the observer feedback. When the results were back, the coach was concerned that the feedback would be devastating to Debbie.

The coach and Debbie took three hours going through the material the first time and, while upset, Debbie was interested in really understanding what it all meant. They went through the report highlighting what were clearly Debbie's strengths and what was perceived to be holding her back. After analyzing the data for over two hours, Debbie's coach encouraged her not to focus on the details but to look for some themes. The remainder of the meeting was spent talking about how she was perceived by her superiors and why the managing partner may not have chosen to complete the report.

It was clear that Debbie's technical competence and commitment were exemplary. All feedback indicated her high standards, but she seemed to lack approachability. Everyone, including those who had good relationships with her, found Debbie to be aloof, cool, and not appreciative of others. Her body language communicated that she wasn't receptive to the concerns of others. While she was often protective of team members, she would publicly criticize them when her standards were not met.

Debbie's first action item was to share her data with all of her current team members and get more input from them. Her motives appeared genuine, but her coach was worried that Debbie's decision lacked some necessary emotional intelligence skills to use this feedback to grow.

Debbie didn't really have a good understanding of her own emotions and how they had a direct negative impact on others, especially when she failed to manage and control those emotions in a positive way. While she did show a lot of personal motivation, Debbie was not skilled at predicting how others would react to her interactions with them. In fact, she often expressed surprise when anyone responded in a manner that was not consistent with how she would choose to behave.

## *What Debbie Discovered—But Her Team Already Knew*

Debbie admitted she really didn't have a good understanding of her own emotions and their impact on others. From the feedback and from the fact that her superior had not completed the report, she knew that many in management had "written her off" as too old to change. She wanted to prove them wrong.

While Debbie worked hard to master the techniques of using her body language more effectively, she still struggles with developing empathy, but she is now self-aware. She is confident about getting more challenging opportunities and her current assignments are showing improvement. In an industry where there was significant downsizing over the past two years, she is grateful for the "wake-up" call that the 360-degree assessment provided.

## *Benefits of 360-Degree Feedback Programs*

The results of using a personal 360-degree process when conducted with a developmental objective (as opposed to a corrective objective) provide the project leader with qualitative and quantitative data for self-reflection and enhanced awareness. This can assist the project leader in gaining the perspectives of others in an objective, non-threatening, confidential manner. If customized, a 360-degree assists in identifying the project leader's development needs and action items that the organization deems important. It can help to expose patterns of behavior, both positive and negative, especially when used in conjunction with other assessment tools. If part of a broader 360-degree feedback process throughout the organization, it creates a platform and language for dialogue between project team members and others. When initiated and implemented properly, it engages the support and encouragement of others in the process.

While the guidelines in Table 26.1 are a good start, the use of a coach or facilitator is considered essential. A professional and neutral third party can assist individuals in introducing the concept to observers, reviewing the output, assessing the meaning, and developing meaningful action plans.

# Theoretical Basis for Multi-Rater Feedback

The 360-degree feedback process is based upon two main theoretical principles. The first is that utilizing multiple sources yields higher quality, more valid, and more reliable information than a single-source appraisal.[1] The information gathered is usually more reliable, since with three or more different raters there is less chance of positive or negative bias. The information is usually more thorough, because when several different sets of feedback are combined, they provide more information than just one. It is also more extensive, since there are different people

**Table 26.1  Tips for Ensuring Success When Utilizing a Multi-Rater Process**

- Determine the intentions and the purpose of the organization.
- Develop a communications strategy to implement and manage both expectations and concerns.
- Allow the client to select the "raters" with guidance from the coach.
- Selected raters who:
  - Have observed the performance of the client on a regular basis.
  - Have first-hand knowledge of the client's work behaviors.
  - Have worked / interacted with the client for a minimum of 6 months (preferably a year).
  - Are open to providing honest and accurate feedback—both positive and developmental.
- Protect the anonymity of individuals and maintain the credibility of the instrument; a minimum of three raters should be used for each category except for superior.
- Make sure a distribution process has been established to protect the confidentiality of the process (e.g., if a paper-based system, provide client with enclosed, self-addressed, stamped envelope to return assessment results to coach or administrator).
- Where possible, incorporate results of the 360 degree with other assessments used as well as a development or action plan.

contributing their perspectives and each interacts with the person being rated in a different manner or capacity.

The second theory that serves as a basis for 360-degree feedback states that individuals can change their behavior by enhancing their self-awareness. By examining the feedback provided by others, individuals can better understand their strengths and weaknesses, others' perceptions of them and their work, and can develop and modify their performance and interaction with others accordingly.[2] In using a multi-rater assessment on a team, it is important to debrief all team members properly. Debriefing is a critical element of making a 360 degree beneficial to the participant. Table 26.2 provides tips on conducting a safe but productive debriefing session.

# The History and Development of the Self-Awareness Movement

Participating in a formal 360-degree assessment can be frightening. Understanding the history of assessments can give the facilitator and participant more confidence in using this tool effectively.

Throughout time, human beings have wanted to understand how they and others function in the world. Assessing personality traits and psychological testing have been around for over 70 years. In actuality, these ideas have been around since

**Table 26.2  Tips for Debriefing a Team Member on a Multi-Rater Instrument.**

1. Re-orient the tool—Before debriefing, provide context to participant and remind them of the purpose assessment.
   Resist the tendency to go directly to comments. Answer questions such as:
   ■ Who was involved?
   ■ How did we set it up?
   ■ Read a sample of one or two questions
   ■ How is it scored/what are the averages?
2. Allow the participant to read it. Ask them to:
   ■ Read and reflect on the feedback
   ■ Note comments on the report
   ■ Look for strengths
   ■ Mark the report as they see fit (agree / disagree / need to clarify or come back to).
3. Help them summarize the experience. Ask them:
   ■ What have they discovered?
   ■ What has this experience been like for them?
   Help them make connections and develop themes.
4. Begin to prepare a plan of action. Ask them:
   ■ What do they want to do with this information?
   ■ What are the costs / benefits / consequences of doing nothing versus doing something?
   ■ What ideas do they have to improve?
   Follow up on progress regularly.

much earlier, and the earliest philosophers often tried to explain human nature from a four-fold system using the basic elements: fire, earth, air, and water. The four temperaments, as they became known, were first used by the Greek writer, Hippocrates, who described them as "humors." He analyzed the four major body fluids Melancholy (black bile), Sanguine (blood), Phlegmatic (phlegm), and Choleric (yellow bile or urine) to sort out different types of men. This was even more popularized a couple of centuries later by the Roman physician Claudius Galen who introduced them to diagnose and treat illness. The four temperaments have remained popular for centuries and remain so to this day. Plato described the four types as artisan, philosopher, guardian, and scientist, and these were more recently modified by David M. Keirsey, who developed the Keirsey Temperament Sorter in 1987.[3] Even the German philosopher Immanuel Kant described the four elements or humors in his 1798 book *Anthropologie in Pragmatischer Hinsicht Abgefasst* as depicted in Table 26.3.[4]

Before World War I, most of the deep thinkers in this area had devoted their minds to analyzing how machines might work, since it was seemingly easier to measure them. The first work to address ability testing was Frank Parsons' *Choosing a Vocation*.[5] It was in 1916 that a psychological test was first used in hiring for an American police department. After the Great War came a leap forward in

**Table 26.3—Kant's Elements of Humors.**

| Element | Humor (Hippocrates) | Physiology | Current Terminology | Keirsey |
|---------|---------------------|------------|---------------------|---------|
| Fire | sanguine | blood | cheerfully confident and optimistic | Dionysian - artisan |
| Water | choleric | yellow bile | easily angered, bad tempered | Apollonian - idealist |
| Earth | melancholic | black bile | depressed, melancholic, unhappy | Epimethean - guardian |
| Air | phlegmatic | phlegm | calm, sluggish, unemotional | Promethean - rational |

understanding the human machine and its creative engine, the mind. The modern phase of psychology and management had begun.

In the 1920s, theories and hypotheses were beginning to be written up in various scientific journals and the refining of test methodology began in earnest. In 1921, Carl Gustav Jung published his book *Psychological Type* and it was translated into English two years later. [6] William Moulton Marston, a psychology professor at Columbia University, completed another major work with his book, *Emotions of Normal People,* published in 1928. [7] A year earlier, L.L. Thurstone created scales for measuring emotion.[8] Then, in his doctoral thesis written at Columbia University, Rensis Likert developed the first forced choice rating scale in 1932.[9] This widely used attitudinal scale that ranges from "strongly agree" to "strongly disagree" is now commonly referred to as The Likert Scale.

The next major move forward was in the 1950s. Recruitment needs of World War II had accelerated the growth of standardized testing and people were taking these theories and models and developing experiments to try to validate the various hypotheses. Massive studies began and lots of data began to be collected. Ability, aptitude, and achievement testing remains a complex and highly technical process that is still only administered by experienced professionals with post-secondary education.

Isabel Meyers, the daughter of Katherine Briggs, is credited for introducing the self-report movement during the fifties.[10] Out of this movement came the best-known assessment tool, the Myers-Briggs Type Indicator® (MBTI®). Other personality instruments quickly followed such as Walter Clark's Activity Vector Analysis in 1954, and the first to be based on Marston's theory and the FIRO-B® by William Schutz in 1958.[11]

In the mid 1970s, these tools became more popular and began to show up frequently in organizations. They were no longer the privy of psychologists and hence, there was no guarantee of proper monitoring of the applications. In 1975, the Association for Psychological Type and Center for Application of Psychological Type established criteria and began to distribute the MBTI®. Not only were career counselors using these instruments, but also human resource departments were becoming interested in using some of these instruments for development, hiring, etc. At the same time, many researchers began to doubt whether psychological testing would in fact be a reliable process for hiring and promoting. This concern is evident in the major court decisions related to employment testing that commenced in 1971.[12]

Today, behavioral and style assessment tools are being widely used by human resource professionals, managers, and coaches to help individuals and teams function at peak performance. There are a number of well-designed instruments and the magic of computers makes the mathematical calculations far superior.

We have now entered the next explosion in the use of "personality tests," due to the accessibility of online assessments—both those that are good and those that are not. This is creating a whole new set of pressures and challenges in the use of assessments. Everyone who uses assessments needs to ensure that he has the proper training and support in order to use the products most effectively.

## Fundamental Theories

To make sense of the numerous assessments on the market today and to choose the right one, it is important to understand two fundamental theories from Jung and Marston.

Jung believed that both conscious and unconscious forces affected behavior and these forces or instincts could help to identify core personality traits that differentiate people. He hypothesized that people are different in fundamental ways even though they all have the same multitude of instincts (archetypes) to drive them from within. One instinct was no more important than another. What is important was how this preference causes individuals to "function." A preference for a given "function" was a characteristic rooted in biology. Thus, Jung invented the "function types," or "psychological types," with the hope of helping individuals discover their natural talents or gifts. Katherine Briggs had been developing her own ideas about people. Upon reading Jung's *Psychological Type*, Briggs began to build her own model based on Jung's work. Later, Briggs's daughter joined her mother in her work to create the Myers-Briggs Type Indicator®. Myers and Briggs added to Jung's three dimensions, a judging-perceiving scale which is designed to measure one's attitude toward the "outer world," or managing one's life.

Marston explored the meaning of normal human emotions by relating how a person perceives himself in relation to the environment and describing how the person is likely to behave in response. Marston's two-dimensional model examines both the environment's perceived favorability or unfavorability and the individual's sense of being more or less powerful than the environment.

In response, the individual either acts on or accommodates to that environment. Marston intended to explain how normal human emotions lead to behavioral differences among people. This also included the observation that changes in a person's behavior will occur from time to time. From his work, he identified four quadrants which he named Dominance, Influence, Steadiness, and Compliance. This was later picked up as the acronym "DISC," by which many of the assessments based on Marston's work are known.

Another popular area in psychology is the Big Five, which represent five broad factors or dimensions of personality traits that have been identified through empirical research. The Big Five is a descriptive model of personality, as opposed to a theory, although psychologists have developed theories to account for the Big Five. The Big Five personality traits are sometimes remembered through the acronym "OCEAN." The letters stand for Openness to experience, Conscientiousness, Extroversion, Agreeableness, and Neuroticism.[13]

## Scientific Studies

When choosing an assessment, you must understand its psychometric rigor—what do the results really tell you.

There are three things to consider when determining psychometric rigor: reliably, validity, and social desirability. Reliability determines how well the items on a scale accurately reflect the scale itself; i.e., if the same person takes it on separate occasions, the results should be the same. Validity determines the extent to which the association among the scores represents the theory and model on which the instrument is based, indicating that the tool measures what it says it measures. Social desirability determines the transparency, or how easy it is to fake the results.[14]

Retest reliability or stability refers to how well an instrument yields consistent results. Scores range between 0.00 and 1.00. A reliability index of 0.85 or higher is generally considered to be effective for all purposes. An index of between 0.65 and 0.85 indicates a good range for groups but is considered less confident in an individual score.[15]

Validity establishes the confidence with which we can interpret any given result on a given test. Validity is obviously a much more complex question than reliability, and is ultimately a more important question. It assumes that we accept the model and the theory upon which the instrument is based or no amount of study will appease. There are at least five different types of validity and reliability, and studies are lengthy and expensive.

It is not critical to analyze and study the scientific studies. The question is: Does the instrument that will be used have sufficient psychometric rigor to satisfy the needs of this particular use and purpose? All the tools and instruments mentioned in this book have met the basic requirements of psychometrics for assessments of this nature. Despite this, researchers often will argue the true validity of all ipsative (self-report) instruments due to their inherent subjectivity.

# Additional Tools
## *FIRO-B*®

The theory underlying the FIRO-B® incorporates ideas from the work of psychologists T.W. Adorno, Erich Fromm, and Wilfred Bion. The FIRO-B® assesses how personal needs affect an individual's behavior toward other people around three interpersonal dimensions: Inclusion, which determines the extent of contact and prominence an individual seeks and wishes from others; Control, which determines the extent of power an individual seeks and wishes from others; and Affection, which determines the extent of closeness that a person seeks and wishes from others.

The FIRO-B® divides each of the three interpersonal dimensions into two subaspects. These are behaviors a person expresses that they feel is appropriate to exhibit toward others, and the actual behavior a person wants from others.

## *Enneagram*

The Enneagram is one of the oldest known personality typing systems, based on Pythagorean sacred geometry and incorporating the esoteric traditions of the Kabala and Islamic Sufi. It was popularized and brought to the Western World by the esoteric teacher and mystic, George Gurdjieff, (a contemporary of Freud) who rediscovered the Enneagram in Afghanistan.

The nine personality types of the Enneagram are based on ancient insights into human nature that have been corroborated by intensive observation and the independent findings of modern psychology (including Freud, Jung, Horney, and others). The types apply to both males and females and are cross-cultural. While originally an oral tradition, more written instruments including those aimed for the organizational setting are appearing on the market.[16]

# Whole Brain Thinking

Ned Herrmann first pioneered the study of the brain in the field of business while working as manager of General Electric Corporation's Management Education. He later wrote a widely acclaimed book, *The Creative Brain*, which traced the scientific and historic roots of his "Whole Brain Thinking" approach. While it looks at behavior, this is a physiological model that focuses on mental (thinking) preferences. The Whole Brain Model emerged as a validated metaphor for describing the four different preference modes. [17]

The metaphor divides the brain into four separate quadrants. Each quadrant is different and of equal importance. The Upper Left Blue A Quadrant specializes in logical, analytical, quantitative, and fact-based thinking. The Lower Left Green B Quadrant focuses on details and specializes in planning, organizing, and sequencing information. The Lower Right Red C Quadrant places a priority on feelings and the interpersonal, emotional, and kinesthetic aspects of a situation. The Upper Right Yellow D Quadrant synthesizes and integrates information and is more intuitive and holistic in its thinking.

### Emotional Intelligence or Emotional Quotient

In 1928, Edward Thorndike gave us the early concept with his discussion of social intelligence, specifically expressing a concern at the over-emphasis on attempts to measure traditional cognitive intelligence.[18] Thorndike believed that social intelligence was equally valid and could be identified, and measured, as a completely separate entity from academic intelligence.

In 1983, Howard Gardner presented the theory that there were seven different kinds of intelligence (linguistic, logical or mathematical, spatial or visual, bodily or kinesthetic, musical, interpersonal, and intrapersonal). What Gardner called interpersonal and intrapersonal would probably be considered emotional intelligence today.[19]

Salovey and Mayer provided us with our first definition when they coined the term Emotional Intelligence in 1990.[20] EQ means "emotional quotient" and was a term apparently first used by Dr. Reuven Bar-On (1998) in an attempt to quantify, or measure, emotional-social intelligence (ESI).[21]

It wasn't until Daniel Goleman's *Working with Emotional Intelligence* that the concept began to really enter the mainstream. Goleman set out a framework of emotional intelligence that reflects how an individual's potential for mastering the skills of self-awareness, self-management, social awareness, and relationship management translates into on-the-job success. This model is based on emotional intelligence competencies that have been identified in internal research at hundreds of corporations and organizations as distinguishing outstanding performers.[22]

Most of the current assessments are based on Goleman's model and work. There is still no universal definition of EI, making comparisons of the various assessments difficult, if not impossible. Some measure skills, while others look at behaviors and competencies. Also, the core model or theory may be looking at different aspects of emotional intelligence. General guidelines that a solid EI assessment should include are the ability to:

■ Perceive the emotions of oneself and others
■ Understand the emotions of oneself and others
■ Express the emotions of oneself and others
■ Manage the emotions of oneself and others
■ Influence the emotions of oneself and others

### Social Styles

Merrill and Reid did not use the research that had been done before when they began their study of social styles in the 1960s, nor did they begin with a specific theory.[23] Merrill and Reid began with a structured adjective checklist developed by Dr. James W. Taylor that could be used reliably to describe behavior precisely. Merrill and Reid adopted this adjective list and asked others to describe the person's behavior. The results were clustered into three scales:

Assertiveness (perceived as tell or ask)
Responsiveness (perceived as emote or control feelings)
Versatility (perceived as adaptable, resourceful, and competent)

Other research into the way humans behave supports these findings. Today, there are a myriad of assessments on the market (some are found in DISC based instruments as well) that were designed around these two scales of assertiveness and responsiveness that then form four primary interaction or communications styles.

## Endnotes

1. Allan H. Church and David W. Bracken, "Advancing the State of the Art of 360-Degree Feedback: Guest Editors' Comments on the Research and Practice of Multi-rater Assessment Methods," *Group & Organization Management*, 22, (1997): 149–161.
2. Simon Hurley, "Application of Team-Based 360° Feedback Systems," Team Performance Management, 4, no. 5 (1998): 202–210.
3. AdvisorTeam®, Inc., s.v. "groups," http://www.advisorteam.org/instruments/ (accessed January 4, 2007).
4. Immanuel Kant, Hans H. Rudnick, and Victor Lyle Dowdell, *Anthropology from a Pragmatic Point of View* (Chicago: Southern Illinois University Press, 1996).
5. Frank Parsons, *Choosing a Vocation* (Boston: Houghton Mifflin, 1909).
6. Carl G. Jung, *Psychological Type* (London: Kegan Paul, 1921).
7. William M. Marston, *Emotions of Normal People*, (New York: Taylor & Francis, 1928).
8. Louis Leon Thurstone, "A Law of Comparative Judgment," *Psychological Review*, 34 (1927): 278–286.
9. Rensis Likert, "A Technique for the Measurement of Attitudes," *Archives of Psychology*, no. 140 (1932): 44–53.
10. Isabel Myers, *Gifts Differing: Understanding Personality Type* (Davies-Black Publishing, 1995).
11. William C. Schutz, W. FIRO: *A Three-Dimensional Theory of Interpersonal Behavior.* (New York: Rinehart, 1958).
12. In the context of project teams, the authors are not going to consider tests to help identify membership of the team for screening purposes—mental or physical ability tests, achievement tests, honesty tests, drug or alcohol examination or other "suitability requirements". Nor is it recommended to use instruments that identify themselves purely as "personality tests". Personality is the complex makeup of the totality of an individual and include but are not limited to behaviors, values, heritage, physical, etc. All of these factors cannot be synthesized into one test. While it is far beyond the scope of this book to review the myriad of assessments on the market, some have found a following in certain markets and industries. Each instrument should always be reviewed to determine how well it meets key criteria.

13. University of Oregon, The Srivastava Lab s.v. "Big Five," http://www.uoregon.edu/~sanjay/bigfive.html (accessed January 4, 2007).

14. J. William Pfeiffer and Arlette C. Ballew, *Using Lecturettes, Theory and Models in Human Resource Development*. (San Diego: Wiley, 1988) chap. 4, 5.

15. American Psychological Association, "The Standards for Educational and Psychological Testing," http://www.apa.org/science/standards.html (accessed January 4, 2007).

16. International Enneagram Association, s.v. "history," http://www.internationalenneagram.org/aboutenn_readmore.php?id=17 (accessed January 4, 2007).

17. Ned Herrmann, *The Creative Brain* (Hartbeespoortdam, Africa: Brain Books, 1988).

18. Edward L Thorndike, *Adult Learning* (New York: Macmillan, 1928).

19. Howard Gardner, *Frames of Mind: The Theory of Multiple Intelligence* (New York: Basic Books, 1983).

20. Peter Salovey and John D. Mayer, "Emotional Intelligence," *Imagination, Cognition, and Personality* 9, (1990): 185–211.

21. Reuven Bar-On and James D. A. Parker, *The Handbook of Emotional Intelligence: Theory, Development, Assessment, and Application at Home, School and in the Workplace* (San Francisco: Jossey-Bass, 2000).

22. Daniel Goleman, *Working with Emotional Intelligence* (New York: Bantam Books, 1998).

23. David W. Merrill and Roger H. Reid, *Personal Styles and Effective Performance* (Radnor, Pennsylvania: Chilton Book Company, 1977).

# Chapter 27

# Team Effectiveness

## Introduction

Several years ago, the scientists at NASA used pictures from the Hubble telescope to confirm a theory they had had for years: that everything in the universe—at an atomic level—is expanding or moving away from everything else, at an ever-increasing rate. They theorized that a mysterious energy exists in the universe that creates this expansion. Some think 80 or 90 percent of the universe is made up of this matter. They have given it the name "dark energy." The pictures from the Hubble allowed scientists to prove this mysterious dark energy does exist.[1]

Most of us have worked on a project where everyone seems to be moving away from each other at an ever-increasing rate. The dark, negative energy repels people, creating chaos. Unfortunately, we can't just blame the nature of the universe for this negative energy. Teams can help themselves. Team leaders are the instigators to team energy and performance—good or bad.

Savvy team leaders can improve performance by paying attention to team dynamics. Project teams have predictable life cycles and consequently will go through very specific developmental stages. Each stage presents its own challenge of growing pains for team members and the project leader. One of the greatest obstacles of teams, including those that work well together, is the ability to have the "tough" conversations about an individual's or the team's performance.

## Carlos's and the IT Team's Story

The project team's task was to coordinate the implementation of a standard portal across a major federal department. They had been together for five months of the nine-month mandate. All six representatives were seasoned project team members and got along

**269**

well. Many had been team leaders on smaller projects. Jean-Pierre, the project leader, encouraged all members to take on leadership roles within the project while he tended to focus on the planning and financial aspects. They regularly conducted team effectiveness surveys to measure their performance. At the end of each meeting, they would ask if the meeting's purpose was clear, if everyone was focused and productive, if there was a good balance between task and process, and if ground rules had been respected.

Carlos, the informal leader of the team, pointed out that they were always giving themselves fours and fives and perhaps were getting rather complacent. A "can of worms" had been opened. One member of the team mentioned how a consultant told him that some teams can fall into "groupthink." Then another member suggested that a more comprehensive assessment be conducted to identify areas in which the team was underperforming. Carlos remembered taking a conflict type assessment and recommended they use one to improve their performance. Everyone thought this was a good idea and Carlos volunteered to initiate it. The team set aside two hours to work through the profile. Each member was willing to put up their personal results on a big chart for all to view and discuss.

## What the Team Discovered—and "Outsiders" Already Knew

Under normal situations, all six of the team members showed a marked desire and interest in collaborating, but when under pressure team dynamics changed. Collaboration was easy when everything was going smoothly. Under stress, three of the six team members became accommodating and less assertive in order to keep the environment harmonious. Carlos became a compromiser, while Jean-Pierre, the project leader, and the remaining team members became less assertive and more combative.

During a particularly stressful time during the project, team members would remain silent in critical discussions and individuals would spend more time justifying their agreement to superiors to accommodate the pressures of project constraints rather than discuss reality or suggest alternatives. They knew they were adverse to conflict and it was hindering team performance and threatening project goals. Jean-Pierre admitted he considered the role of project leader too stressful for him. At the two-thirds point of the project with pressure and stress increasing significantly, a strategy was needed to help meet the challenges of a demanding project and improve team dynamics and performance before it was too late. Everyone looked to Carlos to act as their leader and point out when their desire to avoid conflict was becoming a detriment.

## Outcome

After reviewing the results of their profiles, the group, led by Carlos, defined action items for each member to increase assertiveness and collaboration. This session by itself created energy in the team and others soon noticed a marked improvement in the creativity of the group. There was still a tendency to avoid unpleasant news from outside. A few weeks later, a team member retired, as expected, and was replaced by a young woman, Heather. Initially, the group had difficulty in incorporating Heather's more assertive and competitive style, but they sat down and shared their profiles and action plans with her. Heather was able to immediately recognize her own tendencies and see the tendencies of her teammates. Since Heather was most naturally assertive, Carlos suggested that Heather would play the lead role, but she had to first earn respect and establish credibility with the others prior to taking the lead.

The disclosure of profiles and their potential barriers to team performance were overcome by the group. An outsider did not solve what they had to solve themselves. This allowed them to feel safe and "flex" their own opinions and differences, even with the new team member. The team put forth their deliverables—recommendations for the on-line governmental portal—on time and in budget and received the executive approval. All of the team members were asked to stay on for the implementation project and three were also recruited within the federal government and offered a project leader function on a similar project.

# The Life Cycle of a Project Team

All project teams run into a series of challenges over the course of the project. Some of these could be avoided, but most are the natural process of team development and need to be managed, not denied. Unfortunately, many project leaders operate under the slogan, "If it ain't broke, don't fix it." But productivity is improved when we notice and fix issues before they get broken. Project leaders play a key role in identifying when teams are beginning to go off track—not just from a delivery perspective but also from a development perspective. Early warning systems on how the project team members are operating together can often keep performance and results at a high level.

There is a life cycle of the team itself. Specific timelines are harder to define, as it is not only the quantity but also the quality of interactions over the course of a team. Understanding what stage the project team is experiencing will help to identify the appropriate checklist or assessment to use.

The Forming—Storming—Norming—Performing Model of team development was first proposed by Bruce Tuckman, who maintained that these four phases are all necessary and inevitable in order for the team to grow, face up to challenges, tackle problems, find solutions, plan work, and deliver results.[2] This model has become the basis for subsequent models of team dynamics and frequently used management theory to describe the behavior of existing teams. In 1977, Tuckman added the fifth phase: Adjourning. While presented in a linear manner, it is important to consider this a cyclical process. Many times, projects appear to take two steps forward and one step back as they progress forward toward completion.

It should also be noted that individual team members are often at different stages, especially if they have joined the project at a later date.

## Forming

In the first phase, the forming of the project team takes place. The team meets and learns about the opportunity and challenges, agrees on goals, and begins to tackle the tasks. Team members tend to behave quite independently but are often on their "best behavior" while they determine, "what is in it for them." They may be motivated, but are usually relatively uninformed of the issues and objectives of the project, despite how clear it may seem. A project leader has the opportunity to establish clarity not only around the purpose or goals but also setting roles, expectations, and ground rules (guiding principles). These are critical steps that are sometimes rushed. It is in the forming stage that a project leader sets in motion her plan to build trust-based relationships using credibility, reliability, intimacy, and low self-orientation.

While the project leader may not have significant authority over the other members of the team, the role is one of direction and giving structure to the process. The project leader also needs to ensure that time is taken for members to "get to know" one another. In the forming stage, it is quite common to encourage the team to engage in some form of "team building" activity, which is often a process to help get to know each other's styles. This is where assessments such as MBTI˚, DISC, and The Platinum Rule˚ can be useful—when properly applied. Through these types of activities, the project team leader can help to establish an open and safe space for dialogue.

## Storming

Every group will at some point enter the storming stage where the energy goes down. This is the beginning of the creative or problem-solving phase as the team addresses concerns such as what issues they are really supposed to create, how they will function independently and together, and what leadership model they will accept. The way the team makes decisions might come into question. It is important for team members to be encouraged to open up to one other and confront each other's ideas and perspectives rather than allow covert conflict to develop.

The storming stage is necessary to the growth of the team. It can be contentious, unpleasant, and even painful to members of the team who are averse to conflict. In some cases, storming can be resolved relatively quickly. Often, a project leader will be challenged, particularly if her leadership competency pyramid base is weak. In others, the team never properly resolves issues and conflict continues to arise but is not necessarily "put on the table." Tolerance of each team member and her differences needs to be emphasized. This phase can become destructive

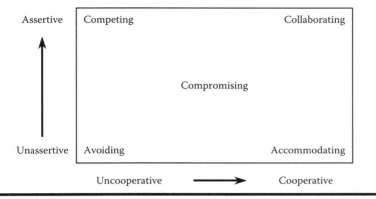

**Figure 27.1 Thomas-Kilmann conflict model.**

to the team and will lower motivation if allowed to get out of control or ignored. The project leader needs courage to "hold the tension" and model that conflict and disagreement are not only fine, but necessary. Using team activities to get at differences is often useful at this stage and can help team members begin the difficult discussions of disagreement.

As with the other assessments presented, there are many established and well-known generic individual and team assessments on the market. One tool shown in Figure 27.1, that has been used easily and very successfully is The Thomas-Kilmann Conflict Mode Instrument (TKI). The Thomas-Kilmann Conflict Mode Instrument is designed to assess an individual's behavior in conflict situations and has been the leader in conflict resolution assessment for more than 30 years.[3]

Research has shown that there are five basic styles or modes for handling conflict—competing where the goal is to "win," avoiding where the goal is to "delay," compromising where the goal is to "find a middle ground," collaborating where the goal is to "find a win-win situation," and accommodating where the goal is to "give in."

## Norming

At some point, the team will enter the norming stage. Team members adjust their behavior to each other as they develop work habits that make teamwork seem more natural and fluid. Team members often work through this stage by acting on previously identified rules, values, professional behavior, shared methods, working tools, and even taboos. During this phase, team members begin to trust each other and a project leader begins to look for opportunities to become a consultative leader. Energy and motivation increase as the team gets more acquainted with the project and members once again want to get on with the task at hand.

Teams in this phase may lose their creativity if the norming behaviors become too strong and begin to stifle healthy dissent and the team begins to exhibit

**Table 27.1   Rating the Project Team.**

| Where do you see our project team right now? (circle rating) | | | | | | |
|---|---|---|---|---|---|---|
| Team's purpose<br>I'm uncertain | 1 | 2 | 3 | 4 | 5 | I'm clear |
| Membership<br>I'm in | 1 | 2 | 3 | 4 | 5 | I'm out |
| Elbow room<br>I'm crowded | 1 | 2 | 3 | 4 | 5 | I'm comfortable |
| Discussion<br>cautious/guarded | 1 | 2 | 3 | 4 | 5 | Open/free |
| Use of skills<br>poor | 1 | 2 | 3 | 4 | 5 | Full |
| Support<br>for self only | 1 | 2 | 3 | 4 | 5 | For all members |
| Conflict<br>avoided | 1 | 2 | 3 | 4 | 5 | Worked on |
| Influence on decisions<br>by few members | 1 | 2 | 3 | 4 | 5 | By all members |

groupthink. Groupthink is a mode of thought whereby individuals intentionally conform to what they perceive to be the consensus of the group.[4] This is more likely to occur in tightly knit and isolated teams. The project leader's role is one of facilitation and that includes challenging complacency and setting higher standards for the team.

Project leaders, like their team members, can often get caught up in activities and may lose sight of the overall picture. It is easy to end up doing things right rather than doing the right things. Reviewing the basic purpose and objectives of the team can often be useful halfway into a project. A team health checklist is a good review tool (See Table 27.1) that teams can use periodically to ensure that they are functioning as a high-performing team.

## *Performing*

Some teams will reach the performing stage, often referred to as the "in the groove" or "flow" state. These high-performing teams are able to function as a unit as they find ways to get the job done smoothly and effectively without inappropriate conflict or the need for external supervision. Team members have become interdependent and each one will take on aspects of the leadership. By this time, they are motivated and knowledgeable. Dissent is expected and allowed as long as it is channeled through means acceptable to the team.

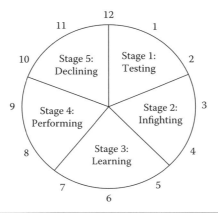

**Figure 27.2   Team clock.**

Even the most high-performing teams will revert to earlier stages in certain circumstances, such as a change in membership. Maintaining flow over the longer term is impossible and even long-standing teams will go through these cycles many times as they react to changing circumstances. This can lead to a return to the forming or storming stage as group membership changes, a new "dorming" stage as the group gets complacent, or adjourning (others call it the phase for mourning) as the group successfully reaches its goal and completes its work.

The project leader's role is participative and non-directive while remaining vigilant to determine when the energy is decreasing. What can often be missed is that one or two team members may feel they are at different levels of commitment at different times. The use of various team assessments can help leaders and teams determine early warning systems and what techniques could be used to be more efficient. One tool based on the principles of the Tuckman Model, in Figure 27.2, but using different terminology is the Team Clock exercise. Over time, teams evolve in their development—events occur that cause a shift forward or backward. Allow team members to record where they see the team based on these stages.

## *Adjourning*

Bringing closure to a team is often a challenge. By the time the project is completed, few want to make the extra effort to celebrate the successes and "say goodbyes." As unnecessary is it may seem, team members may have an unstated sense of being vulnerable. If members of the group have been closely bonded, this is a time to acknowledge everyone's contributions so that members can move on to new things, feeling good about what's been achieved. It is the project team leader's responsibility to build this aspect into the project tasks and recognize the work well done.

## Endnotes

1. Hubblesite.org s.v. "dark energy," http://hubblesite.org/newscenter/archive/releases/2006/52/full/ (accessed January 4, 2007).
2. Bruce Tuckman, "Developmental Sequence in Small groups," *Psychological Bulletin* 63, (1965): 384–399.
3. Irving L. Janis, *Victims of Groupthink*: *A Psychological Study of Foreign-Policy Decisions and Fiascoes* (Boston: Houghton Mifflin, 1972).

# Appendix A

## Leadership Theories for Project Management

### Trait and Behavioral Theories

There is extensive research on how one becomes an effective leader. All of the competing theories flow from either *Trait* theories or *Behavioral* theories.

**The Trait Theory** indicates that leadership is inherited. Many people still believe that leaders are born possessing innate qualities that make them more likely to be good leaders. After all, history is full of leaders who descended from aristocracy or privileged families, who were in a position of cultural leadership. We see this in athletics where children of great sports figures grow up to become accomplished athletes on the playing field. Of course, this could also be a result of growing up in an environment conducive to athletics or exposure to the best teaching and training.

Trait theories researched in the first half of the 1900s insisted that one must possess a sufficient number of key traits and skills in order to become a good leader. Ralph M. Stogdill, in *Handbook of Leadership: A Survey of Theory and Research*, distilled the findings from a selection of these studies addressing characteristics of leaders. Findings in previous research indicated that while physical stamina was a characteristic of a leader, physical disability was not necessarily a limiting factor; disabled persons with high energy were just as likely to lead as their able-bodied counterparts.[1] Social status was a prominent characteristic of American leaders; more than half of the presidents, vice presidents, and cabinet members from 1789 to 1934 were born into families where the father held a position of status.[2]

Stogdill listed key traits of task-related characteristics and social characteristics that were found in leaders as identified in these studies. Table A.1 lists those sets of characteristics for comparison.[3]

Most people working on a project team would probably agree that these traits and skills are necessary for a project manager to lead effectively. When determining

## Table A.1 Leadership Traits and Skills

| *Task-Related Characteristics* | *Social Characteristics* |
| --- | --- |
| Need for achievement, desire to excel | Ability to enlist cooperation |
| Drive for responsibility | Administrative ability |
| Enterprise, initiative | Attractiveness |
| Responsible in pursuit of objectives | Cooperativeness |
| Task orientation | Nurturance |
| | Popularity, prestige |
| | Sociability, interpersonal skills |
| | Social participation |
| | Tact, diplomacy |

*Adapted from Stogdill 1974, pp 80–81.*

which traits are more important than others, one can think of specific project situations that certain traits or skills might be valued more than others. During the planning and scope definition of a project, the business analyst's writing requirements may benefit from persistent leadership that roots out the real needs of the customer, as well as decisiveness in managing scope creep. On the other hand, during the testing phase, ambition and persuasion may not be of great importance to a team of methodical testers working with software programmers. Instead, knowledge of task, organization, patience, and diplomacy may allow the project leader to be effective.

Trait theory research does not satisfactorily explain leadership because a person does not necessarily become an effective leader just by possessing certain traits or skills, nor is there any solid evidence that any combination of traits consistently produces effective leaders. **As scientists continually decode human genetics, maybe they will find that "leadership gene." Until then, many, like me, continue to believe leadership can be learned if one truly desires to lead.**

**The Behavioral Theory** of leadership was developed through observation of the actions and behaviors of leaders. Behaviorists attempt to measure the actions and behaviors of leaders by observing how they lead.[4] Then, aspiring leaders can mimic or learn these actions and become effective. Within behavioral theory is role theory, which suggests that people within teams will send messages to their leaders indicating expectations based on their needs; these messages are based on an individual's understanding of leadership. Leaders will then conform to these roles if they are socially aware of the people around them and their needs.

A project leader who has knowledge of follower preferences can accelerate this role development and enhance project team performance. However, it is common for team members to challenge a project leader's role, creating conflict until each develops into his preferred roles.

Behavioral theories state that a leader's ability to adapt himself to learned behaviors through the progression of a team's role development is an essential component of becoming an effective leader. Lewis's Law of Requisite Variety applies: "In any system of humans or machines, the element in the system with the greatest flexibility in its behavior will control the system."[5] In project management terms, the person who exhibits the most variation in his behavior will control the system. Watch a group of children at play. The child whose behavior varies the most often dominates the group, to the approval or disappointment of the watching parents. The project leader who exhibits the most flexible behavior will control the project organization.

But these theories are really just the beginning of understanding leadership. A project leader must have insight into an extended project environment. He must be able to examine a situation and how it impacts his customer and team members. Some environments foster top-down decision making while others prefer consensus-driven decisions, and either one will influence and impact the effectiveness of the project leader. These unique circumstances play an enormous role in leader effectiveness and team behavior. What is at stake? Who is impacted by the outcome? Who is accountable? What are the perceptions of influential stakeholders? These questions and many more create a myriad of circumstances that influence a project leader.

All of these known and unknown variables combine at frightening speeds to create a treacherous environment for project managers who are thrust into leadership roles, particularly on visible, strategic project or program initiatives.

Leadership is complex; there is no set formula and project leadership is arguably more unique due to its temporary structure and the lack of authority. Success is often temporary at best. **Attempting to lead in project management requires knowledge of self, awareness of stakeholder preferences and their messages, while quickly interpreting, synthesizing, and acting upon the changing dynamics of the project environment.**

The history of leadership research really begins where trait and behavioral theories leave off. The groundwork laid by these theories has given rise to many additional theories of leadership. In this appendix, participative, situational, contingency, transactional, or transformational leadership are all briefly reviewed within the context of project management.

A project leader improves his odds of achieving leader effectiveness if he has awareness and predictability of self, his environment, his followers, and co-leaders. Figure A.1 illustrates the intersection of these variables, creating a maximum opportunity for effective leadership in projects. As a leader becomes more aware of these variables and anticipates or predicts them with more accuracy, he expands the opportunities for effective leadership.

These variables are unique to the environment, the project, and the day-to-day circumstances that arise. There are many other micro-variables, such as award systems and internal politics that influence a leader's ability to lead effectively. With so many variables out of the leader's grasp, leadership success is often temporary and borne out of unique temporary factors that align at the right time, or just pure luck. However, self-knowledge, environment, follower, and co-leader awareness can all be increased by having a general understanding of leadership theory.

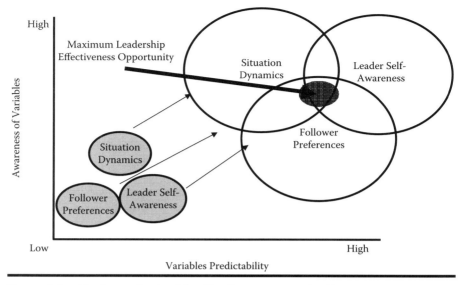

**Figure A.1    Maximum leadership effectiveness opportunity.**

# Participative Leadership in Project Management

Participative leadership acknowledges the effect of the participation of followers in decision making. Generally, the more leaders include followers in the decision-making process, the more likely they will accept the decision and act upon it. This premise sounds logical and can be applicable to project leaders even in situations where they lack authority. If a project leader wants team members to execute a plan and customers to accept the resulting deliverables, success is more likely if all parties are included in developing the plan.

Lewin, Lippitt, and White's influential 1939 study with children[6] is useful for its exploration of leadership decision making. The study identified three types of leadership decision making: Autocratic, Democratic, and Laissez-faire.[7] In autocratic decision-making, the leader makes a decision without consulting others. Most of us are either guilty of this or have witnessed project leaders making decisions on their own. Autocratic decision making is not universally destructive. Where input from others would not have changed the decision and when the motivation of the followers carrying out the actions resulting on the decision is not affected, autocratic decision making can be effective and efficient.

Democratic decision making can vary from pure democratic majority rule to decision making strongly facilitated by the leader. Most people like the democratic style because they want to be heard, even if they do not get their way. Not surprisingly, Lewin, Lippitt, and White found this to be the most accepted style, but it is subject to lengthy delays and may contribute to raising conflicts among members with strong opinions.

Lastly, they defined the laissez-faire decision making style in which the leader takes a hands-off approach to decision making. Followers make their own decisions, often accompanied with the delegation of accountability for the outcome. Laissez-faire works best when followers are very capable and do not rely on each other for input. Each one of these styles can be appropriate given the project circumstances at hand.

Rensis Likert describes four types of leadership behavior: exploitive authoritative, benevolent authoritative, consultative, and participative group.[8]

The exploitive authoritative leader has no concern for people and uses fear to achieve compliance and influence behavior. Communication is always from the top down.

The benevolent authoritative leader has some regard for people and uses reward systems to influence behavior. Because of his authoritative position, however, he is told what he wants to hear. He holds onto critical decision making and only delegates minimally. It may appear from the outside that a benevolent authoritative leader is listening to followers, but in reality he is usually not, and the final decision always resides with him.

The consultative style leader reaches out more to followers and actively encourages an upward flow of information, but decisions are still closely held and centrally made.

Lastly, the participative leader engages both followers and peers, fostering collaboration. The success of participative leadership comes through the creation of supportive relationships based on mutual trust, loyalty, and respect, including the recognition of the personal worth of others. Decision making is done with a perspective on the relationships that bind the entire group or organization. These relationships facilitate open communication and willingness to help others through non-binding, reciprocal agreements.

Likert's models help explain why project teams are unlikely to succeed if they hold team members hostage to the exploitive or benevolent authoritative leadership styles. **Today's knowledge workers or team members are likely to be non-compliant because the project leader does not have the express or implied authority or expertise to effectively make all decisions.** Success is more likely if the project leader nurtures a supportive and participative environment in which trust, a level of decentralized decision making, and open communication are the norms.

# Situational Leadership in Project Management

Challenge in the environment and the variables that impact leadership gave birth to new theories. Over time, the research gravitates from how a leader makes decisions toward a leader's decision-making capability as a measurement of leadership qualities. Situational leadership and participative leadership theories both relate environment and decision making to leadership effectiveness.

The premise of situational leadership is that the environment or situation impacts leadership results. Conditions surrounding the organization's structure, its climate, team member roles, and their characteristics influence a leader's actions. Models that have gained recognition in situational leadership research are Vroom's and Yetton's Normative Model, which explains the relationship of the leader to decision quality,[9] and the Path-Goal theory,[10] which explains the leader's role in assisting followers to achieve their goals.

Experienced project managers are familiar with the various follower traits and are usually adept at changing their style. A skilled, experienced, and independent team member may prefer to be left alone to complete work and make decisions as to how to best complete the work. However, the project environment with its ambiguous nature and constant changes can mislead a project manager to assume that his team members are motivated, knowledgeable, and capable project decision makers, when in reality, they are not. In a competitive environment, team members can be motivated to oversell themselves and their capabilities. This requires a project leader to coach, facilitate, and create an environment conducive to shared decision making and collaboration.

The Vroom and Yetton's Normative Model[11] focuses on decision quality and decision acceptance. A project leader is in a position to make or impact many project decisions. The ability to facilitate good decision making is directly linked to his perceived value by team members, sponsors, and stakeholders.

This model is based on three decision procedures: autocratic, consultative, and group, similar to Lewin, Lippitt, and White's study of leadership decision making mentioned earlier. The Vroom and Yetton model can be applied to various situations illustrating the importance of quality decisions. For example, autocratic decisions are not best when decision quality is important and followers have critical information, or when followers are not likely to be receptive to an autocratic decision. Group decision making is more appropriate when decision acceptance is more important than quality, or when decision quality must be high, ambiguity exists, and the leader does not have all the information. A group decision would not be appropriate when the leader sees the need for a quality decision, but the followers do not.

Of course it is difficult for a project manager to measure the importance of decision quality to followers or to be certain of their knowledge, perceptions, and required level of acceptance. Once attuned to the strategic nature and the daily ebb and flow of the project and his team members, he can get a sense of the importance of one decision over another, but this is far from a scientific process. It is logical that in order to gain a sense of followers' feelings toward decision quality, and their need to accept the decision, a project leader would need a relationship with these followers. Complicating the matter more is each individual follower may have different feelings toward these situations. Assessing seemingly countless variables at project speed is challenging and can contribute to unpredictable leadership behavior. Evidence is emerging that intuition may be a leader's best guide when he is in tune with the events and people around him.

Participative leadership, in Vroom and Yetton's Normative Model, recognizes the importance of working closely with subject matter experts who provide valuable insight to decisions and actions. Getting team member participation and com-mitment up front is the duty of the project leader and requires relationships with these experts. This can be difficult, particularly with remote team members. Thus, **a project leader must carefully consider his first impressions on team members to gain maximum trust and credibility.**

A project leader finds himself in an environment that requires excellence among all team members to achieve success. Vroom and Yetton's achievement-oriented leadership style promotes setting high standards for both self-development and task completion in an environment that is complex and challenging. The achievement-oriented leader relies heavily on follower preferences and their willing participation. This leader demonstrates a strong belief in his followers, ensures commitment to excellence and ethical standards, and encourages them to become better people.

The Path-Goal theory,[12] based on research by Robert J. House, describes leader adaptation to the situation to use various degrees of identifying or clarifying a clear path for followers. He removes roadblocks and provides incentives to accelerate movement down the path. This theory is appropriate when the leader possesses supportive and directive styles.

In supportive leadership, the leader demonstrates a high concern for the follower as a person, not just as a worker, and helps create a more pleasant environment with enticing work. When work is stressful, boring, or repetitive, a leader's creativity can improve the worker satisfaction and productivity. Many projects involve work that is stressful and tedious; awareness to this type of need—high concern for the fol-lower as a person—is valuable.

The directive leadership style provides direct instructions on what to do and how to do it, while providing assistance along the way. This is beneficial when tasks are unstructured and followers are inexperienced. Project start-up phases can be prone to ambiguity and unstructured tasks. Team members may be inexperienced with volatile project start-up phases and new subject matter addressed by the proj-ect. Projects tend to get behind early and then struggle to catch up. A project leader can use a more directive leadership style to help minimize unproductive time and establish credibility. There are risks associated with this style; not everyone likes to be told what to do nor do they like the idea of needing assistance.

These situational leadership theories highlight the importance of a project lead-er's awareness of their environment, including follower competence and preferred style, decision quality, and the type of work being performed.

# Contingency Leadership in Project Management

Contingency leadership is similar to situational leadership; however, it introduces a new variable by considering the leaders' preferences in addition to the follower preferences.

This theory focuses on leaders' preferences for dealing with relationships over tasks or tasks over relationships. Fred E. Fiedler pioneered this research on leadership, stating that both the leadership style and situational factors combine to determine leadership effectiveness. [13] An effective leader in one situation may prove quite ineffective in another situation. The skills used successfully on one project can be seemingly ineffective on other projects.

Fiedler's work should be of great interest to project leaders. He used his "least preferred co-worker scale" to determine if a leader naturally focuses on relationships or tasks. The method is simple; the leader thinks of a person with whom he would least like to work, perhaps someone who annoyed him to no end. The leader then answers a series of descriptors regarding this annoying co-worker on a scale from 1 to 8. The questions focus on the perceptions of this person in terms of friendliness, openness, and cooperativeness. The upper end of the scale indicates this least preferred co-worker is friendly, supportive, open, etc. and the lower end indicates this person is unfriendly, hostile, uncooperative, and so forth. Table A.2 depicts some of Fiedler's least preferred co-worker descriptors; think of your least preferred co-worker and rate them.

A high score shows the leader made the relationship work, indicating a preference for relationships over tasks; a low score indicates this relationship soured and the leader prefers task completion over relationship quality. Since project leaders cannot normally select their dream team, they must turn difficult relationships into productive relationships.

A leader's style preference is also reflected in other theories, such as the Managerial Grid defined by Blake and Mouton in the 1960s.[14] By comparing the level of concern for people versus the concern for production (task), Blake and Mouton defined five managerial styles: Impoverished Management (low concern for both), High Performance Team Management (high concern for both), Country Club management (high concern for people, but low concern for production), Authority-compliance (high concern for production, but low concern for people), and the Middle of the Road style. Many of these styles can be found in projects and their leaders.

**Table A.2    Fiedler's Least Preferred Co-Worker Descriptors.**

| *Fiedler's Least Preferred Co-Worker Descriptors* | | | | | | | | | *Answer* |
|---|---|---|---|---|---|---|---|---|---|
| Pleasant | 8 | 7 | 6 | 5 | 4 | 3 | 2 | 1 | Unpleasant |
| Friendly | 8 | 7 | 6 | 5 | 4 | 3 | 2 | 1 | Unfriendly |
| Close | 8 | 7 | 6 | 5 | 4 | 3 | 2 | 1 | Distant |
| Warm | 8 | 7 | 6 | 5 | 4 | 3 | 2 | 1 | Cold |
| Supportive | 8 | 7 | 6 | 5 | 4 | 3 | 2 | 1 | Hostile |
| Harmonious | 8 | 7 | 6 | 5 | 4 | 3 | 2 | 1 | Quarrelsome |
| Open | 8 | 7 | 6 | 5 | 4 | 3 | 2 | 1 | Closed |
| Considerate | 8 | 7 | 6 | 5 | 4 | 3 | 2 | 1 | Inconsiderate |
| Agreeable | 8 | 7 | 6 | 5 | 4 | 3 | 2 | 1 | Disagreeable |
| Kind | 8 | 7 | 6 | 5 | 4 | 3 | 2 | 1 | Unkind |

*Adapted from Bedeian, 1983, p. 505.*

According to Fiedler, "a leader's style depends on his or her personality and is, thus, fixed."[15] Our leadership success or failure is subject to the present variables and situations. Thus, leadership effectiveness is determined by a leader's ability to control the environment and its people, or by dumb luck.

Like most leaders, a project manager has little control over the many variables present in projects. He may be able to select certain team members, but has little control over their preferences, competencies, attitudes, and behaviors. Attempting to control too many of these variables is dangerous. But he can create and foster a structure within project teams that is more conducive to producing favorable situations.

Fiedler defines three factors that significantly help a leader. The first and most important factor is the leader-member relationship. The degree to which he is accepted by the team members creates a favorable or unfavorable situation. The second factor is the task structure of the work being performed. Fiedler claims that more structured tasks help create a favorable situation for the leader. The least important factor is the leader's formal position. The more formal power he possesses, the more favorable the situation is for him.[16] A project leader who is well accepted by his team, has very structured work for them, and can fire them on the spot theoretically has the ideal situation!

A project leader rarely operates in this environment; work is usually unstructured and ambiguous. Each project by definition is unique and has never been done before. He usually does not hold formal power over his team members; he has accountability with little authority. However, large projects and programs, such as government and military programs, executed over many years typically have more formal power to be assigned to the leader.

**Fiedler's Contingency Theory of Effective Leadership can and should be a wake-up call for a project manager. He will typically have only one favorable situational factor to rely on, and that is the degree to which his team accepts him as their leader.**

A project leader, who finds task structure and formal power in his favor, should be careful not to rely too much on these factors. The good news is Fiedler claims this is the most important situational factor for effective leadership. It is also the factor over which we have the most control!

# Transactional Leadership in Project Management

Have you ever heard someone say, "He is paid to do a job". The idea that a subordinate exists only to do what his superior wants occurs on projects as much as it does in general management. This idea is known as Transactional Leadership.[17] Transactional Leadership assumes a clear contractual relationship between the leader and follower. A follower agrees to an implied contract and expects a reward, typically financial, for satisfactorily completing the job, but does not expect to have a say in the way it gets done. The Transactional Leader distributes work to the follower and holds him accountable for getting it done. Blame associated with failure is placed on the follower.

Working with a project leader who uses this type of leadership style can be frustrating and reduce motivation of team members; however, this contractual paradigm is very prevalent in organizations. Statements such as, "Just get it done!" and "What are we paying these people to do?" are indicative of a transactional leadership style that can exist at almost any level of an organization. A subordinate who expects a bad outcome—getting written up, damaged reputation, or being fired—is likely to complete the work without asking questions.

A project leader loses trust and then power by prolonged or extreme use of transactional leadership. He can mitigate this risk by surrounding himself with an inner circle of trusted team members who pay for this privileged position by working harder. Being on the inside lets them become more influential, make decisions, and become leaders themselves. This is called the Leader-Member Exchange Theory. It describes how a leader maintains his position by forming informal agreements with his members. With little authority and much accountability, the project leader feels the need to surround himself with people on whom he can rely to perform at a high level, tell the truth, cover his back, and so on. These relationships are formed when both parties have something to gain. The project leader has confidence in his inner circle and the team member has the opportunity to be on the inside and gain additional opportunities.

## Leadership from Heart and Mind

Knute Rochne asking his Notre Dame football team to win one for the Gipper, President Kennedy asking the nation to put a man on the moon by the end of the decade, and Martin Luther King asking Americans to share his dream of equality, are all examples of leadership through the heart and mind. Influencing the heart and the mind forms the essence of transformational leadership, which assumes that a compelling vision, passion, excitement, and energy will lift the follower, creating a positive experience that will motivate them to act willingly toward the accomplishment of the leadership objective.

Note the particular word used in the first sentence describing Rochne, Kennedy, and King. They were asking, not telling or demanding. They successfully framed the need, articulated a vision, and inspired others to act, but also recognized the free will of the human spirit. The follower emotionally and rationally attached themselves to a transformational leader and his vision. By doing so, they believe in being a part of something bigger than themselves. Transformational leadership attempts to ignite the spirit and appeal to need for self fulfillment. Transformational leadership is powerful, but also potentially dangerous. It focuses on the big picture and leaves the details to others. Great projects can be accomplished by transformational leaders, but those who rely heavily on transformational leadership methods can also lose sight of reality.

## *Transformational Leadership*

Transformational leadership has been described and explored by authors such as Bernard Bass, James Burns, and Warren Bennis. A common characteristic is that development of the relationship between the leader and follower is different than that described by other leader and follower models. A transformational leader has a high level of concern not just for the accomplishment of her vision, but also for the individual's identity. She desires to see the individual transform himself into something better as a result of the journey, by participating and connecting himself with a higher moral purpose. By appealing to individuals' needs and intellectual capability, transformational leaders align followers toward their idealistic vision and use charismatic appeal to inspire them. The acceptance of these leaders' actions, which are steeped in strong moral principles, is an entrance criterion that followers must accept or reject.

Projects come in all shapes and sizes and many projects have a higher purpose, or a social value through which leaders can successfully exercise transformational leadership. Many of these projects gain recognition in our industry—safe disposal of nuclear reactors, building power plants in Third World countries, or providing relief to victims of natural disasters. Any project can be an ideal situation for transformational leaders to engage the hearts and minds of individuals and ask them to participate in and contribute to this higher purpose. Invoking a higher purpose makes people excited to come to work and take pride in what they do. It inspires people to collaborate with one another, rather than work individually.

However, there are millions of projects that happen behind the scenes, projects that are mundane, that just need to be done. **Many information technology projects require replacement or upgrades of hardware or software; the customer may not even perceive any real change. These projects can be transformational by instilling a sense of community, shaping stakeholders' views of the importance of project management, or allowing others to experience project leadership and sharpen their leadership skills.** Every project requires the integration of people and tasks, and something wonderful happens to the heart when people experience meaningful growth.

## *Emotional Intelligence*

Daniel Goleman's ground breaking book, *Emotional Intelligence: Why it can matter more than IQ,* has created an industry of coaches and trainers dedicated to helping leaders become more effective through understanding themselves, their emotions, and how they play out on the leadership field. The theory behind emotional intelligence (EI) is that emotions are just as important or even more important, in leadership effectiveness than raw intelligence. The theory involves brain chemistry and its influence of emotions that impact a leader's effectiveness.[18] Emotional intelligence includes both personal competence—self-awareness and management—as well as social competence—social awareness and relationship management.

Self-awareness essentially means sensing your own emotions and recognizing their impact on yourself and on others. Self-management is keeping control of emotions and impulses and adapting yourself to situations to consistently promote transparency, honesty, integrity, and trustworthiness among peers and subordinates. Social competence focuses on being familiar with organizational cultures and recognizing the needs of followers, clients, and customers. The fourth domain is relationship management, which includes providing inspiration to team members, using healthy means of influence, developing subordinates, managing conflicts, building strong interdependent relationships among team members, and working collaboratively.[19]

Goleman found in his studies of executive leaders that their self-awareness, including openness to feedback, was critical to their ability to develop trust-based relationships with their peers. This trust was a common trait among the executives who were more effective at leading.[20] Emotional intelligence is an important part of the leadership material influencing an entire generation of leaders.

Project management has long suffered from the view that it is a purely technical skill; planning, scheduling, budgeting, tracking, and reporting. Some project managers recognize the stereotypes senior management, sponsors, and stakeholders hold of project managers when it comes to leadership but they continue to reinforce the stereotypes, to the detriment of all. Enhancing emotional intelligence is critical to overcoming these stereotypes.

## Servant Leadership

In 1970, Robert Greenleaf, a manager at AT&T, was inspired by Hermann Hesse's *A Journey East*, a fictional story of a group of people on a spiritual endeavor, led by a servant, Leo, who along with doing menial chores, sustains them with his spirit and song. Once Leo leaves the group, the journey loses its direction.[21] This story helped inspire Greenleaf to write an essay entitled *The Servant as Leader*. Greenleaf spent 40 years at AT&T and then consulted with organizations on the benefits of servant leadership. Servant leadership has gained the recognition of leadership authors and thought-leaders around the world. Greenleaf's belief was that one's greatness as a leader is first experienced in acting as a servant.

Servant leadership embraces many leadership themes already discussed. Larry Spears summarized ten themes of servant leadership:[22]

- Listening—Servant leaders listen intently to others, no matter how busy they are.
- Empathy—They strive to understand people's feelings, sincerely, and not just as business.
- Healing—They seek to heal themselves and others.
- Awareness—Servants leaders seek to continually understand themselves.
- Persuasion—They don't rely on formal authority but rather strive to influence in a positive, healthy manner.

- Conceptualization—They think beyond today and create realistic dreams about tomorrow.
- Foresight—They anticipate the reality of today as well as the promise of tomorrow, and learn from the lessons of yesterday.
- Stewardship—They create a trust, much like a promissory note, when guiding the actions of projects and institutions, for the good of society.
- Commitment to the growth of people—Servant leaders believe all people, not just the highest performers, have intrinsic value.
- Building community—Servant leaders value people coming together to bond emotionally and intellectually for each other's benefit.

The concept of servant leadership is radical for business management and project management. It holds no promises for a successful project but is a practice of ideals that commits one's entire spiritual, emotional, and intellectual being to seeking perpetual clarity.

## Summary

We've exposed the project leader to numerous leadership theories that apply to project management. The project environment is unique and is exposed to numerous influencing variables, including but not limited to the project leader's traits and preferences, the follower's background, experiences, preferences, and skills, the cultural or political environment of the organization, the type of project, its urgency, risks, location of team members, etc. All of these factors converge on a leader's specific project and the circumstances present weekly, daily, or even hourly.

At a minimum, a project leader should increase his awareness of self, of situational dynamics, and of follower preferences and increase the predictability of each. As awareness and predictability increase, so does the opportunity for effective project leadership. This awareness and predictability can be increased by understanding a broad range of leadership theories and how they apply to project work.

## Endnotes

1. Ralph M. Stogdill, *Handbook of Leadership: A Survey of Theory and Research* (New York: Free Press, 1974),76.
2. Ibid., 77.
3. Ibid., 80–81.
4. Arthur G. Bedeian and William F. Gleuck, *Management 3rd ed.* (Chicago: Dreyden Press, 1983), 498.
5. James P. Lewis, *Project Leadership* (Boston: McGraw Hill, 2003), 71.
6. Kurt Lewin, Ron Lippitt, and Robert White, "Patterns of Aggressive Behavior in Experimentally Created Social Climates," *Journal of Social Psychology*, 10 (1939): 271–301.

7. Ibid.

8. Rensis Likert, *The Human Organization: Its Management and Value* (New York: McGraw-Hill, 1967), 14.

9. Arthur G. Bedeian and William F. Gleuck, *Management 3rd ed.* (Chicago: Dreyden Press, 1983), 404–512.

10. Robert J. House, "A Path Goal Theory of Leader Effectiveness," *Administrative Science Quarterly*, 16 (1971): 321–338.

11. Arthur G. Bedeian, ibid.

12. Robert J. House, ibid.

13. Arthur G. Bedeian, ibid.

14. Arthur G. Bedeian, ibid.

15. Arthur G. Bedeian, ibid.

16. Arthur G. Bedeian, ibid.

17. Fred Dansereau Jr., George Graen, and William J. Haga, "A Vertical Dyad Linkage Approach to Leadership within Formal Organizations: A Longitudinal Investigation of the Role Making Process," *Organizational Behavior and Human Performance*, 13 (1975): 46–78.

18. Daniel Goleman, Richard Boyatzis, and Annie McKee, *Primal Leadership: Learning to Lead with Emotional Intelligence* (Boston: Harvard Business School Press, 2004) 102.

19. Ibid., 39.

20. Daniel Goleman, *What Makes a Leader*, Harvard Business Review, January 2004, 82–86.

21. Robert K. Greenleaf, *The Servant as Leader*, (1970; repr., Westfield, IN: The Robert K. Greenleaf Center, 1991) 1.

22. Larry C. Spears, "Tracing the Growing Impact of Servant-Leadership," in *Insights on Leadership: Service, Stewardship, Spirit, and Servant-Leadership* (New York: Wiley & Sons 1998) 4–6.

# Appendix B

## Self-Directed Project Leadership Workbook

### Part One: Establishing Commitment

1. List 5–10 dream jobs you wish to experience. (Consider athletics, entertainment, religion, politics, medicine, etc. Consider working in other parts of the world; let your imagination go.)

   _____       _____
   _____       _____
   _____       _____
   _____       _____
   _____       _____

2. Choose 2–3 jobs that seem most exciting and describe what about them makes them so appealing.

   _____
   _____

3. Try to identify your value system by evaluating your convictions. Below is a list of words. Use your hand or something suitable to cover the words and uncover one word at a time. Read each word out loud and take a few minutes to record the thoughts, places, people, images, and feelings associated with each one. Make a list of the values that generate the strongest thoughts, images, and feelings.

   _____
   _____
   _____
   _____

| | | | |
|---|---|---|---|
| Adventure | Assisting others | Belonging | Challenge |
| Comfort | Competitiveness | Conformity | Control |
| Creativity | Economic Security | Equality | Physical Security |
| Freedom | Health | Independence | Improving Society |
| Integrity | Intellect | Order | Peace |
| Power | Recognition | Respect | Spirituality |
| Success | Wealth | | |

4. Make of list of 10 or more things you wish to do or experience before you die. Don't worry about the practicality or priorities.

_____    _____
_____    _____
_____    _____
_____    _____
_____    _____

5. Your Ideal Life

   Do some free writing on what your ideal life looks like 10 years from now. What people are you around? What does the environment look like? What are you doing? Do not worry about the feasibility.

6. What themes arise in each of these exercises?

7. Begin drafting a personal vision statement and enhance it over the next 30 days. Include your values (convictions) and purpose (outcome). (See Chapter 8 for examples.)

8. Make a list of people needed to help you achieve this vision or people who are impacted by your personal vision.

| | |
|---|---|
| _____ | _____ |
| _____ | _____ |
| _____ | _____ |
| _____ | _____ |
| _____ | _____ |

9. Commit to Action
   What action can I take in the next 30–60 days to move toward my personal vision?

   _____
   _____
   _____
   _____
   _____

10. Make a list of 3 people you will tell about your new commitment to your person vision.

    _____
    _____

# Part Two: Leadership Competency Self Assessment
## *Evidence of Trust-Based Relationships*

1. You have talked to your sponsor in the last seven days.
   ☐ True      ☐ False

2. On your current project(s), the client or sponsor has involved you in pre-initiation project vision and strategy discussions for your current assignment.
   ☐ True      ☐ False

3. On your current assignment, you have found out indirectly that the client or sponsor is considering new approaches to addressing the business need of the project.
   ☐ True      ☐ False

4. In the past month, your client or sponsor has asked you to justify cost and schedule status.
   ☐ True      ☐ False

5. You know the name of your sponsor's or client's spouse.
   ☐ True      ☐ False

6. In the past month, a significant stakeholder has called you in the last week just to talk, with no specific agenda.
   ☐ True      ☐ False

7. In the past month, a project team member discussed awkward or bothersome situations with you.
   ☐ True      ☐ False

8. In the last week, a team member approached you to discussion a concern or problem.
   ☐ True      ☐ False

9. In the last week, a team member, customer, or sponsor has solicited your advice.
   ☐ True      ☐ False

10. On your last project, users of the project's product personally thanked you for your involvement.
    ☐ True      ☐ False

|    | *T* | *F* | *Score* |
|----|-----|-----|---------|
| 1. | 3   | 2   | —       |
| 2. | 5   | 0   | —       |
| 3. | −5  | 0   | —       |
| 4. | −3  | 2   | —       |
| 5. | 3   | 1   | —       |
| 6. | 3   | 0   | —       |

|  |  |  |  |
|---|---|---|---|
| 7. | 4 | 0 | — |
| 8. | 2 | 0 | — |
| 9. | 5 | 0 | — |
| 10. | 3 | 0 | — |

Total                  —

25 to 30—Strong and broad evidence of trust-based relationships

20 to 24—Some strong evidence of trust-based relationships, but pockets of weakness

10 to 19—Some evidence of trust-based relationships, but significant pockets of weakness

Less than 9—Minimal evidence of trust-based relationships

## *Evidence of Consultative Leadership*

1. You have asked a team member today, "How can I help you?"
   ☐ True      ☐ False

2. On your current project, a project team member personally thanked you for your support or guidance.
   ☐ True      ☐ False

3. This week when walking the halls, a team member stopped what he/she was doing to ask for help or advice.
   ☐ True      ☐ False

4. On your current project, a sponsor or client called you to ask for your assistance or opinion on a matter outside the scope of the current project.
   ☐ True      ☐ False

5. This month, you heard stakeholders discussing delicate project topics that you are unaware of.
   ☐ True      ☐ False

6. A project team member volunteered to work on your current project.
   ☐ True      ☐ False

7. On your current project, you have evidence a team member has promoted your current project to others not directly involved.
   ☐ True      ☐ False

8. On your current project, you heard someone else use your "near" exact words to frame (bring new insight) to project issues.
   ☐ True      ☐ False

9. You have made 2 or more recommendations to team members, sponsors, or customers this week.
   ☐ True      ☐ False

10. A team member has made a decision this week on executing a project task this week.
    ☐ True    ☐ False

|      | T   | F   | Score |
|------|-----|-----|-------|
| 1.   | 3   | −2  | —     |
| 2.   | 5   | 0   | —     |
| 3.   | 2   | 0   | —     |
| 4.   | 3   | 0   | —     |
| 5.   | −3  | 2   | —     |
| 6.   | 3   | 0   | —     |
| 7.   | 3   | −1  | —     |
| 8.   | 3   | 0   | —     |
| 9.   | 3   | −3  | —     |
| 10.  | 3   | −1  | —     |
| Total |    |     | —     |

25 to 30—Strong and broad evidence of consultative leadership
20 to 24—Some strong evidence of consultative leadership, but pockets of weakness
10 to 19—Some evidence of consultative leadership, but significant pockets of weakness
Less than 10—Minimal evidence of consultative leadership

## Evidence of Courage

1. On your current project, you have shared a personal failure with a stakeholder and taken accountability.
   ☐ True    ☐ False
2. You have performance incentives associated with your current project results.
   ☐ True    ☐ False
3. A stakeholder has given you direct feedback on your performance in the past 30 days.
   ☐ True    ☐ False
4. In the past 6 months, you have taken on new work that you have never done before.
   ☐ True    ☐ False

5. In a meeting this month, you have initiated the discussion of difficult topics.
   ☐ True    ☐ False

6. This past month, you have initiated a lunch, dinner, coffee, etc. with a team member, peer, or stakeholder you wished to get to know better.
   ☐ True    ☐ False

7. On your current project, you have taken a position on an issue that upholds a personal value.
   ☐ True    ☐ False

8. In the past year, a team member has been recognized or promoted by someone other than you for work on your project.
   ☐ True    ☐ False

9. You have introduced new knowledge, concepts, or tools to your project team in past month.
   ☐ True    ☐ False

10. You have initiated a self-assessment in the past year.
    ☐ True    ☐ False

|      | T  | F   | *Score* |
|------|----|-----|---------|
| 1.   | 3  | −1  | —       |
| 2.   | 3  | 0   | —       |
| 3.   | 2  | −1  | —       |
| 4.   | 3  | −3  | —       |
| 5.   | 4  | −1  | —       |
| 6.   | 2  | 0   | —       |
| 7.   | 3  | −1  | —       |
| 8.   | 3  | 0   | —       |
| 9.   | 3  | −2  | —       |
| 10.  | 4  | −2  | —       |

Total                      —

25 to 30—Strong and broad evidence of courage
20 to 24—Some strong evidence of courage, but pockets of weakness
10 to 19—Some evidence of courage, but significant pockets of weakness
Less than 9—Minimal evidence of courage

# Part Three: Desired Supportive Relationship Checklist

Answer these YES and NO questions as a guide to find candidates for a supportive relationship. The more YES answers, the more the person is a candidate for a supportive relationship.

| Question | Yes | No |
|---|---|---|
| 1. Does this person have a vested interest in my development? | | |
| 2. Is he or she a sponsor or customer on a current project or assignment? | | |
| 3. Does this person currently benefit from my project leadership services? | | |
| 4. Is this person readily accessible? | | |
| 5. Do I feel at ease when around this person? | | |
| 6. Is this a person I have known for sometime? | | |
| 7. Does this person have quality that I would like to possess? | | |
| 8. Is this person well respected by their peers? | | |
| 9. Does this person have coaching or mentoring experience? | | |
| 10. Does this person show a strong interest in developing others? | | |

# Part Four: Leadership Competency Pyramid Acquisition Plan

Review the MyProjectAdvisor® Leadership Competency Pyramid and consider the following questions to acquire project leadership competencies.

Review each question with regard to your environment, current project, and career.

## *Knowledge, skills, experience*

1. What knowledge, skills, and experience can I acquire that benefit my project team and customers? (Discuss with a person you identified in Part Three as a desired supportive relationship.)

   _____

   _____

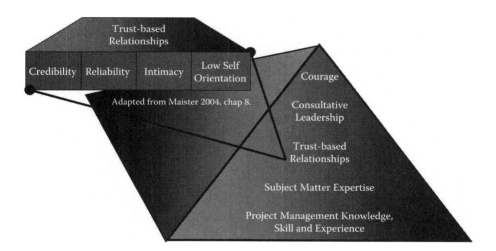

2. What knowledge, skills, or experience would make my job more fun or exciting?

   _____

   _____

3. What can I do immediately to acquire needed knowledge, skills, or experience?

Immediately (within 30 days)          Longer range (6 months to 1 year)

_____          _____

_____          _____

_____          _____

_____          _____

_____          _____

## *Trust-Based Relationships*

Discuss each question with a person you identified in Part Three as a desired supportive relationship.

What is the status of my relationships with key project team members and customers? Do I have positive, healthy, and trust-based relationships with key customers?

_____

_____

Which relationships are causing me emotional discomfort? What is the source of this pain? (Fear, confrontation, incompatibility)

_____

_____

What are the benefits of healing these relationships, to the project, me, and others?

_____

_____

_____

What specific actions can I take to turn these relationships into positive, healthy relationships.

How can I adapt my behavior to increase my compatibility?

1. _____

2. _____

What content can I gain that will enhance my credibility?

1. _____

2. _____

What actions can I take that will enhance my reliability?

1. _____

2. _____

What risks can I take that will enhance my intimacy?

   1. _____

   2. _____

What values can I display to enhance my low self-orientation?

   1. _____

   2. _____

## *Consultative Leadership*

Answer each question individually with regard to a project.

1. How do you feel when you attempt to advise co-workers? (Confident, nervous, I rarely advise).
2. What type of visioning activities do you want to participate in?
3. What advice can I provide today? To whom?
4. What outcomes can I assign to my consultation?

Answer each question individually with regard to your experience of being a consultative leader.

1. What can I do to improve my engagement process?
2. What can I do to improve my listening skills?
3. What can I do to improve my ability to frame complexity?
4. What can I do to improve my ability to develop a vision for my team and customers?
5. What can I do to improve my ability to get team members to commit to act?

Discuss each question with a supportive relationship.

On what topics have I been able to effectively consult, advise, and influence?

_____

_____

Whom have I served and what have I done to improve their well-being?

_____

_____

What opportunities should I have to be a consultative leader?

_____

_____

## *Courage*

Discuss each question with a person you identified in Part Three as a desired supportive relationship.

What risks can I take to improve my project's performance?

_____

_____

What risks can I take to improve my career?

_____

_____

What fears do I have about my project management career?

_____

_____

What components of the pyramid can be strengthened to bolster my courage?

_____

_____

# Part Five: Active Leadership Experience™ (ALE)

1. Write down a list of specific conditions, situations, or events you care deeply about in your job, which you desire to transform. List them in the left-hand column of the table below. (See Chapter 22).
2. Write down your results from Exercise 1 that helped uncover your values and convictions.
3. Try to pare down these items to the top 5, ranking them from highest to lowest. List them in the right-hand column of the table below.

| Transformable conditions, situations, or events in your job | List of top 5 related values and convictions |
| --- | --- |
|  |  |
|  |  |
|  |  |
|  |  |
|  |  |

4. Try to align a value or conviction with the event, condition, or situation you care deeply about. Here are some questions to help you find the alignment.

■ How would I feel if I could successfully impact the condition, situation, or event?
■ Who benefits from a change in the event, condition, or situation?
■ What are the consequences if nothing changes?

## *ALE Statement*

Because of my desired value _____ I will begin an Active Leadership Experience™ in my job by (creating/transforming) _____.

5. Identify a list of behaviors you can exhibit daily and weekly to reflect your ALE statement.

_____
_____
_____
_____

6. List the people who need to be involved to make this happen.

_____
_____
_____
_____

7. List actions you can take to build trust-based relationships with them and establish a consultative leadership role. (Credibility, reliability, intimacy, low self-orientation).

   _____
   _____
   _____
   _____

8. List actions you can take to remove their fear of failure.

   _____
   _____
   _____
   _____
   _____

9. List key milestones in your ALE.

   _____
   _____
   _____
   _____
   _____

# Part Six: Risk Tolerances—Facts and Feelings

When contemplating a risk one can determine how he personally perceives the risk by answering two questions. On a scale of 1 to 10 (1 being definitely and 10 being not at all), how certain are you of this event or change? And on a scale of 1 to 10 (1 being definitely and 10 being not at all), how comfortable are you with this event or change?

This Facts/Feelings Model of Risk Taking as shown below blends in the two key components of risk—an analytical predictability analysis along with the emotional component of a belief in our ability to control the outcomes.

■ On a scale of 1 to 10 (1 completely certain and 10 completely uncertain), how well can I calculate with some certainty the outcome?
■ On a scale of 1 to 10 (1 being completely comfortable and 10 completely uncomfortable), how comfortable am I with this choice?

Because the continuums are normally scored from high to low, the questions have been reversed to compensate and make it easier to plot.

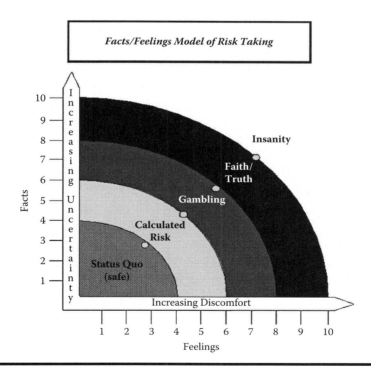

**Figure B-1 Fact/feeling model. (Courtesy of Roberta F. Hill, copyright 1990, 1997.)**

Example: *I will go skydiving this weekend.*

| I can calculate the outcome with _____: (Select a number) | | | |
|---|---|---|---|
| Complete Certainty | Moderate Certainty | Moderate Uncertainty | Complete Uncertainty |
| • 1 2 3 | 4 5 6 | 7 8 9 | 10 |
| I feel _____ with this choice. (Select a number) | | | |
| Completely Comfortable | Moderately Comfortable | Moderately Uncomfortable | Completely Uncomfortable |
| • 1 2 3 | 4 5 6 | 7 8 9 | 10 |

If you are uncertain, (a score of 7) or high on discomfort (a score of 9), that would place you on the chart in the "Trust/Faith" Zone. In this zone, you are highly unlikely to skydive this weekend unless you have strong trust/faith in the outcome. Even if you chose a score of 3, completely certain of the outcome but still high on discomfort (a score of 9), this is still in the same zone "Trust/Faith" Zone and we would predict—you may show up but you won't jump (unless pushed). Based on your answers, select where you generally fall on the Fact/Feeling Model of Risk Taking.

## Determine Your Certainty and Comfort

Read each question and develop the specifics for each question before assessing your certainty and comfort.

1. I will advise my customer to modify his approach or process to increase the chances of project success. Write down specifics _____

| I can calculate the outcome with _____: (Select a number) | | | |
|---|---|---|---|
| Complete Certainty | Moderate Certainty | Moderate Uncertainty | Complete Uncertainty |
| • 1 2 3 | 4 5 6 | 7 8 9 | 10 |
| I feel _____ with this choice. (Select a number) | | | |
| Completely Comfortable | Moderately Comfortable | Moderately Uncomfortable | Completely Uncomfortable |
| • 1 2 3 | 4 5 6 | 7 8 9 | 10 |

2. I will articulate specific content knowledge to my project sponsor that is relevant to a critical project issue next week. Write down specifics

| I can calculate the outcome with _____: (Select a number) | | | |
|---|---|---|---|
| Complete Certainty | Moderate Certainty | Moderate Uncertainty | Complete Uncertainty |
| • 1 2 3 | 4 5 6 | 7 8 9 | 10 |
| I feel _____ with this choice. (Select a number) | | | |
| Completely Comfortable | Moderately Comfortable | Moderately Uncomfortable | Completely Uncomfortable |
| • 1 2 3 | 4 5 6 | 7 8 9 | 10 |

3. I will make a commitment to a team member to remove ambiguity from our project next week. Write down specifics _____

| I can calculate the outcome with _____: (Select a number) | | | |
|---|---|---|---|
| Complete Certainty | Moderate Certainty | Moderate Uncertainty | Complete Uncertainty |
| • 1 2 3 | 4 5 6 | 7 8 9 | 10 |
| I feel _____ with this choice. (Select a number) | | | |
| Completely Comfortable | Moderately Comfortable | Moderately Uncomfortable | Completely Uncomfortable |
| • 1 2 3 | 4 5 6 | 7 8 9 | 10 |

4. I will link my bonus to the performance of the entire project team. Write down specifics _____

| I can calculate the outcome with _____: (Select a number) | | | |
|---|---|---|---|
| Complete Certainty | Moderate Certainty | Moderate Uncertainty | Complete Uncertainty |
| • 1 2 3 | 4 5 6 | 7 8 9 | 10 |
| I feel _____ with this choice. (Select a number) | | | |
| Completely Comfortable | Moderately Comfortable | Moderately Uncomfortable | Completely Uncomfortable |
| • 1 2 3 | 4 5 6 | 7 8 9 | 10 |

Feel free to generate additional questions which apply to your environment and current situation.

1. Where did you tend to fall in the Fact/Feeling bands?
2. What makes you uncomfortable about these choices?
3. What steps can you take to increase certainty and comfort?

# Part Seven: Service-based Project Leader 360-degree Evaluation

Review these questions and assess yourself on a scale from 1 to 10.

| Strongly Disagree | Disagree | Agree | Strongly Agree |
|---|---|---|---|
| 1 2 | 3 4 5 | 6 7 8 | 9 10 |

## *Project Management Performance*

### *Project Initiation*

1. Conducts fearless needs analysis, business case, and project charter development.
2. Thoroughly and accurately identifies and defines all stakeholders.
3. Defines current and future states that can be easily interpreted by stakeholders.

### *Project Planning*

1. Ensures the development of well-defined project scope, including WBS and requirements documentation.
2. Effectively defines resource needs, resource roles and responsibilities, project team organizational charts, and clear reporting structures among the project team.
3. Develops meaningful project baselines to measure performance for project cost, time, and scope.
4. Conducts effective risk assessments and creates usable risk response plans.
5. Defines quality criteria and acceptance criteria for project deliverables.

### *Project Execution*

1. Creates a productive working environment for all project team members.
2. Fosters interdependent, uninhibited communication channels between stakeholders and team members.
3. Gains quick acceptance for project deliverables in a manner consistent with project plans.
4. Works in advance to create unimpeded work streams for team members.

### *Project Control*

1. Actively monitors new needs and validates customer benefits.
2. Initiates corrective action to improve project performance (cost, schedule, quality, scope).

3. Enforces project quality measures and implements continuous improvement processes.

## Project Closure

1. Maintains accurate project records that are accessible to stakeholders and future project teams.
2. Is asked to start new project work with the customer.

# Trust-Based Relationships

## Credibility

1. Articulates the fundamentals of project management concepts, tools, and technical knowledge in a meaningful way—applicability and use.
2. Runs productive project meetings.
3. Exhibits a thorough understanding of stakeholder expectations; including team members, sponsors, customers, vendors, etc.

## Reliability

1. Sets priorities, proactively initiates work, regularly follows up, links promises to actions.
2. Behaves consistently in managing personnel, making decisions, and dealing with stress and adversity.
3. Responds to stakeholders' emotions and feelings concerning the project.

## Intimacy with stakeholders

1. Is always open and honest with stakeholders.
2. Invests time in developing meaningful relationships with key stakeholders.
3. Uses good judgment when dealing with sensitive issues.

## Self-Orientation

1. Shows absence of prejudice and stereotypical thinking.
2. Resists jumping to conclusions, does not feel the need to always have an answer.
3. Allows others share the spotlight for successes.

### Consultative Leadership Behaviors

#### Communication

1. Conveys a positive "can do" attitude in discussions.
2. Focuses on key project issues appropriate for the stakeholder.
3. Values face-to-face discussions, eliminates distractions.
4. Prepares and presents high-quality, high impact presentations.
5. Listens for clarity with non-verbal signals, then confirms what has been received, and shows an understanding of the depth and magnitude of what has been discussed.

#### Advisory

1. Solicits ideas, suggestions, and opinions from others.
2. Researches and presents project facts accurately, in a timely manner, and well-summarized.
3. Explores multiple scenarios and outcomes of project recommendations.
4. Demonstrates insight, articulates numerous complex business and project issues into clear, concise statements.
5. Educates stakeholders on a potential course of action or options and lets them decide.

#### Visioning

1. Creates a unified vision to the creation of the product or services of the project.
2. Inspires innovation and creativity, focuses on long-term solutions versus short-term problem solving.
3. Gains rational and emotional commitment and consensus on vision and generates excitement and energy with project team and customer.
4. Links project vision to strategic business goals.

#### Result Orientation

1. Takes initiative and risks to build confidence of project stakeholders.
2. Knows when to stop planning the project and start implementing; creates and sustains momentum.
3. Takes action to reduce resistance though removing project unknowns.

#### Service and Development of Others

1. Is patient, encourages development, delegates effectively, and provides objective feedback.
2. Looks for ways to help others, puts stakeholders' priorities ahead of self interests.

3. Sets high standards, helps others achieve them.
4. Creates a comfortable project environment in which team members can share emotions and feelings.

## *Courage*

### *Confidence*

1. Attitudes, behaviors, and demeanor reflect one who has self confidence.
2. Maintains a high energy level, takes care of physical health and mind.
3. Thirsts for constructive criticism, identifies and follows through on opportunities to improve performance.

### *Risk Tolerance*

1. Willing to make recommendations to stakeholders and influence project outcomes.
2. Accepts responsibility, admits mistakes, learns from them, and moves on.
3. Aligns personal stake (reputation, monetary, perks etc.) with expected project outcomes.

# Part Eight: Active Leadership Experience Scorecard

| Self assessed score | Yes | No | Stakeholder assessed score | Yes | No |
|---|---|---|---|---|---|
| **Alignment** | | | **Alignment** | | |
| I feel energized when I think about my ALE | | | I am energized by their interest in this project | | |
| I often envision the result of my ALE | | | I clearly see your vision and understand its purpose and significance | | |
| I often think of new ideas or extensions of my ALE | | | We discuss new ideas frequently | | |
| **Behaviors** | | | **Behaviors** | | |
| I speak regularly about the importance of my ALE | | | You speak regularly about the importance of your ALE | | |
| I model ALE behaviors daily | | | You model the behaviors consistent with the values | | |
| Trust-based relationship— name: _____ | | | Trust-based relationship— name:_____ | | |
| This trust-based relationship seeks my direction on the ALE | | | I am comfortable with you setting direction | | |
| This trust-based relationship actively contributes to the ALE transformation | | | I actively contribute | | |
| **Progress** | | | **Progress** | | |
| Milestones on my ALE have been met | | | Milestones on your ALE have been met | | |
| The progress is generating interest and excitement among a larger community | | | The progress is generating interest and excitement among a larger community | | |
| I believe we will be successful | | | I believe we will be successful | | |

# Part Nine: Questions to Help Align Your Talent, Time and Resources

1. What strengths can I lend to a cause? It could be simple things such as organizing, creating, inspiring, listening, contacting etc.

   _____

   _____

2. What type of organization do I feel comfortable associating myself with? List the specific organizations.

   ■ Local community: _____
   ■ Government: _____
   ■ Religious: _____
   ■ Youth: _____
   ■ Social Causes: _____
   ■ Other: _____

3. What type of people do I wish to work with?

   ■ Professionals: _____
   ■ Non professionals: _____
   ■ Children: _____
   ■ Adults: _____
   ■ Handicapped: _____
   ■ Disadvantaged: _____
   ■ Other: _____

4. How much time a week or month do I have to give? _____

5. What resources can I offer?

   ■ Skills: _____
   ■ Knowledge: _____
   ■ Materials: _____

6. What is my motivation to serve? _____

# Index